A LIFE OF TOTAL PRAYER

Selected Writings of
CATHERINE OF SIENA

Upper Room Spiritual Classics® — Series 3

Selected, edited, and introduced by
Keith Beasley-Topliffe

**A Life of Total Prayer:
Selected Writings of Catherine of Siena**

Copyright © 2000 by Upper Room Books™
All rights reserved.

No part of this book may be used or reproduced in any manner whatsoever without written permission of the publisher except in the case of brief quotations embodied in critical articles or reviews. For information, write Upper Room Books,™ 1908 Grand Avenue, Nashville, Tennessee 37212.

The Upper Room® Website: http://www.upperroom.org

UPPER ROOM,® UPPER ROOM BOOKS™ and design logos are trademarks owned by the Upper Room,® Nashville, Tennessee. All rights reserved.

Scripture quotations are from the New Revised Standard Version of the Bible Copyright © 1989 by the Division of Christian Education of the National Council of Churches of Christ in the USA. Used by permission. All rights reserved.

Excerpts from *I, Catherine* Edited and Translated by Kenelm Foster and Mary John Ronayne, 1980. Published by HarperCollins Publishers Ltd., London, England. Used by permission.

Excerpts from *The Letters of Catherine of Siena, Volume 1*, translated by Suzanne Noffke, O.P., MRTS vol. 52 (Binghampton, NY, 1988), pp. 73–78, 122–124, 148–150, 226–228. Copyright Arizona Board of Regents for Arizona State University.

Cover design: Gore Studio, Inc.
Interior design and layout: Nancy J. Cole

First printing: 2000

Library of Congress Cataloging-in-Publication Data

Catherine, of Siena, Saint, 1347–1380.
    [Selection. English. 2000]
    A life of total prayer : selected writings of Catherine of Siena / selected, edited, and introduced by Keith Beasley-Topliffe.
      p. cm. — (Upper Room spiritual classics. Series 3)
    ISBN 0-8358-0903-X
    1. Spiritual life—Catholic authors. I. Beasley-Topliffe, Keith.
II. Title. III. Series.
BX2349.C37213 2000   99-40407
248.4'82—dc21   CIP

Printed in the United States of America

TABLE OF CONTENTS

Introduction	5
Learning to Love	12
Loving God, Not Things	16
Armor Against Evil	21
Clothed in the Fire of Love	24
The Cell of Self-Knowledge	28
Prayer	32
Love and Service	36
The Bridge	40
River and Thorns	44
Beginning to Climb	47
From Vocal to Mental Prayer	51
Going On to Perfection	55
Perfect Purity	60
Final Prayer	63
Appendix: Reading Spiritual Classics for Personal and Group Formation	68

INTRODUCTION

Saint Paul urged Christians, "Present your bodies as a living sacrifice, holy and acceptable to God" (Rom. 12:1). Thirteen centuries later, Catherine of Siena tried to live according to Paul's word. She drove herself tirelessly for the reconciliation of enemies and the reform of the church, offering her physical sufferings as atonement for the sins of others. With Paul, she could truly say, "In my flesh I am completing what is lacking in Christ's afflictions for the sake of his body, that is, the church" (Col. 1:24).

This self-sacrifice was driven by a burning desire to submit her will completely to God's will for her. This, in turn, was fueled by a prayer life so intense that she often lost all consciousness of the world around her. Even in the midst of dictating letters, she sometimes burst into prayer and praise.

Fortunately Catherine was very good at putting her experiences into words. She wrote hundreds of letters to friends and religious and government leaders. Whatever the occasion, her writing always moved on to deeper matters, urging her correspondents to turn away from sin and draw nearer to God. Her teaching earned her the title of Doctor of the Church, one of the first two women (the other was Teresa of Avila) to be so honored.

CATHERINE'S WORLD

The fourteenth century was a tumultuous time in Italy and throughout Europe. Several years of poor crops were followed in 1348 by the Black Death, an epidemic of bubonic plague that killed one-third of the people of Europe. Bands of mercenary soldiers that helped cities to pursue feuds with neighbors turned to banditry when no one would hire them. Many cities in central Italy, though officially subject to either the pope or the Holy Roman emperor, had a great amount of self-government and very turbulent politics. One of these city-republics was Siena, about 180 miles north of Rome and 43 south of Florence.

The church reached a high point in the twelfth century. The pope was powerful enough to demand and receive penance from kings, but his power declined drastically by the early fourteenth century. In 1303 the king of France forced the election of a French pope, the first of several. In 1309 Pope Clement V moved his headquarters from Rome to Avignon in southern France. That was the beginning of the so-called Babylonian Captivity of the church. For nearly seventy years the papacy was controlled by the French monarchy, and the pope's territory in central Italy was ruled by proxies, often French bishops. Several cities, led by Florence and Milan, rebelled against papal authority.

At the end of the twelfth century, Dominic and Francis founded orders of friars who helped to revitalize the church with enthusiasm and scholarship.

Both orders established universities and produced outstanding theologians in the Franciscan Bonaventure and the Dominican Thomas Aquinas. By the fourteenth century, the orders became institutionalized and scholarship stagnated. Still, the Dominicans in Siena maintained a standard of theological training and preaching through which Catherine absorbed a first-rate education.

CATHERINE'S LIFE

Catherine Benincasa was born March 25, 1347, the twenty-third of twenty-four children born to Giacomo di Benincasa, a cloth dyer, and his wife, Lapa. A twin sister died in infancy. The next year the Black Death came to Siena, killing half the people. When she was six, Catherine had a vision of Christ that led her to dedicate her life to God. As a child she practiced a variety of devotions, tempered somewhat by the desire to be a typical girl.

In 1362, when she was fifteen, Catherine cut her hair to discourage her parents' plans for her marriage, and she began to live as a servant in her home. Two years later she became one of the Mantellate, a Dominican lay order of women (primarily older widows) who took special vows and who were named for the cloaks (*mantella*) they wore in public. As an unmarried teenager, Catherine needed special permission to join the order. For the next three years she remained primarily in her room in prayer. She left each morning to attend Mass, where she sometimes

8 — A Life of Total Prayer

each morning to attend Mass, where she sometimes went into ecstasy and had to be carried out at the end of the service. Often she did housework while her family slept. By this time she ate only bread, water, and raw vegetables. She wanted to be able to read, but struggled to learn her letters. She prayed for help and found she could read from then on.

At the beginning of Lent in 1368, Catherine had a vision in which Christ took her as his bride. At the same time, Christ sent her out of solitude to a life of service. At first she worked in the hospitals of Siena. By that point, she had gathered a circle of friends—male and female, clergy and lay—who looked to her for guidance, calling her "Mama." As her prayer life intensified, she became less able to tolerate earthly food. She stopped eating bread in 1370 and could not keep down any solid food after 1372.

After the return of the Black Death to Siena in 1374, Catherine felt called to go beyond service to individuals to serve the church as a whole and the people of Italy in particular. She had three overriding concerns. She supported a call for a new crusade in the hope that those who wanted to fight would do so in the Holy Land and for a holy cause. She urged the pope to return to Rome. And she called for the reform of the church. The crusade never happened. But in 1376, Catherine traveled to Avignon to meet with Pope Gregory XI. Her attempt to mediate the dispute with Florence and its allies failed, but the pope left Avignon for Rome in September. Catherine returned to Siena. She learned to write and began to work on her book, the *Dialogue*, which she completed by October 1378.

In the meantime, Gregory XI died. His successor, Urban VI, pushed so strongly for sweeping reforms that many of the cardinals turned against him and elected their own pope, Clement VII. Urban called Catherine to Rome to lend her support to his cause. She and her large group of disciples lived as a community under her direction. Catherine's health was in a precarious condition. She had to spend much of the time in bed, though she still rallied her strength to walk to Mass at Saint Peter's each day. She was completely unable to eat or drink water by January 1380. Yet she lived through Lent, continuing to dictate letters supporting reform and unity in the church. She died in Rome on April 29, 1380, at the age of thirty-three. She was buried in a tomb in the church of Santa Maria sopra Minerva, though her head was later removed and taken to Siena. She was declared a saint in 1461.

FURTHER READING

See the "Note on the Texts" for information on Catherine's writings.

The first biography of Catherine was written by her confessor, Raymondo da Capua, soon after her death. A couple of recent translations are available. The best modern biographies are by Johannes Jörgenson (translated by Ingeborg Lund) and Sigrid Undset (translated by Kate Austin-Lund), though both may be hard to find. Suzanne Noffke's *Catherine of Siena: Vision Through a Distant Eye* (Liturgical Press, 1996) is an excellent introduction to Catherine's life and thought and includes a travelogue of places in Italy connected with Catherine.

Barbara Tuchman's *A Distant Mirror: The Calamitous Fourteenth Century* offers a thorough look at Catherine's time, including a discussion of the Avignon "captivity" and Catherine's part in ending it.

Catherine's theology was greatly influenced by the writings of Thomas Aquinas, available in a variety of editions. Spiritual writers who were contemporaries include Julian of Norwich and the author of *The Cloud of Unknowing*.

Note on the Texts

The selections from the *Dialogue* are taken from the 1907 translation by Algar Thorold, available on the Internet at the Christian Classics Ethereal Library. It omits more than one-third of the book. These selections have been edited for modern grammar, vocabulary, and inclusive language. Paulist Press has published a complete and modern translation by Suzanne Noffke.

Noffke is the translator for the first five selections from Catherine's letters, taken from the first of a projected four-volume annotated set from the Center for Medieval and Early Renaissance Studies at SUNY Binghamton. When completed, it will be the first complete English translation of Catherine's letters, but only one volume has been published. The final selection from a letter was translated by Kenelm Foster and Mary John Ronayne in *I, Catherine*, published by Collins. These letters have been edited for length only. Catherine's letters were numbered in an edition of 1860 by Niccola Tomaseo. These numbers are given (as T29, etc.) for cross-reference with other collections.

Catherine's use of Scripture is very free. The translators have followed her own Italian. No attempt has been made to conform with a standard translation.

LEARNING TO LOVE

From a letter (T29) to Regina della Scala of Milan (late 1373)

In 1373, Bernabo Visconti, the tyrant of Milan, sent ambassadors to urge Siena to join an antipapal league. Catherine wrote to Visconti urging him to give up this plan and submit to the authority (secular as well as spiritual) of the pope, whom she refers to as "Christ on earth." She also wrote a long letter to his wife, Regina della Scala, in hopes that she might persuade her husband to a more holy life. This selection and the next come from that letter.

In the name of Jesus Christ crucified and of gentle Mary.

Revered mother in Christ Jesus,

I Caterina, servant and slave of the servants of Jesus Christ, am writing to you in his precious blood. I long to see you so clothed in the garment of blazing charity that you may be the means and instrument of reconciling your husband with Christ gentle Jesus and with his vicar, Christ on earth. I am certain that if charity is strong in you, your husband cannot fail to feel its warmth. This is what First Truth wants: that the two of you share one spirit, one affection, one holy desire. And without the love of charity this is beyond your reach.

But you will say to me, "Since I have no such love, and without it I am powerless, how can I get it?" I will tell you. Love is had only by loving. If you want love, you must begin by loving—I mean you must want to love. Once you want it, you must open the eye of your understanding to see where and how love is to be found. And you will find it within your very self. How? When you recognize your nothingness. And once you see that of yourself you do not even exist, you will recognize and appreciate that God is the source of your existence and of every favor above and beyond that existence—God's graces and gifts both temporal and spiritual. For without existence, we would not be able to receive any grace at all. So everything we have, everything we discover within ourselves, is indeed the gift of God's boundless goodness and charity.

This discovery and sight of our Creator's tremendous goodness to us makes us rise to such a growth of love and desire that we count as nothing— even despise—ourselves and the world and all the world's pleasures. This doesn't surprise me, because this is love's way, that when we see ourselves loved we love in return. And because we love, we would rather die than offend the one we love. We are fed in love's fire because we realize how loved we are when we see that we ourselves were the soil and the rock that held the standard of the most holy cross. For you know very well that neither earth nor rock could have held the cross, nor could cross or nails have held God's only-begotten Son, had not love held him fast. So God's love for our souls was the rock and the nails that held him fast.

This then is how we find love. And how are we to love once we have discovered where love is? Oh dearest revered mother, he himself is the rule and the way. There is no other. If we would walk in the light and receive the life of grace, the way he teaches us to follow—his way—is to go the path of suffering, the path of disgrace, derision, torment, ridicule, and persecution. It is by such suffering that we become conformed with Christ crucified. He is the spotless Lamb who scorned the world's wealth and power. He was the God-Man; yet, as our rule and our way, he teaches us by becoming himself a fulfiller, not an abolisher, of the Law. He is humble and meek, for never a cry or complaint is heard from him. In the greatness of his love he has opened himself up. Our salvation becomes his food and delight as he neither considers nor seeks himself but only the Father's honor and other people's welfare. He does not evade suffering but walks right up to it.

It is an awesome thing to see the good gentle Jesus, the one who rules and feeds the whole universe, in such great want and need that no one else has ever been as poor as he. He is so poor that Mary hasn't a blanket to wrap him in. In the end he dies naked on the cross so that he might reclothe us and cover our nakedness. Our sin had left us naked; we had lost the garment of grace. So Jesus gave up his own life and with it clothed us. I tell you, then, the soul who has discovered love in the love of Christ crucified will be ashamed to pursue it in any other way than that of Christ crucified. She will not want pleasure, status, or pomp, but will prefer to be like a pilgrim or traveler in this life, with her attention focused wholly on reaching her journey's goal. And if she is a good pilgrim, neither any prosperity she may encounter along the way nor any difficulty will slow her down. No, she will go forward bravely in love and in eagerness for the goal she hopes to reach.

Loving God, Not Things

From a letter (T29) to Regina della Scala of Milan (continued)

This selection is a later portion of the letter. Here she addresses the subject of avarice, for which Regina della Scala was notorious.

Use the things of this world as nature needs them, but not with excessive attachment. For it would be very displeasing to God if you were to set your heart on something of less value than yourself. That would be nothing but a surrender of your dignity. For people become like what they love. If I love sin, which is nothingness, I too become a nothing. I cannot fall any lower than that.

Sin arises simply from loving what God hates and hating what God loves. So if you love the passing things of this world and love yourself with a sensual love, you sin. For this is what God hates; in fact, it so displeases him that he willed to work out vengeance and punishment for it upon his own body. He made himself an anvil, and on this anvil hammered out our sins.

How great, then, is our wretched blindness! We see that we were created in God's image and likeness and later formed anew in grace. (He formed his image in us anew by the outpouring of his blood after we had lost it by deadly sin.) Yet we are so blind as to abandon God's affection and love which in his goodness made us so great, and give ourselves over to loving things apart from God! I mean we take our affection and love away from God to love ourselves and created things without God! It is not that prestige and worldly pleasure and other people are evil in themselves; what is evil is our attachment to them when by such attachment we disregard the sweet commandment of God. When, on the other hand, our affection and love are turned away from ourselves and centered entirely in Christ crucified, we achieve the greatest dignity possible to us, because we become one with our Creator. What greater good could there be than union with him who is all good? We cannot attribute the dignity of that union to ourselves, however; love is responsible for it. A servant maid would become a great lady should the emperor make her his wife. By her union with him she would become an empress—not by her own merit (for she was only a servant), but because of his dignity as emperor. Just think, dearest mother in Christ gentle Jesus! The soul who has fallen in love with God, she who is a servant and slave ransomed by the blood of God's Son, attains such great dignity that she cannot be called a servant now, but an empress, spouse of the eternal emperor! How well this agrees with the words of First Truth: "To serve God is not to be a slave but to reign"! For God rescues her from the servitude of sin and makes her free. This perfect union is indeed powerful, for it completes the basic dignity of being, of having been created by God, by uniting the soul in love and virtue with her Creator. Such a soul has been stripped of her old self and has been clothed in a new self, in Christ gentle Jesus. Then she is open to receive and hold that grace by which she experiences God in this life, and in the end enjoys the sight of him eternally. There she is at peace, in perfect rest and quiet, for her desires are fulfilled.

The reason we cannot have this sort of peace in this life is that our desire is not completely satisfied until we reach this union with the divine Being. As long as we are pilgrim travelers in this life we have only desire and hunger: desire to follow the right path, and hunger to reach our final destination. This desire makes us run along the way, the road cemented by Christ crucified. For if we had no love for God as our destination, we would have no concern for wanting to know the way.

I want you, then, to have an ever greater true holy desire to follow this way, the road that will bring you to your destination. Know that this road is not dark and gloomy or overgrown with thorns. It is lighted by the true light, Jesus Christ, who cemented this road with his own blood. There are no thorns here because this road is fragrant with a profusion of flowers and delicious fruits—so much so that once a person sets out along that pleasant roadway, she experiences such delight there that she would rather die than deliberately leave it. And though thorns may appear on this road (the seeming thorns of the devil's frequent annoyances and deceits), and though the world may flaunt itself before us with its inflated pride, yet I say the soul who finds her delight on this road is not bothered by these things. Rather she does as one who goes to a rosebush and picks the rose, letting the thorns be. So she leaves behind the troubles and anxieties of the world and picks the fragrant rose of true holy patience, setting before her mind's eye the life-giving blood of the Lamb, set before us on this road.

So run, mother! And let all true faithful Christians run to this blood, attracted by its fragrance. Then we will get really drunk on this blood, afire and consumed in gentle divine charity, made one with him. We will be like a heavy drinker, who thinks not of himself but only of the wine he has drunk and of what he still has left to drink. Get drunk on the blood of Christ crucified! Don't let yourself die of thirst when you have it right there before you! And don't take just a little, but enough to make you so drunk that you will lose yourself. Love yourself not selfishly but for God's sake. Love other people not for their sake but only for the praise and glory of God's name. Love God not for your own sake, for your own profit, but love him for his sake, because he is the highest Good and is worthy of being loved. Then your love will be perfect and not mercenary. You will be unable to think of anything except Christ crucified and the wine you have drunk—that is, the perfect charity which you see God has shown and given you before the creation of the world, since he was in love with you before you even came to be. If he had not so fallen in love with you he would never have created you. But because of the love he had for you as he saw you within himself, he was moved to grant you being. How your thoughts will be stretched when you drink this charity! I mean you will be thinking about what there is still to drink, eagerly desiring to taste and possess the supreme eternal beauty of God.

ARMOR AGAINST EVIL

From a letter (T148) to Pietro del Monte Santa Maria of Siena (summer 1375)

Pietro del Monte Santa Maria was one of the leading citizens of Siena. In this letter Catherine plays upon the traditionally "masculine" virtues (courage, boldness, etc.) to urge Pietro to be a knight for Christ on the spiritual battlefield.

In the name of Jesus Christ crucified and of gentle Mary.

Very revered and dearest father and son in Christ gentle Jesus,

I Caterina, servant and slave of the servants of Jesus Christ, am writing to you in the precious blood of God's Son. I long to see you a courageous and fearless knight. A man who knows he is well armed ought not be afraid. Oh dearest son, we see that God has equipped us with armor so strong that it cannot be pierced by the devil or anyone else. That armor is our free will, and this is the freedom God refers to when he says, "I created you without your help, but I will not save you without your help."

Now God wants us to make use of the armor he has given us; he wants us to deflect with it the blows our enemies inflict on us. We have three specific enemies: the world, the flesh, and the devil. But let's not be afraid, because divine providence has outfitted us so well that we have no reason for fear. Our armor is good, and our helper the best. For our helper is God, and he is such that no one can withstand him. As long as we continue to look to this strong loving helper, we cannot be weakened by the thought of our own frailty. It seems this is what that dear lover Paul saw when he said, "I can do all things in Christ crucified, who is in me and strengthens me." For when Paul felt the annoyance and pricking of the flesh, he found strength not in himself, because he knew he was weak, but in Christ Jesus. It was because of Christ Jesus and that fine strong armor God had given him, his strong freedom, that he could say, "I can do all things." For neither the devil nor anyone else can force me to commit a single deadly sin against my will. We can never be overcome unless we give up this armor and turn it over to the devil by our willing consent. The temptations and wiles of the devils, the flesh, and the world may come shooting poisoned arrows—the flesh with ugly thoughts and sensations, the devil with his assorted temptations and deceit and trickery, the world with its pretentiousness and pride. But unless lady freedom consents to these disordered suggestions, she never sins, because sin is in the will alone. And God has given us this as a favor, not as our due.

I don't want you to be afraid, no matter what you may experience, my dear son in Christ Jesus, because God has so favored us that he himself is our helper, and he has given us good armor. Even more: he was in the end dead yet victorious on the battlefield—dead because he died on the wood of the most holy cross, victorious because by his death he gave us life. He returned to the city of his eternal Father with his spouse as his spoils, I mean with our souls, whom God espoused when he took our human nature. Well may we focus our mind's eye, wide open, on such a fire of love! Our enemies have been conquered! We have been snatched from the hands of the devils who possessed us and held our souls as their own. Christ conquered the world and pride by stooping down to our humanity. And the flesh has been conquered by his enduring suffering and disgrace, insults and wrongs, torments and ridicule, abuse and death for us. So we may well be encouraged, since our enemies have been conquered!

Let us follow in his footsteps, driving out vice by virtue: pride by humility, impatience by patience, injustice by justice, impurity by perfect chastity and continence, vainglory by God's honor and glory—so that whatever we do and accomplish may be for the glory, praise, honor, and spread of our Jesus' name. Let a sweet holy war be waged against these vices!

CLOTHED IN THE FIRE OF LOVE

From a letter (T108) to Monna Giovanna di Capo
and Francesca in Siena (late 1375)

Giovanna and Francesca were two of the Mantellate of Siena. Catherine urges them to increase their devotion until they are consumed in the fire of divine love.

In the name of Jesus Christ crucified and of gentle Mary.

My dearest and very loved daughters,

I Caterina, servant and slave of the servants of Jesus Christ, am writing to you in his precious blood. I long to see you so thoroughly ablaze and consumed in the fire of divine charity that all selfish love, all coldheartedness, all spiritual darkness must be driven out. What is divine charity like? It is always working, never gets tired. It is like the money lender, always making a profit on time: if he sleeps, he is making a profit; if he eats, he is making a profit. Whatever he does, he is making a profit; he never wastes time. It isn't the money lender who does the work; it is his treasure, time. This is how the loving spouse of Christ acts when she is ablaze with divine charity: she is always making a profit, and is never idle. She sleeps and charity does the work. Eating, sleeping, keeping vigil — everything she does is fruitful for her. Oh charity, full of joy! You are a mother nourishing the virtues as children at your breast. You are rich beyond all wealth, so rich that the soul clothed in you cannot be poor. You give her your beauty because you make her one with you. For, as Saint John says, God is charity, and those who live in charity live in God, and God lives in them.

Oh dearest daughters, my soul's gladness and joy, consider your excellence and dignity, which you received from God through this mother charity! For God's love for his creatures was so strong that it moved him to draw us out of himself and give us, us, his own image and likeness—just so we might experience and enjoy him, and share in his eternal beauty. He did not make us animals without memory or understanding, but gave us memory to hold fast his benefits, and understanding to comprehend his supreme eternal will—his will that seeks nothing else but that we be made holy. And he gave us our will to love that will of his.

The will of the Word wants us to follow him on the way of the most holy cross by enduring every pain, abuse, insult, and reproach for Christ crucified, who is in us to strengthen us. And as soon as our understanding's eye perceives this, our will gets up at once. Warmed by the fire of this mother charity, it runs to love what God loves and hate what God hates, wanting to seek and desire and clothe itself in nothing but God's eternal will. Once we have seen and understood that God wants only our good, we see that it is God's will and pleasure to be followed on the way of the cross. We rejoice and are content with whatever God permits: sickness or poverty, insult or abuse, intolerable or unreasonable commands. We rejoice and are glad in everything, and we see that God permits these things for our profit and perfection. I'm not surprised that we are, then, free from suffering, since we have shed the cause of suffering — I mean self-will grounded in self-centeredness — and have put on God's will grounded in charity.

If you should say to me, "Mother, how shall we clothe ourselves?" I answer, "With hatred and with love." For love makes us put on love. It is just like a person who changes clothes, who is quick to take off old clothes in dislike for them, and with love put on new ones. My daughters, is it really the clothes the person is putting on? No, it is love, because clothes wouldn't get changed of their own accord. The person had to choose them out of love. And this hatred — where can we get it? Only from knowledge of ourselves, from recognizing that we are nothing. This is what banishes all pride and infuses true humility. This knowledge lets us discover the light and the generosity of God's goodness and boundless charity. This is not hidden from us. It was, of course, hidden to our coarseness until the Word, God's only-begotten Son, became incarnate. But once he had chosen to be our brother, clothing himself in the coarseness of our humanity, it was revealed to us. Then he was lifted up so that the fire of love might be revealed to all people and their hearts be attracted by love's power. So it is certainly true that love transforms and makes the beloved one with the lover.

So be eager, my daughters, to reach out with arms of love to seize and store away in your memory what your understanding has grasped. This is how God's desire and mine for you will be fulfilled. I mean I shall see you ablaze and consumed, clothed in the fire of divine charity. See to it, please do, that you nourish yourselves on blood, so that our time may come soon.

Don't be surprised that we haven't come. We will come soon, if it so pleases divine Goodness. I have delayed my coming a bit for the sake of a certain service to the Church and because the holy father wanted it. I beg you, I command you all, daughters and sons, to pray, to offer holy prayers and fervent desires to God for holy Church for she is much persecuted. I'll say no more. Keep living in God's holy and tender love.

Gentle Jesus! Jesus love!

The Cell of Self-Knowledge

From a letter (T241) to Monna Giovanna di Corrado
From Maconi in Siena (summer 1376)

Giovanna was the mother of one of Catherine's disciples, Stefano Maconi. Stefano went with Catherine to Avignon. Apparently Giovanna wrote to protest this separation from her son. Catherine responded by urging her to go beyond her motherly love to true love for God, a love she could find only in the "cell of self-knowledge."

In the name of Jesus Christ crucified and of gentle Mary.

Dearest mother in Christ gentle Jesus,

I Caterina, servant and slave of the servants of Jesus Christ, am writing to you in his precious blood. I long to see you making your home in the cell of self-knowledge, so that you may attain perfect love, for I know that we cannot please our Creator unless we love him, because he is love and wants nothing but love. If we do know ourselves we find this love. Why? Because we see our own nothingness, that our very existence is ours by grace and not because we have a right to it, and every grace beyond our existence as well—it is all given to us with boundless love. Then we discover so much of God's goodness poured out on us that words cannot describe it. And once we see ourselves so loved by God, we cannot help loving him. And within ourselves we love God and our rationality, and hate the sensuality that would take inordinate pleasure in the world.

Some people delight in wealth or status, or would rather please creatures than the Creator. These build their foundation in worldly appearance, pleasure, and enjoyment. Then there are some who love their children or spouse or mother or father excessively, with too sensual a love. Such a love gets between their soul and God and keeps them from a clear knowledge of the truth of real heavenly love. This is why gentle First Truth said, "Unless you leave father and mother, sisters and brothers, and your very self, you are not worthy of me." God's true servants have always been very conscious of this, and quickly strip their heart, soul, and affection of the world and its pleasures and ostentation, and of loving anyone apart from God. Not that they don't love other people, but they love them only for God's sake, as creatures boundlessly loved by their Creator. But just as they hate in themselves the sensuality that rebels against God, so they hate this in their neighbors, for they see that it offends supreme eternal Good.

Here is what I want you to do, dearest mother in Christ gentle Jesus: to love God's goodness within yourself, and his immeasurable charity, which you will find in the cell of self-knowledge. In this cell you will find God. For just as God holds within himself everything that shares in being, so you will find within yourself memory, which holds and is well-suited to hold the treasure of God's blessing. There too you will find understanding, which makes us sharers in the wisdom of God's Son by understanding and knowing his will, a will that wants nothing but that we be made holy. When we see this, our soul cannot be sad or shaken, no matter what happens, for we know that everything is done with God's providence and tremendous love.

I want you, I beg you for love of the slain Lamb, to use this knowledge to assuage the grief and heartache you have felt because of Stefano's departure. Be glad; be happy! For this will surely make his soul and yours grow in grace. And by God's grace you will see him soon.

Getting back to self-knowledge: I tell you, you will also find there the gentle mercy of the Holy Spirit, the aspect of God that gives and is nothing but love. Whatever the Spirit does is done because of love. And this movement of love you will find within your own soul, because our will is nothing but love, and its every affection and movement comes from nothing but love. It loves or hates whatever the eye of understanding has seen and understood. How true it is then, dearest mother, that within the cell of your soul you will find the whole of God. And he bestows such sweetness, refreshment, and consolation that no matter what may happen we cannot be shaken, because we have been made big enough to hold God's own will. How? By getting rid of all selfish love, by getting rid of everything that is not God's will.

Then right away our soul is transformed into a garden filled with fragrant blossoms of holy desire.

And in the center of the garden is planted the tree of the most holy cross, the resting place of the spotless Lamb. He bathes and waters this glorious garden, irrigating it with his blood; and he himself bears the mature fruit of true solid virtues. If you want patience, he is the bedrock of meekness, since not a murmur of complaint was heard from the Lamb. He is the bedrock of deep humility, since God stooped down to humanity, and the Word stooped to the shameful death of the cross. If you want charity, he is that charity—and even more, for it was the power of love and charity that kept him nailed fast to the cross. The cross and nails could never have held the God-Man, had not the power of charity held him. I'm not surprised that those who make of themselves a garden through self-knowledge are strong in the face of the whole world, for they are conformed and made one with supreme strength. They truly begin in this life to have a foretaste of eternal life. They control the world by making light of it. The devils are afraid to get near a soul on fire with divine charity.

So up, dearest mother! I don't want you sleeping any more in irresponsibility and sensual love. No, with a boundless blazing love get up and take a bath in Christ's blood, hide in the wounds of Christ crucified. I'll say no more. I'm sure that if you live in the cell I've been talking about you will discover none other than Christ crucified. And tell Corrado to do the same. Keep living in God's holy and tender love.

Gentle Jesus! Jesus love!

PRAYER

From a letter (T353) to Monna Catella and others in Naples (spring 1379)

Little is known of the group of women to whom this letter was addressed. Catherine wrote a similar letter to a niece about the same time, so perhaps it is general advice she felt moved to send to various disciples. In this section, she talks about various kinds of prayer.

There are three ways of praying. The first is that abiding holy desire which prays to God in everything we creatures do, for it directs all our spiritual and bodily actions in his honor, and so is called continuous. The glorious Saint Paul seems to have meant this kind of prayer when he said: "Pray without ceasing." Then there is vocal prayer, as when the tongue is used in reciting the Office or other vocal prayers. This is a preparation for the third kind of prayer, namely mental, which the soul comes to when it practices vocal prayer prudently and humbly; that is when, as the tongue prays, the heart is not far from God.

But one must endeavor to establish the heart firmly in a love for divine Charity. And whenever one feels God visiting one's mind, drawing it in some way to think of the Creator, one should stop praying vocally and rest lovingly in whatever one feels this visitation to be. If there is still time when this has passed, the soul should resume its vocal prayer so that the mind will always be full and not empty. And even if the prayer abounds in battles of all kinds, in darkness and great confusion of mind, with the devil suggesting that our prayer is not pleasing to God, we must not give up prayer on this account, but persist with fortitude and unfailing perseverance, realizing that this is the devil's way of enticing us away from our mother, prayer; and that God permits this to test in us our fortitude and constancy and also so that, in the struggles and darkness, we may know our own nothingness, while in the good will that we perceive in ourselves we know the goodness of God, who gives and upholds our good and holy desires, and will not refuse this gift to those who ask him.

The soul thus comes to the third and last kind of fully mental prayer, in which it receives the fruit of the efforts it has put into the less perfect vocal prayer, for it now savors the milk of fidelity to prayer. It lifts itself above the crude level of feeling and with the mind as of an angel is made one with God by love; by the light of its understanding it sees, knows and is clothed with the Truth. Made now sister to the angels, seated with the Bridegroom at the table of crucified desire, it delights in seeking God's honor and the salvation of souls for which, it now sees clearly, the eternal Bridegroom ran to meet the shameful death of the cross and, in so doing, obeyed his Father's will and achieved our salvation. Such prayer is indeed a mother, conceiving her children, the virtues, in God's love, and giving birth to them in love for others. Where do you find the light that guides you in the way of truth? In prayer. And where do you display love, faith, hope and humility? Again, in prayer. You would not be doing these things unless you loved them, and it is because a creature loves that it seeks to be one with the thing it loves, that is, with God. By prayer you ask him for what you need. Knowing yourself — and true prayer is founded on this knowledge — you see you are in great need and feel surrounded by your enemies: the world with its hurts; the devil, with all his temptations; and the flesh, ever warring against the spirit by rebelling against reason. You see, too, that of yourself you are not; and since you are not, you cannot help yourself; so you turn with faith, to him who IS; who knows your needs and can and will help you in them. You ask with hope, then wait for his help. This is how we must pray if we are to get what we desire. No right thing will ever be denied us if we ask the divine Goodness for it in this way, but we would get very little benefit from praying in any other.

Where shall we sense the fragrance of obedience, if not in prayer? Where strip ourselves of the self-love that makes us impatient when insulted or made to suffer? Or put on a divine love that will make us patient, and ready to glory in the cross of Christ crucified? In prayer. And where shall we sense the sweet perfume of virginity and purity, and a hunger for martyrdom that will make us ready to give our lives for the honor of God and the salvation of souls? In this sweet mother, prayer. She will make us obey God's holy commandments, and seal her counsels into our hearts and minds by imprinting on us the desire to keep them until death. She withdraws us from the company of creatures and gives us the Creator as companion. She fills the vessel of our heart with the blood of the humble spotless Lamb and clothes it in Fire, for by the fire of Love was it shed.

 LOVE AND SERVICE

From *Dialogue*, Chapter 7

The Dialogue *is Catherine's only book, a summary of all her teaching, presented as a dialogue between an ardent soul and God. At least the core of the book was dictated while Catherine was caught up in ecstatic prayer. The soul begins with a series of questions and occasionally offers a prayer of thanksgiving, but in most of the book, including all but the last of these selections, God is the speaker. Here God speaks about service to neighbors. Note that Catherine always refers to the soul as "she."*

The soul sees that she can become grateful and acceptable to me in no other way than by conceiving hatred of sin and love of virtue. When she has thus conceived by the affection of love, she immediately gives birth to fruit for her neighbors. There is no other way that can she act out the truth she has conceived in herself except by loving me in truth. And in the same truth, she serves her neighbors.

And it cannot be otherwise because love of me and love of her neighbors are one and the same thing. So far as the soul loves me, she loves her neighbors because love toward them issues from me. This is the means that I have given you, so that you may exercise and prove your virtue. Since you can do me no service, you should do it to your neighbors. This proves that you possess me by grace in your soul: bearing much fruit for your neighbors and making prayers to me, seeking with sweet and loving desire my honor and the salvation of souls. The soul that is enamored of my truth never ceases to serve the whole world, both in general and in particular cases, according to the situation of the recipient and the ardent desire of the donor. As I showed you earlier, the endurance of suffering alone, without desire, was not enough to atone for sin.

When she has discovered the advantage of this unitive love in me, by means of which she truly loves herself, she extends her desire to the salvation of the whole world and seeks to come to the aid of its neediness. Just as she has done good to herself by the conception of virtue, from which she has drawn the life of grace, now she strives to fix her eye on the needs of her neighbor in particular. So when, through the affection of love, she has discovered the state of all rational creatures in general, she helps those who are at hand, according to the various graces that I have entrusted to her to administer. One she helps with doctrine, that is, with words, giving sincere counsel without any respect of persons. She helps another with the example of a good life. Indeed all can give their neighbors this much: the edification of a holy and honorable life. These virtues and many others—too many to list—are brought forth in the love of the neighbor. I have given them in different ways, that is to say not all to one, but to one, one virtue, and to another, another. But really it is impossible to have one, without having them all, because all the virtues are bound together. Understand, then, that in many cases I give one virtue, to be like the chief of the others. That is to say, to one I will give principally love, to another justice, to another humility, to one a lively faith, to another prudence or temperance or patience, to another fortitude. I place these and many other virtues in the souls of many creatures. So it happens that the particular one so placed in the soul becomes the principal object of its virtue. The soul disposes herself to this rather than to other virtues for her primary rule of conduct. By the effect of this virtue, the soul draws to herself all the other virtues, since they are all bound together in the affection of love. So it is with many gifts and graces of virtue—not only in the case of spiritual things but also of temporal. I use the word *temporal* for the things necessary to the physical life. All these I have given so that no one soul should have them all. Therefore you must show love, at least in material things, for one another. I could easily have created people possessed of all that they should need for both body and soul. But I wish one to have need of the other so that they should all be my ministers to administer the graces and the gifts that they have received from me. Whether they will or not, they cannot help making an act of love. It is true, however, that unless that act is made through love of me, it does them no good so far as grace is concerned.

Love and Service — 39

See, then, that I have made people my ministers and placed them in various stations and ranks so that they may make use of the virtue of love. In my house are many mansions. I wish for nothing other than love, for love of me is fulfilled and completed in the love of the neighbors, and in this love the law is observed. For only those who are bound to me with this love can be of use, whatever their state of life.

 THE BRIDGE

From *Dialogue*, Chapter 26

The central image in the Dialogue *is of Christ as a Bridge connecting earth and heaven, crossing the river that human sin has caused to divide the two. People reach the Bridge by three steps that Catherine compares at various times to Christ's feet, wounded side, and mouth; to human memory, intellect, and will; and to stages of spiritual growth, which Catherine calls the imperfect, the perfect, and the more perfect.*

I will now explain to you the nature of this Bridge. I have told you, my daughter, that the Bridge reaches from heaven to earth. It does this through the union I have made with humanity, whom I formed of the clay of the earth. Now learn that this Bridge, my only begotten Son, has three steps. Two were made with the wood of the most holy cross, and the third still retains the great bitterness he tasted when he was given gall and vinegar to drink. In these three steps you will recognize three states of the soul, which I will explain to you below. The feet of the soul, signifying her affection, are the first step, for the feet carry the body as the affection carries the soul. So my Son's pierced feet are steps by which you can arrive at his side. His side shows you the secret of his heart because the soul, rising on the steps of her affection, commences to taste the love of his heart by gazing into that open heart of my Son with the eye of the intellect and finds it consumed with unspeakable love. I say consumed because he does not love you for his own benefit. You can be of no benefit to him, since he is one and the same thing with me. Then the soul is filled with love, seeing herself so much loved. Having passed the second step, the soul reaches out to the third. This is to the mouth, where she finds peace from the terrible war she has been waging with her sin. On the first step, then, lifting her feet from the affections of the earth, the soul strips herself of vice. On the second she fills herself with love and virtue. And on the third she tastes peace. So the Bridge has three steps, so that by climbing past the first and the second, you may reach the last. This is lifted high so that the water running beneath may not touch it. That is, there was no venom of sin touching my Son. This Bridge is lifted high and yet, at the same time, joined to the earth. Do you know when it was lifted high? When my Son was lifted up on the wood of the most holy cross. His divine nature remained joined to the lowliness of the earth of your humanity.

For this reason I said to you that even when he was lifted high, he was not lifted out of the earth. The divine nature is united and kneaded into one thing with it. And there was no one who could go on the Bridge until it had been lifted high. That is why he said, "If I am lifted high I will draw all things to me." When my goodness saw that in no other way could you be drawn to me, I sent him so that he should be lifted high on the wood of the cross. I made of it an anvil on which my Son, born of human generation, could be remade. I did this to free you from death and to restore you to the life of grace. And so he drew everything to himself by this means: by showing the unspeakable love with which I love you. For the human heart is always attracted by love. Greater love, then, I could not show you than to lay down my life for you. So my Son had to be treated in this way by love so that ignorant people should be unable to resist being drawn to me.

In very truth, then, my Son said that when he was lifted high, he would draw all things to himself. And this is to be understood in two ways. First, when the human heart is drawn by the affection of love, as I have said, it is drawn together with all the powers of his soul—with the memory, the intellect, and the will. Now, when these three powers are harmoniously joined together in my name, all the other operations that the soul performs—whether in deed or thought— are pleasing. They are joined together by the effect of love because love is lifted on high, following the sorrowful Crucified One. So my Truth said well, "If I am lifted high I will draw all things to me." If the heart and the powers of the soul are drawn to him, all the actions are also drawn to him. Second, everything has been created for the service of humanity, to serve the necessities of rational creatures. The rational creatures have not been made for them but for me, to serve me with all their hearts and with all their affection. See, then, that when you are drawn, everything else is drawn with you because everything else has been made for you. It was therefore necessary that the Bridge should be lifted on high and have steps, so that it might be climbed more easily.

RIVER AND THORNS

From *Dialogue*, Chapter 44

Here God speaks of how Satan tempts souls to avoid the Bridge—and so drown in the river. In another metaphor, these souls are scared away from the Tree of Life for fear of thorns that seem to surround it.

I have told you that the devil invites people to the water of death since that is what he himself has. Blinding them with the pleasures and conditions of the world, he catches them with the hook of pleasure under the pretense of good. There is no other way could he catch them, for they would not allow themselves to be caught if they saw that they would get no good or pleasure from it. The soul naturally always desires the good. But indeed the soul, blinded by self-love, does not know and discern what is truly good and profitable to the soul and to the body. So the devil, seeing them blinded by self-love, evilly places before them various kinds of delights, colored so as to have the appearance of some benefit or good. He gives to all according to their condition and those principal vices to which he sees them to be most disposed. He gives one kind to the laity, another to the religious, and others to priests and noblemen, according to their different conditions. I have told you this because I now speak to you of those who drown themselves in the river and care for nothing but themselves. They love themselves to my injury. Now I will tell you their end.

I want to show you how they deceive themselves and how, wishing to flee troubles, they fall into them. Because it seems to them that following me — that is, walking by the way of the Bridge, the Word, my Son — is great toil, they draw back. They fear the thorns because they are blinded and do not know or see the truth. You know that I showed you this in the beginning of your life, when you prayed for me to have mercy on the world and draw it out of the darkness of mortal sin. You know that I then showed you myself under the figure of a tree, of which you saw neither the bottom nor the top. You could not see that the roots were united with the earth of your humanity. At the foot of the tree, if you remember well, there was a certain thorn. All those who loved their own sensuality kept away from it. Instead, they ran to a mountain of chaff that you recognized as a figure for all the delights of the world. That chaff mountain seemed to be of wheat. But it was not, and so, as you saw, many souls died of hunger on it. Many others recognized the deceits of the world and returned to the tree and passed the thorns, which is the decision of the will. Before this decision is made, it is a thorn that appears to stand in the way of following the truth. Conscience always fights on one side and sensuality on the other. But as soon as they, with hatred and displeasure toward themselves, bravely make up their minds, saying, "I wish to follow Christ crucified," they immediately break through the thorns and find inestimable sweetness, as I showed you then. Some find more and some less, according to their disposition and desire. And you know that then I said to you, "I am your God, unmoving and unchangeable. I do not draw away from any creature who wants to come to me."

I have shown them the truth, making myself visible to them. I have shown them what it is to love anything apart from me. But they, as if blinded by the fog of disordered love, know neither me nor themselves. You see how deceived they are. They choose to die of hunger rather than to pass a little thorn bush. But they cannot escape enduring pain. No one can pass through this life without a cross. How much less those who travel by the lower way! Not that my servants pass without pain. But their pain is eased. And because—by sin, as I said to you above—the world brings forth thorns and tribulations, and because this river flows with tempestuous waters, I gave you the Bridge, so that you might not be drowned.

BEGINNING TO CLIMB

From *Dialogue*, Chapters 59–60

In this selection, God explains the three steps as stages in the spiritual life. They are described here as imperfect, perfect, and more perfect and seem to correspond with the more traditional stages of purgation, enlightenment, and union. Here the emphasis is on the pitfalls of the first two stages.

I told you that no one could go by the Bridge or come out of the river without climbing the three steps. This is the truth. There are some who climb imperfectly, and some perfectly, and some climb with the greatest perfection. The first are those who are moved by slavish fear. Though they have climbed this far, they are imperfectly gathered together. That is to say, the soul has seen the punishment that follows her sin. So she climbs and gathers together her memory to recollect her vice, her intellect to see the punishment she expects to receive for her fault, and her will to move her to hate that fault. Let us consider this to be the first step and the first gathering together of the powers of the soul. It should be taken by the light of the intellect. The mind's eye, whose pupil is holy faith, looks not only at the punishment of sin, but at the fruit of virtue and the love that I bear to the soul. So she may climb with love and affection, stripped of slavish fear. In doing so, such souls will become faithful and not unfaithful servants. They serve me through love and not through fear. If, with hatred of sin, they employ their minds to dig out the root of their self-love with prudence, constancy, and perseverance, they will succeed in doing so. But there are many who begin their course climbing so slowly and render their debt to me by such small degrees and with such negligence and ignorance that they suddenly faint. Every little breeze catches their sails and turns their prow backward. Since they imperfectly climb to the first step of the Bridge of Christ crucified, they do not arrive at the second step of his heart.

There are some who have become faithful servants, serving me with fidelity and love rather than slavish fear of punishment. But if they serve me with a view to their own profit or the delight and pleasure that they find in me, even this love is imperfect. Do you know what proves the imperfection of this love? The withdrawal of the consolations that they found in me, and the insufficiency and short duration of their love for their neighbor. It grows weak bit by bit and sometimes disappears. Their love toward me grows weak when, on occasion, in order to test them in virtue and raise them above their imperfection, I withdraw my consolation from their minds and allow them to fall into battles and confusion. I do this so that they may come to perfect self-knowledge and know that they are nothing and have no grace of themselves. Accordingly in time of battle they will fly to me, their benefactor, seeking me alone with true humility. That is why I treat them this way, withdrawing consolation from them indeed but not grace. At such a time these weak ones of whom I speak relax their energy and impatiently turn backward. Sometimes they abandon many of their exercises and call this virtue. They say to themselves, *This labor does me no good.* They do all this because they feel themselves deprived of mental consolation. Such a soul acts imperfectly, for she has not yet unwound the bandage of spiritual self-love. Had she unwound it she would see that, in truth, everything comes from me. No leaf of a tree falls to the ground without my providence, and what I give and promise to my creatures, I give and promise to them for their sanctification. This is the good and the end for which I created them. My creatures should see and know that I wish nothing but their good, through the blood of my only begotten Son, in which they are washed from their iniquities. By this blood they are enabled to know my truth: how, in order to give them eternal life, I created them in my image and likeness and re-created them by grace with the blood of my Son, making them my children by adoption. But since they are imperfect, they make use of me only for their own benefit, relaxing their love for their neighbor. So those in the first state come to nothing through the fear of enduring pain. Those in the second also come to nothing because they slacken their pace, cease to render service to their neighbor, and withdraw their charity if they see their own profit or consolation withdrawn from them. This happens because their love was originally impure. They gave to their neighbor the same imperfect love that they gave to me: a love based only on desire for their own advantage. If, through a desire for perfection, they do not recognize their imperfection, it is impossible that they should not turn back. For those who desire eternal life, a pure love without any selfish regard is necessary. It is not enough for eternal life to fly from sin out of fear of punishment or to embrace virtue from the motive of one's own advantage. Sin should be abandoned because it is displeasing to me, and virtue should be loved for my sake.

fROM VOCAL TO MENTAL PRAYER

From *Dialogue*, Chapter 66

In this selection, God speaks of the need to go beyond saying written or memorized prayers (vocal prayer) to prayer that comes from one's own heart and mind (mental prayer). Only such prayer can truly stir and illuminate the soul.

Do not think that the soul receives such ardor and nourishment from prayer if she prays only vocally, as do many souls whose prayers are words rather than love. These only care about completing psalms and saying many Our Fathers. Once they have completed their appointed tally, they do not appear to think of anything further. They seem to place devout attention and love in merely vocal recitation. The soul is not required to do this. And in doing only this she bears but little fruit, and that pleases me very little. But if you ask me whether the soul should abandon vocal prayer (since it does not seem to all that they are called to mental prayer), I should reply, "No." The soul should advance step by step. I know well that, just as the soul is at first imperfect and afterward perfect, so it is with her prayer also. She should still continue in vocal prayer while she is imperfect, so as not to fall into idleness. But she should not say her vocal prayers without joining them to mental prayer. That is, while she is reciting she should endeavor to raise her mind in my love, considering her own sins and the blood of my only begotten Son, in which she finds the breadth of my charity and the remission of her sins. She should do this so that self-knowledge and the consideration of her defects will make her recognize my goodness in herself and continue her exercises with true humility. I do not wish sins to be considered in particular but in general so that the mind may not be contaminated by the remembrance of particular and hideous sins. But, as I said, I do not wish the soul to consider her sins, either in general or in particular, without also remembering the blood and the broadness of my mercy. Otherwise she might be brought to confusion. And together with confusion would come the devil, who has caused it, under guise of remorse and displeasure for sin. So she would arrive at eternal damnation, not only on account of her confusion, but also through the despair that would come to her because she did not seize the arm of my mercy.

The soul, therefore, should season the knowledge of herself with the knowledge of my goodness. Then vocal prayer will be of use to the soul who makes it, and pleasing to me. And she will arrive from the vocal imperfect prayer, exercised with perseverance, at perfect mental prayer. But if she simply aims at completing her tally and abandons mental prayer for vocal, she will never arrive at it. Sometimes I may visit the soul's mind, sometimes in one way, and sometimes in another, in a flash of self-knowledge or of contrition for sin, sometimes in the broadness of my charity. Sometimes I may place the presence of my truth before her mind, in various ways and according to my pleasure and the desire of the soul. But the soul will be so ignorant that, having resolved to say so many prayers vocally, she will abandon my visitation (that she feels by conscience), rather than abandon what she had begun. She should not do so, for, in so doing, she yields to a deception of the devil. The moment she feels her mind disposed by my visitation (in the many ways I have told you), she should abandon vocal prayer. Then when my visitation is past and if there is time, she can resume the vocal prayers that she had resolved to say. But if she has not time to complete them, she ought not on that account to be troubled or suffer annoyance and confusion of mind.

You see, then, that perfect prayer is reached not through many words, but through affection of desire. The soul raises herself to me with knowledge of herself and of my mercy, each one adding to the flavor of the other. Thus she will engage in both mental and vocal prayer. For just as the active and contemplative life are one, so are they. Of course, vocal or mental prayer can be understood in many different ways. I have told you that a holy desire is a continual prayer. A good and holy will disposes itself with desire to the occasion actually appointed for prayer in addition to the continual prayer of holy desire itself. So vocal prayer will be made at the appointed time by the soul who remains firm in a habitual holy will. Sometimes it will even be continued beyond the appointed time, as love commands for the salvation of others (if the soul sees them to be in need), and also her own necessities according to the state in which I have placed her. Each soul, according to her condition, ought to exert herself for the salvation of souls, for this exercise lies at the root of a holy will. Whatever she may contribute, by words or deeds, toward the salvation of her neighbors is virtually a prayer. This is what my glorious standard-bearer Paul said, in the words, "Whoever does not stop working does not stop praying." It was for this reason that I told you that prayer was made in many ways, that is, that actual prayer may be united with mental prayer if made with the affection of love. And this love is itself continual prayer.

GOING ON TO PERFECTION

From *Dialogue*, Chapters 99–100

Here the discussion moves to the third stage of spiritual growth, as the soul moves to ever greater perfection and union with God. This means moving from the light of reason that sees the transitory nature of the world to the light of faith that sees God's love and goodness. Here, too, there are pitfalls.

When the soul has attained this general light, of which I have spoken, she should not remain contented. As long as you are pilgrims in this life, you are capable of growth. Whoever does not go forward, by that very fact is turning back. The soul should either grow in the general light, which she has acquired through my grace, or anxiously strive to attain to the second and perfect light, leaving the imperfect and reaching the perfect. For if the soul truly has light, it will wish to arrive at perfection. In this second perfect light are to be found two kinds of perfection—for those who have abandoned the general way of living of the world may be called perfect. One perfection is that of those who give themselves completely to subduing bodily desires by doing great and severe penance. These, in order that their sensuality may not rebel against their reason, have placed their desire rather in the mortification of the body than in the destruction of their self-will, as I have explained to you in another place. They feed their souls at the table of penance and are good and perfect, if their penance is illuminated by discretion and founded on me — that is, if they act with true knowledge of themselves and of me, with great humility, and are wholly conformed to the judgment of my will, and not to the human will's judgment. But if they were not thus clothed with my will and in true humility, they would often offend against their own perfection, esteeming themselves the judges of those who do not walk in the same path. Do you know why this would happen to them? Because they have placed all their labor and desire in the mortification of the body rather than in the destruction of their own will.

Such as these wish always to choose their own times and places and consolations, after their own fashion, and also the persecutions of the world and of the devil. They cheat themselves with the delusion of their own "spiritual" self-will when they say, "I wish to have that consolation, and not these battles, or these temptations of the devil, not, indeed, for my own pleasure, but in order to please God more and in order to hold him more in my soul through grace. It seems to me that I should possess him more and serve him better in that way than in this." And this is the way the soul often falls into trouble and becomes tedious and unbearable to herself. In this way she injures her own perfection. She still does not perceive this injury or that the stench of pride lurks within her. And there she lies.

Now if the soul were not in this condition but were truly humble and not presumptuous, she would be illuminated to see that I, the First Sweet Truth, grant condition and time and place and consolations and tribulations as they may be needed for your salvation and to complete the perfection I have chosen for the soul. And she would see that I give everything through love. Therefore, she should receive everything with love and reverence. That is what the souls in the second state do. By doing this, they arrive at the third state. I will now speak to you about them, explaining to you the nature of these two states, which stand in the most perfect light.

The third state immediately follows the last, and those who belong to it and have arrived at this glorious light are perfect in every condition in which they may be. They receive every event that I permit to happen to them with due reverence, as I have mentioned to you when speaking of the third and unitive state of the soul. These deem themselves worthy of the troubles and stumbling blocks caused them by the world and of the privation of their own consolation and indeed of whatever circumstance happens to them. Since they deem themselves worthy of trouble, so also do they deem themselves unworthy of the fruit, which they receive after their trouble. In the light they have known and tasted my eternal will that wishes nothing else but your good and gives and permits these troubles so that you should be sanctified in me. So the soul that has known my will clothes herself with it and fixes her attention on nothing else except seeing in what way she can preserve and increase her perfection to the glory and praise of my name. She opens the eye of her intellect and fixes it in the light of faith upon Christ crucified, my only begotten Son. She loves and follows his teaching, which is the rule of the road for perfect and imperfect alike. And see how my Truth, the Lamb, who became enamored of her when he saw her, gives the soul the doctrine of perfection. She knows what this perfection is since she has seen it practiced by the sweet and amorous Word, my only begotten Son, who was fed at the table of holy desire, seeking honor and your salvation from me, the eternal Father. And inflamed with this desire, he ran with great eagerness to the shameful death of the Cross, and accomplished the obedience that was imposed on him by me, his Father. He did not shun labors or insults or withdraw on account of your ingratitude or ignorance of so great a benefit or because of the persecutions of the Jews or on account of the insults, derision, grumbling, and shouting of the people. But all this he passed through like the true captain and knight that he was. For I had placed him on the battlefield to deliver you from the hands of the devil so that you might be set free and drawn out of the most terrible slavery in which you could ever be and also to teach you his road, his doctrine, and his rule. In this way you might open the door of me, Eternal Life, with the key of his precious blood, shed with such fire of love and such hatred of your sins. It was as if the sweet and loving Word, my Son, had said to you: "Behold, I have made the road and opened the door with my blood." So do not be negligent to follow, laying yourselves down to rest in self-love and ignorance of the road, presuming to choose to serve me in your own way, instead of in the way that I have made straight for you by means of my Truth, the incarnate Word, and built up with his blood. Rise up then promptly, and follow him, for no one can reach me, the Father, if not by him; he is the Way and the Door by which you must enter into me, the Sea of Peace.

PERFECT PURITY

From *Dialogue*, Chapter 100

As the discussion of perfection continues, Catherine is reminded of an earlier vision in which Christ had pointed the way to purity through refusing to judge others.

Do you want to arrive at perfect purity and be freed from stumbling blocks so that your mind may not be scandalized by anything? Unite yourself always to me by the affection of love, for I am the Supreme and Eternal Purity. I am the Fire that purifies the soul. The closer the soul is to me, the purer she becomes. The farther she is from me, the more her purity leaves her. This is why people of the world fall into such iniquities, for they are separated from me. But the soul who, without any intermediary, unites herself directly to me participates in my purity.

Another thing is necessary for you to arrive at this union and purity: that you should never judge the human will in anything that you may see done or said by any creature whatsoever, either to yourself or to others. You should consider my will alone, both in them and in yourself. And if you should see evident sins or defects, draw the rose out of those thorns. That is to say, offer them to me with holy compassion. In the case of injuries done to yourself, judge that my will permits this in order to prove virtue in yourself and in my other servants, figuring that the one who acts thus does so as the instrument of my will. You should also realize that such apparent sinners may frequently have a good intention. No one can judge the secrets of a person's heart. What you do not see you should not judge in your mind, even though it may evidently be open mortal sin. See nothing in others but my will—not in order to judge but, as has been said, with holy compassion.

In this way you will arrive at perfect purity because when you act this way, your mind will not be scandalized either in me or in your neighbors. Otherwise you fall into contempt of your neighbors if you judge their evil will toward you instead of my will acting in them. Such contempt and scandal separate the soul from me and prevent perfection and, in some cases, deprive her of grace, more or less according to the gravity of her contempt and the hatred her judgment has conceived against her neighbor.

A different reward is received by the soul who perceives only my will. As has been said, it wishes nothing else but your good so that everything I give or permit to happen to you, I give so that you may arrive at the end for which I created you. And because the soul remains always in the love of her neighbor, she remains always in my love and thus remains united to me. So in order to arrive at purity you must entreat me to grant you three things: to be united to me by the affection of love, retaining in your memory the benefits you have received from me; to see the affection of my love (with which I love you inestimably) with the eye of your intellect; and to discern my will only in the will of others and not their evil will. For I am their judge, not you, and in doing this you will arrive at all perfection.

FINAL PRAYER

From *Dialogue*, Chapter 167

The Dialogue *concludes with the soul's great outpouring of thanks for all that God has showed her and done for her.*

Thanks, thanks to you, O eternal Father, for you have not despised me, the work of your hands, or turned your face from me, or despised my desires. You, the Light, have not regarded my darkness. You, True Life, have not regarded my living death. You, the Physician, have not been repelled by my grave infirmities. You, the Eternal Purity, have not considered the many miseries of which I am full. You, who are the Infinite, have overlooked that I am finite. You, who are Wisdom, have overlooked my folly. Your wisdom, your goodness, your clemency, your infinite good, have overlooked these infinite evils and sins and the many others that are in me. Having known the truth through your clemency, I have found your charity and the love of my neighbors. What has constrained me? Not my virtues but only your charity. May that same charity constrain you to illuminate the eye of my intellect with the light of faith so that I may know and understand the truth that you have manifested to me. Grant that my memory may be capable of retaining your benefits and that my will may burn in the fire of your charity. May that fire so work in me that I give my body to be wounded, and that by my blood given for love of the blood of Christ, the key of obedience, I may unlock the door of heaven. I ask this of you with all my heart, for every rational creature, both in general and in particular, in the mystical body of the holy church. I confess and do not deny that you loved me before I existed. Your love for me is unspeakable, as if you were mad with love for your creature. Oh, eternal Trinity! O Godhead that gave value to the blood of your Son! You, O eternal Trinity, are a deep Sea. The deeper I enter the more I find, and the more I find the more I seek. The soul cannot be filled in your abyss, for she continually hungers after you, the eternal Trinity, desiring to see you with light in your light. As the deer desires the spring of living water, so my soul desires to leave the prison of this dark body and see you in truth.

How long, O eternal Trinity, fire and abyss of love, will your face be hidden from my eyes? Melt at once the cloud of my body. The knowledge that you have given me of yourself in your truth constrains me to long to abandon the heaviness of my body and to give my life for the glory and praise of your name. I have tasted and seen with the light of the intellect in your light, the abyss of you, the eternal Trinity, and the beauty of your creature. Looking at myself in you, I saw myself to be your image. My life was given me by your power, O eternal Father. Your wisdom, which belongs to your only begotten Son, shines in my intellect and my will, being one with your Holy Spirit, who proceeds from you and your Son and by whom I am able to love you. You, eternal Trinity, are my Creator, and I am the work of your hands. And I know through the new creation you have given me in the blood of your Son that you are enamored of the beauty of your workmanship.

O Abyss, O eternal Godhead, O deep Sea! What more could you give me than yourself? You are the fire that ever burns without being consumed. You consume in your heat all the soul's self-love. You are the fire that takes away all cold.

With your light you illuminate me so that I may know all your truth. You are the light above all light that supernaturally illuminates the eye of my intellect, clarifying the light of faith so abundantly and so perfectly that I see that my soul is alive and in this light receives you, the true Light. By the light of faith I have acquired wisdom in the wisdom of the Word, your only begotten Son. In the light of faith I am strong, constant, and persevering. In the light of faith I hope. Do not allow me to faint by the way. This light, without which I should still walk in darkness, teaches me the road. For this I said, O eternal Father, that you have illuminated me with the light of holy faith.

Truly this light is a sea, for the soul revels in you, eternal Trinity, the Sea of Peace. The water of the sea is not murky and causes no fear to the soul, for she knows the truth. It is a deep that manifests sweet secrets so that where the light of your faith abounds, the soul is certain of what she believes. This water is a magic mirror into which you, the eternal Trinity, bid me gaze. You hold it with the hand of love so that I may see myself, your creature, there represented in you and yourself in me through the union that you made of your Godhead with our humanity. For this light I know to represent to myself you—the supreme and infinite Good, Good blessed and incomprehensible, Good inestimable. Beauty above all beauty; Wisdom above all wisdom—for you are Wisdom itself. You, the food of the angels, have given yourself in a fire of love to people. You, the garment that covers all our nakedness, feed the hungry with your sweetness. Oh! Sweet, without any bitter, O eternal Trinity!

In your light you have given me with the light of holy faith I have known the many and wonderful things you have declared to me. You explained to me the path of supreme perfection so that I may no longer serve you in darkness, but with light, and that I may be the mirror of a good and holy life, and arise from my miserable sins, for through them I have hitherto served you in darkness. I have not known your truth and have not loved it. Why did I not know you? Because I did not see you with the glorious light of the holy faith; because the cloud of self-love darkened the eye of my intellect. But you, the eternal

Trinity, have dissipated the darkness with your light. Who can attain to your greatness? Who can give you thanks for such immeasurable gifts and benefits as you have given me in this doctrine of truth? It has been a special grace over and above the ordinary graces that you give also to your other creatures. You have been willing to condescend to my need and to that of your creatures—the need of introspection. Having first given the grace to ask the question, you reply to it and satisfy your servant, penetrating me with a ray of grace so that in that light I may give you thanks. Clothe me, clothe me with you, O eternal Truth, so that I may run my mortal course with true obedience and the light of holy faith. I feel that my soul is about to become drunk again with that light. Amen.

APPENDIX

Reading Spiritual Classics for Personal and Group Formation

Many Christians today are searching for more spiritual depth, for something more than simply being good church members. That quest may send them to the spiritual practices of New Age movements or of Eastern religions such as Zen Buddhism. Christians, though, have their own long spiritual tradition, a tradition rich with wisdom, variety, and depth.

The great spiritual classics testify to that depth. They do not concern themselves with mystical flights for a spiritual elite. Rather, they contain very practical advice and insights that can support and shape the spiritual growth of any Christian. We can all benefit by sitting at the feet of the masters (both male and female) of Christian spirituality.

Reading spiritual classics is different from most of the reading we do. We have learned to read to master a text and extract information from it. We tend to read quickly, to get through a text. And we summarize as we read, seeking the main point. In reading spiritual classics, though, we allow the text to master and form us. Such formative reading goes more slowly, more reflectively, allowing time for God to speak to us through the text. God's word for us may come as easily from a minor point or even an aside as from the major point.

Formative reading requires that you approach the text in humility. Read as a seeker, not an expert. Don't demand that the text meet your expectations for what an "enlightened" author should write. Humility means accepting the author as another imperfect human, a product of his or her own time and situation. Learn to celebrate what is foundational in an author's writing without being overly disturbed by what is peculiar to the author's life and times. Trust the text as a gift from both God and the author, offered to you for your benefit—to help you grow in Christ.

To read formatively, you must also slow down. Feel free to reread a passage that seems to speak specially to you. Stop from time to time to reflect on what you have been reading. Keep a journal for these reflections. Often the act of writing can itself prompt further, deeper reflection. Keep your notebook open and your pencil in hand as you read. You might not get back to that wonderful insight later. Don't worry that you are not getting through an entire passage— or even the first paragraph! Formative reading is about depth rather than breadth, quality rather than quantity. As you read, seek God's direction for your own life. Timeless truths have their place but may not be what is most important for your own formation here and now.

As you read the passage, you might keep some of these questions running through your mind:

- How is what I'm reading true of my own life? Where does it reflect my own *experience*?

- How does this text challenge me? What new *direction* does it offer me?

- What must I change to put what I am reading into practice? How can I *incarnate* it, let this word become flesh in my life?

You might also devote special attention to sections that upset you. What is the source of the disturbance? Do you want to argue theology? Are you turned off by cultural differences? Or have you been skewered by an insight that would turn your life upside down if you took it seriously? Let your journal be a dialogue with the text.

If you find yourself moving from reading the text to chewing over its implications to praying, that's great! Spiritual reading is really the first step in an ancient way of prayer called *lectio divina* or "divine reading." Reading leads naturally into reflection on what you have read (meditation). As you reflect on what the text might mean for your life, you may well want to ask for God's help in living out any new insights or direction you have perceived (prayer). Sometimes such prayer may lead you further into silently abiding in God's presence (contemplation). And, of course, the process is only really completed when it begins to make a difference in the way we live (incarnation).

As good as it is to read spiritual classics in solitude, it is even better to join with others in a small group for mutual formation or "spiritual direction in common." This is *not* the same as a study group that talks about spiritual classics. A group for mutual formation would have similar goals as for an individual's reading: to allow the text to shine its light on the *experiences* of the group members, to suggest new *directions* for their lives and practical ways of *incarnating* these directions. Such a group might agree to focus on one short passage from a classic at each meeting (even if members have read more). Discussion usually goes much deeper if all the members have already read and reflected on the passage before the meeting and bring their journals.

Such groups need to watch for several potential problems. It is easy to go off on a tangent (especially if it takes the focus off the members' own experience and onto generalities). At such times a group leader might bring the group's attention back to the text: "What does our author say about that?" Or, "How do we experience that in our own lives?" When a group member shares a problem, others may be tempted to try to "fix" it. This is much less helpful than sharing similar experiences and how they were handled (for good or ill). "Sharing" someone else's problems (whether that person is in or out of the group) should be strongly discouraged.

One person could be designated as leader, to be responsible for opening and closing prayers; to be the first to share or respond to the text; and to keep notes during the discussion to highlight recurring themes, challenges, directives, or practical steps. These responsibilities could also be shared among several members of the group or rotated.

For further information about formative reading of spiritual classics, try *A Practical Guide to Spiritual Reading* by Susan Annette Muto. *Shaped by the Word* by Robert Mulholland (Upper Room Books®) covers formative reading of the Bible. *Good Things Happen: Experiencing Community in Small Groups* by Dick Westley is an excellent resource on forming small groups of all kinds.

WALKING HUMBLY WITH GOD

Selected Writings of
JOHN WOOLMAN

Upper Room Spiritual Classics® — Series 3

Selected, edited, and introduced by
Keith Beasley-Topliffe

**Walking Humbly with God:
Selected Writings of John Woolman**

Copyright © 2000 by Upper Room Books™
All rights reserved.

No part of this book may be used or reproduced in any manner whatsoever without written permission of the publisher except in the case of brief quotations embodied in critical articles or reviews. For information, write Upper Room Books,™ 1908 Grand Avenue, Nashville, Tennessee 37212.

The Upper Room® Website: http://www.upperroom.org

UPPER ROOM,® UPPER ROOM BOOKS™ and design logos are trademarks owned by the Upper Room,® Nashville, Tennessee. All rights reserved.

Scripture quotations are from the New Revised Standard Version of the Bible Copyright © 1989 by the Division of Christian Education of the National Council of Churches of Christ in the USA. Used by permission. All rights reserved.

Cover design: Gore Studio, Inc.
Interior design and layout: Nancy J. Cole

First printing: 2000

Library of Congress Cataloging-in-Publication Data
Woolman, John, 1720–1772.
    Walking humbly with God : selected writings of John Woolman / selected, edited, and introduced by Keith Beasley-Topliffe.
      p. cm. — (Upper Room spiritual classics. Series 3)
    ISBN 0-8358-0900-5
    1. Woolman, John, 1720–1772. 2. Spiritual life—Society of Friends. I. Beasley-Topliffe, Keith. II. Title. III. Series.
BX7795.W7A3 2000   99-37742
289.6'092—dc21   CIP

Printed in the United States of America

TABLE OF CONTENTS

Introduction	5
Childhood	12
Youthful Struggles	15
Learning to Listen	19
Growing Concern	23
Thoughts on Business, Liquor, and Luxury	27
Receiving the Fruits of Slavery	31
Thoughts on Slavery	35
Tax Scruples	40
Speaking Out	44
Dyed Clothing	47
Visit to the Native Americans	51
Empathy	55
The Tyranny of Self-Love	59
Identification with the Poor	64
Appendix: Reading Spiritual Classics for Personal and Group Formation	68

INTRODUCTION

Many Christians feel drawn from time to time toward a particular social concern. Some may send money or sign a petition. A few will take further action—volunteering to help in a local project or contacting a legislator. And a very few will allow the concern to reorder their lives.

John Woolman was one of the very few. As a Quaker (a member of the Society of Friends), he was taught to pay particular attention to the interior movements of God's Spirit. A reluctance to write a bill of sale for a slave grew into a concern about slavery in general that sent him visiting other Quakers throughout the British colonies in America in the mid-1700s. He spoke at large Meetings and in private with individual slave owners, explaining why he believed slavery was wrong.

As Woolman's concern grew, it branched out into concerns for Native Americans, for Africans, and ultimately for all who were poor, oppressed, or exploited. In solidarity with the poor, he lived simply—even turning away customers when business demanded too much of his time.

Because he wanted his actions to be understood, he wrote a journal in which he explained the development of his special concerns and their effect on his way of life. He wrote pamphlets and essays that set out more systematic and objective views of slavery and other forms of economic exploitation. But the *Journal* stands as a spiritual classic, a look at the growth and development of a Christian soul seeking to know and do God's will in all things.

WOOLMAN'S WORLD

The Society of Friends grew out of the experiences of George Fox, who was born in Fenny Drayton, England, in 1624. After years of seeking a deeper experience of God, he had a series of insights, or *openings*, in the late 1640s. He felt called to be a religious reformer, to rid the church of dependence on ancient symbols and external authority in favor of the direct experience of the Holy Spirit, the Inner Light. Worship in the societies he founded emphasized silent prayer until someone was prompted by the Spirit to share some word with the assembly.

Fox's attacks on traditional religion met with strong counterattacks, including prosecution for blasphemy. At one defense, he told the judge that he ought to tremble before God, leading the judge to call him a quaker. The nickname stuck and was eventually embraced.

In 1652, several similar groups joined with Fox in the Society of Friends. Many others were *convinced* (a term the Quakers preferred to *converted* or *convicted*). One of them was William Penn, in 1667. Penn and others bought proprietary rights to the colonies of New Jersey and what became Pennsylvania. Many Quakers settled in these colonies, though when George Fox visited America in 1671–73, he found Quakers from New England to the Carolinas. Penn came to America in 1682 to help found Philadelphia.

The Society of Friends was organized in a structure of Meetings. The local society or perhaps a few banded together met monthly for business as a Monthly Meeting. This was related to a regional Quarterly Meeting and a much larger Yearly Meeting. Though local societies did not have pastors, gifted and Spirit-filled speakers could be given credentials as ministers with authority to visit other Meetings and even preach revivals. Woolman was such a minister.

Their religious convictions and experiences led Quakers to adopt a special vocabulary. Since the names of the days of the week and months of the year were often based on names of pagan gods, Quakers preferred to speak of First-day and Second-day, of First-month and Second-month, and so on. In addition to convincement (mentioned above), other special terms applied to the movements of the Spirit. Two are particularly important in reading Woolman. A moral objection or reservation about some action or possession was a *scruple*. The word could also be used as a verb, so that Woolman writes of scrupling to do such and such. The other term is *exercise*, which might refer to a strong pull to perform some action or to the inward struggle that came from resisting such a pull. Woolman compares some of his own exercises to the prophetic "burden of the Lord" often mentioned in the Old Testament prophets (translated as *oracle* in some modern translations) or to Jeremiah's description of God's message as "like a burning fire shut up in my bones."

Slavery, which was a fixture in all of the British colonies, took a variety of forms. Some slaves, both white and black, were set free after a fixed term of service. Others (almost exclusively black) were slaves for life. Many Quakers owned slaves, though as early as 1675 some had expressed misgivings about the practice. Still, there was an agreement to disagree peacefully. The few antislavery resolutions passed by Meetings in the early 1700s were advisory only, not binding.

WOOLMAN'S LIFE

John Woolman was born in Northampton (near what is now Rancocas), New Jersey, on October 19, 1720. He was the fourth of six children of Samuel and Elizabeth Woolman to survive infancy. At age twenty-one he moved to Mount Holly, about twenty miles east of Philadelphia, where he worked in a shop and later apprenticed himself to a tailor. By 1746 he was working on his own as a tailor and shopkeeper. Three years later he married Sarah Ellis. Their only surviving child, Mary, was born the next year.

In 1742, Woolman began to speak out in Meetings and was chosen as a minister of the Mount Holly Meeting. The next year he went on his first set of religious visits. As his concern about slavery grew, his visits became more extensive. In 1746, he spent three months visiting in Pennsylvania, Maryland,

Virginia, and North Carolina. The next year he spent four months in Long Island and New England.

In 1754, Woolman organized his thoughts about slavery into a pamphlet: *Some Considerations on the Keeping of Negroes*. A much longer *Consideration on Keeping Negroes, Part Second* followed in 1762. He also began to write his *Journal*, edited from less formal records. In the meantime, he was largely responsible for convincing the Philadelphia Yearly Meeting to adopt a resolution (a "formal minute") urging Quakers to free their slaves and excluding those who bought or sold slaves from participating in Society business.

Woolman's visits continued. He made some of them on foot in order to better appreciate the condition of the poor. In 1761 he decided to give up dyed clothing, in part because he believed dyeing harmed the material (so that clothes wore out more quickly) and in part because he believed dye served mainly to hide dirt and so encouraged lack of cleanliness. In 1763 he visited Native American villages in north-central Pennsylvania. He began to write another pamphlet, *A Plea for the Poor*, though it was not published until after his death. Over the next few years he wrote several other pamphlets and essays and continued to prepare his *Journal* for publication.

In 1772, Woolman sought affirmation from his Monthly and Quarterly Meetings for a trip to the London Yearly Meeting in England. He left for England on May 1, traveling in steerage while other Quakers stayed in elegant staterooms. When he arrived in London on June 8, the London Yearly

Meeting was in session. Woolman hurried over in his strange clothes, without taking time to wash, and was met with a less-than-enthusiastic welcome. A few Friends took the time to listen to him, and soon he was asked to address the whole Meeting. For the next several months he traveled to Meetings throughout England. In late September he contracted smallpox and died in York on October 7, 1772.

By 1784, Yearly Meetings in Virginia, Philadelphia, New York, and New England had all passed resolutions disowning members who still held slaves. In 1790, Quakers sent a memorandum to the first session of Congress urging the abolition of slavery throughout the United States.

Further Reading

Although Woolman had edited parts of his journal with an eye to publication, it was not published until two years after his death. An editorial committee made many changes, most fairly minor, but often complicating sentence structure. A later edition made substantial cuts. A reprint of this edition in 1871 with a new introduction by John Greenleaf Whittier became the basis for most later editions, including several now in print. In 1971, Oxford University Press published *The Journal and Major Essays of John Woolman*, edited by Phillips P. Moulton and based on the original manuscripts. It includes many helpful notes on Woolman's editing as well as a glossary and biographical sketches of people mentioned by Woolman.

For further information about Quakers, *The*

Faith and Practice of the Quakers by Rufus M. Jones (Friends United Press) is the classic introduction. The journal of George Fox is available in various editions. Recent Quaker writers include Thomas Kelly (particularly *A Testament of Devotion*) and Douglas Steere, who wrote many books on the spiritual life including *Dimensions of Prayer* and *On Listening to Another*.

Woolman constantly quotes or alludes to the Bible. The only other book he mentions significantly is *Foxe's Book of Martyrs*. In 1567, John Foxe, an Oxford scholar, published this history of Christian witness from the first Christians through the early Reformation. His title was *History of the Acts and Monuments of the Church*. Later editions added further stories to bring the history forward another two and a half centuries and make Foxe a sort of brand name. It is readily available in a variety of editions.

Note on the Text

The underlying text for these selections is the Whittier edition of 1871, sometimes expanded in light of Moulton's edition of Woolman's manuscript. Selections have been edited for length and inclusive language. Punctuation, grammar, spelling, and in some cases, vocabulary have been modernized. Woolman's sentences sometimes run on to great length with complex systems of subordinate clauses. These have been untangled and broken into shorter sentences. Direct quotes from Scripture and some allusions have been conformed to the language of the New Revised Standard Version.

# childhood

From *Journal*, Chapter 1

Woolman began writing his Journal when he was thirty-six, so the first three chapters are a spiritual autobiography rather than a day-to-day account. This selection about events of his childhood is the beginning of his story.

I have often felt a motion of love to leave some hints in writing of my experience of the goodness of God. Now, in the thirty-sixth year of my age, I begin this work.

I was born in Northampton, in Burlington County, West Jersey, in the year 1720. Before I was seven years old I began to be acquainted with the operations of divine love. Through the care of my parents, I was taught to read nearly as soon as I was capable of it. I remember that as I went from school one day and my companions were playing by the way, I went forward out of sight. Sitting down, I read the twenty-second chapter of Revelation: "Then the angel showed me the river of the water of life, bright as crystal, flowing from the throne of God and of the Lamb." In reading it, my mind was drawn to seek after the pure habitation that I then believed God had prepared for his servants. The place where I sat and the sweetness that attended my mind remain fresh in my memory. This and similar gracious visitations had such an effect upon me that when boys used ill language, it troubled me. And through the continued mercies of God, I was preserved from that evil.

The pious instructions of my parents were often fresh in my mind and of use to me when I happened to be among wicked children. Having a large family of children, they would often, on First-days after Meeting, set us one after another to read the Holy Scriptures or some religious books. The rest would sit by without much conversation. I have since often thought it was a good practice. From what I had read and heard, I believed there had been, in past ages, people who walked in uprightness before God in a degree exceeding any that I knew or heard of now living. The apprehension of there being less steadiness and firmness among people in the present age often troubled me while I was a child.

I may here mention a remarkable circumstance that occurred in my childhood. On going to a neighbor's house, I saw on the way a robin sitting on her nest. As I came near she went off. But having young ones, she flew about and with many cries expressed her concern for them. I stood and threw stones at her. When one struck her, she fell down dead. At first I was pleased with the exploit, but after a few minutes was seized with horror at having, in a playful way, killed an innocent creature while she was caring for her young. I beheld her lying dead and thought those young ones, for which she was so full of care, must now perish for want of their mother to nourish them. After some painful considerations on the subject, I climbed up the tree, took all the young birds, and killed them. I supposed that better than to leave them to pine away and die miserably. In this case I believed that scriptural proverb was fulfilled, "the mercy of the wicked is cruel." I then went on my errand. For some hours I could think of little else but the cruelties I had committed and was greatly troubled. Thus the One whose tender mercies are over all his works has placed a principle in the human mind that incites us to practice goodness toward every living creature. If they only pay attention to this, people become tender-hearted and sympathizing. But when it is frequently and totally rejected, the mind becomes shut up in a contrary disposition.

About the twelfth year of my age, while father was out, my mother reproved me for some misconduct, to which I made an undutiful reply. The next First-day, as I was returning with my father from Meeting, he told me that he understood I had behaved amiss to my mother and advised me to be more careful in future. I knew myself blamable and in shame and confusion remained silent. Being thus awakened to a sense of my wickedness, I felt remorse in my mind. On getting home I retired and prayed to the Lord to forgive me. I do not remember that I ever afterward spoke unhandsomely to either of my parents, however foolish I was in some other things.

 YOUTHFUL STRUGGLES

From *Journal*, Chapter 1

As Woolman continues to tell the story of his early years, he turns to the distractions of an active social life during his adolescence.

As I advanced in age, the number of my acquaintances increased. This made my way grow more difficult. Though I had found comfort in reading the Holy Scriptures and thinking on heavenly things, I was now estranged from them. I knew I was going from the flock of Christ and had no resolution to return. Hence serious reflections were uneasy to me, and youthful vanities and diversions were my greatest pleasure. In this road I found many like myself, and we associated in what is adverse to true friendship.

In this swift race it pleased God to visit me with sickness, so that I doubted of recovery. Then darkness, horror, and amazement seized me with full force, even when my pain and distress of body were very great. I thought it would have been better for me never to have had being than to see the day I now saw. I was filled with confusion. In great affliction, of both mind and body, I lay and bewailed myself. I did not have the confidence to lift up my cries to God, whom I had so offended. But in a deep sense of my great folly I was humbled before God. At length the word that is like a fire and a hammer broke and dissolved my rebellious heart. My cries were sent up in repentance. In the multitude of God's mercies I found inward relief and felt a firm assurance that if God were pleased to restore my health, I would walk humbly before God.

After my recovery, this awareness remained with me a considerable time. But by degrees I lost ground, giving way to youthful vanities and associating with wanton young people. The Lord had been very gracious and spoke peace to me in the time of my distress. I most ungratefully turned again to folly. At times I felt sharp reproof, but I did not get low enough to cry for help. I was not so daring as to do scandalous things. But my chief design was to excel in vanity and to promote mirth. Still I retained a love and esteem for pious people, and their company brought awe upon me. My dear parents several times admonished me in the fear of the Lord. Their admonition entered into my heart and had a good effect for a season. But since it did not get deep enough to lead me to pray rightly, the tempter found entrance when he came. Once I spent a part of a day in wantonness. When I went to bed at night, there lay in a window near my bed a Bible. I opened it and first cast my eye on the text, "Let us lie down in our shame, and let our dishonor cover us." This I knew to be my case and was somewhat affected meeting with so unexpected a reproof. I went to bed under remorse of conscience that I soon cast off again.

Thus time passed; my heart was refilled with mirth and wantonness. Pleasing scenes of vanity were presented to my imagination until I attained the age of eighteen years. Near that time I felt the judgments of God in my soul like a consuming fire. As I looked over my past life, the prospect was moving. I was often sad and longed to be delivered from those vanities. Then again my heart was strongly inclined to them. There was a sore conflict in me. At times I turned to folly, and then again sorrow and confusion took hold of me. In a while I resolved totally to leave off some of my vanities. But there was a secret reserve in my heart of the more refined part of them. I was not low enough to find true peace. Thus for some months I had great troubles. My will was unsubjected, and that rendered my labors fruitless. At length, through the merciful continuance of heavenly visitations, I was made to bow down in spirit before the Lord. One evening I had spent some time in reading a pious author. Walking out alone, I humbly prayed to the Lord for help that I might be delivered from all those vanities that so ensnared me. Since I was brought low, God helped me. As I learned to bear the cross, I felt refreshment come from God's presence. But I did not keep in the strength that gave victory, and so I lost ground again. The sense of this greatly affected me. I sought deserted and lonely places. There with tears I confessed my sins to God and humbly longed for God's help. And I may say with reverence that God was near to me in my troubles and in those times of humiliation opened my ear to discipline. I was led to look seriously at the means by which I was drawn from the pure truth. I learned that if I wanted to live such a life as the faithful servants of God lived, I must not go into company as before, according to my own will. But all the cravings of sense must be governed by a divine principle. In times of sorrow and abasement these instructions were sealed upon me. I felt the power of Christ prevail over selfish desires, so that I was preserved in a good degree of steadiness. Since I was young and believed at that time that a single life was best for me, I was strengthened to keep from such company as had often been a snare to me.

 Learning to Listen

From *Journal*, Chapter 1

As a young adult, Woolman began to pay more attention to the movements of the Holy Spirit in his heart. Here he writes about learning how and when to speak at Meetings and about the beginning of his lifelong concern over slavery.

After a while my former acquaintances gave over expecting me as one of their company, and I began to be known to some whose conversation was helpful to me. Now I experienced the love of God through Jesus Christ redeeming me from many pollutions and helping me through a sea of conflicts, with which no person was fully acquainted. As my heart was often enlarged in this heavenly principle, I felt a tender compassion for the youths who remained entangled in snares like those that had entangled me. From one month to another this love and tenderness increased, and my mind was more strongly engaged for the good of my fellow creatures.

I went to Meetings in an awe-filled frame of mind and endeavored to be inwardly acquainted with the language of the True Shepherd. One day, being under a strong exercise of spirit, I stood up and said some words in a Meeting. But not keeping close to the divine opening, I said more than was required of me. Being soon aware of my error, I was afflicted in mind for some weeks without any light or comfort, even to the degree that I could take satisfaction in nothing. I remembered God and was troubled. And in the depth of my distress God had pity upon me and sent the Comforter. I then felt forgiveness for my offense. My mind became calm and quiet. I was truly thankful to my gracious Redeemer for his mercies. And after this I felt the spring of divine love opened and a concern to speak, and I said a few words in a Meeting in which I found peace. This I believe was about six weeks from the first time. As I was thus humbled and disciplined under the Cross, my understanding became more strengthened to distinguish the language of the pure Spirit, which inwardly moves upon the heart. I was taught to wait in silence sometimes many weeks together until I felt the rise that prepares the creature to stand like a trumpet through which the Lord speaks to his flock.

About the time called Christmas I observed many people, both in town and from the country, resorting to public houses and spending their time in drinking and vain sports, tending to corrupt one another; on which account I was greatly troubled. At one house in particular there was much disorder. I believed it was my duty to speak to the master of that house. I considered that I was young and that several elderly friends in town had opportunity to see these things. But though I would gladly have been excused, yet I could not feel my mind clear.

As I was reading what the Almighty said to Ezekiel respecting his duty as a watchman, the matter was set home more clearly. With prayers and tears I asked the Lord for assistance, and he, in loving-kindness, gave me a resigned heart. At a suitable opportunity I went to the public house. Seeing the man in a large group, I called him aside. In the fear and dread of the Almighty I expressed to him what rested on my mind. He took it kindly and afterward showed more regard to me than before. A few years later he died, middle-aged. I often thought that if I had neglected my duty in that case, it would have given me great trouble. I was humbly thankful to my gracious Father, who had supported me in this.

My employer had a Negro woman and sold her. He asked me to write a bill of sale while the man who bought her was waiting. The thing was sudden. Though I felt uneasy at the thoughts of writing an instrument of slavery for one of my fellow creatures, yet I remembered that I was hired by the year, that it was my master who directed me to do it, and that it was an elderly man, a member of our Society, who bought her. So through weakness I gave way and wrote it. But at the executing of it I was so afflicted in my mind that I said before my master and the Friend that I believed slaveholding to be a practice inconsistent with the Christian religion. This, in some degree, abated my uneasiness. Yet as often as I reflected seriously upon it, I thought I should have been clearer if I had desired to be excused from it, as a thing against my conscience. Some time after this a young man of our Society spoke to me to write an instrument of slavery, since he had lately taken a Negro into his house. I told him I was uneasy about writing it. Even though many of our Meeting and in other places kept slaves, I still believed the practice was not right. I asked to be excused from the writing. I spoke to him in goodwill. He told me that keeping slaves was not altogether agreeable to his mind, but that since the slave was a gift made to his wife, he had accepted her.

GROWING CONCERN

From *Journal*, Chapter 3

By 1756 Woolman was in his midthirties, married with one daughter, and working as a tailor, shopkeeper, and farmer. He had already made several extensive trips throughout New Jersey and Pennsylvania and into other colonies, both north and south. His scruple against doing anything that might support slavery had grown into an exercise that demanded stronger action to oppose it. Here he talks about some ways he addressed the issue.

Scrupling to do writings relative to keeping slaves has been a means of various small trials to me. In these I have so evidently felt my own will set aside that I think it good to mention a few of them. Those who practice a trade and retailers of goods depend on their business for a living. They are naturally inclined to keep the goodwill of their customers. Nor is it a pleasant thing for young people to be under any necessity to question the judgment or honesty of elderly people—and more especially of such as have a fair reputation. Deep-rooted customs, though wrong, are not easily altered. But it is the duty of all to be firm in what they certainly know is right for them. A charitable, benevolent man, well acquainted with a Negro, may, I believe, under some circumstances, keep him in his family as a servant, on no other motives than the Negro's good. But we, as people, do not know what shall be after us. We have no assurance that our children will attain to that perfection in wisdom and goodness necessary rightly to exercise such power. So it is clear to me that I ought not to be the scribe where wills are drawn in which some children are made absolute masters over others during life.

About this time an ancient man of good esteem in the neighborhood came to my house to get his will written. He had young Negroes, and I asked him privately how he intended to dispose of them. He told me. I then said, "I cannot write your will without breaking my own peace," and respectfully gave him my reasons for it. He signified that he had preferred that I should have written it. But as I could not consistent with my conscience, he did not desire it. And so he got it written by some other person. A few years later, there being great alterations in his family, he came again to get me to write his will. His Negroes were still young. And since he first spoke to me, his son, to whom he intended to give them, was turned from a libertine to a sober young man. He supposed that I would have been free on that account to write it. We had much friendly talk on the subject and then deferred it. A few days later he came again and directed their freedom. I then wrote his will.

Near the time that the last-mentioned Friend first spoke to me, a neighbor received a bad bruise in his body and sent for me to bleed him. When I had done this, he desired me to write his will. I took notes. Among other things he told me to which of his children he gave his young Negro. I considered the pain and distress he was in and did not know how it would end. So I wrote his will except for the part concerning his slave. Carrying it to his bedside, I read it to him. I then told him in a friendly way that I could not write any instruments by which my fellow creatures were made slaves without bringing trouble on my own mind. I let him know that I charged nothing for what I had done and asked to be excused from doing the other part in the way he proposed. We then had a serious conference on the subject. At length, he agreed to set her free, and I finished his will.

Having felt drawn to visit Friends on Long Island, I set off twelfth of Fifth month, 1756, after obtaining a certificate from our Monthly Meeting. When I reached the island, I lodged the first night at the house of my dear friend Richard Hallett. The next day being the first of the week, I was at the Meeting in New Town. There we experienced the renewed manifestations of the love of Jesus Christ to the comfort of the honest-hearted. I went that night to Flushing, and the next day I and my beloved friend Matthew Franklin crossed the ferry at White Stone. We were at three Meetings on the mainland and then returned to the island, where I spent the remainder of the week in visiting Meetings. The Lord, I believe, has a people in those parts who are honestly inclined to serve him.

But I fear many are too much clogged with the things of this life and do not come forward bearing the cross in such faithfulness as the Almighty calls for.

My mind was deeply engaged in this visit, both in public and in private. At several places where I was, on observing that they had slaves, I found myself under a necessity in a friendly way to labor with them on that subject. When a way opened, I expressed the inconsistency of that practice with the purity of the Christian religion and its ill effects manifested among us.

tboughts on business, liquor, and luxury

From *Journal*, Chapter 3

Here Woolman talks about the struggle between the demands of Christ and the demands of business. This leads him into consideration of strong drink and other luxuries.

Until this year, 1756, I continued to retail goods, besides following my trade as a tailor. About this time I grew uneasy on account of my business growing too cumbersome. I had begun with selling trimmings for garments. From there I proceeded to sell cloths and linens. At length, having gotten a considerable shop of goods, my trade increased every year. The way to large business appeared open, but I felt a stop in my mind.

Through the mercies of the Almighty, I had, to a good degree, learned to be content with a plain way of living. I had but a small family. On serious consideration, I believed truth did not require me to engage much in encumbering affairs. It had been my general practice to buy and sell things really useful. I was not easy to trade in things that served chiefly to please the vain mind in people. I seldom did it. And whenever I did, I found it weakened me as a Christian.

The increase of business became my burden. Though my natural inclination was toward merchandise, yet I believed truth required me to live more free from outward encumbrance. There was now a strife in my mind between the two. In this exercise my prayers were put up to the Lord, who graciously heard me and gave me a heart resigned to his holy will. Then I lessened my outward business. As I had opportunity, I told my customers of my intentions so that they might consider what shop to turn to. In a while I wholly laid down merchandise and followed my trade as a tailor by myself, having no apprentice. I also had a nursery of apple trees, in which I employed some of my time in hoeing, grafting, trimming, and inoculating. In merchandise it is the custom where I lived to sell chiefly on credit, and poor people often get in debt. When payment is expected and they do not have wherewithal to pay, their creditors often sue for it at law. Having frequently observed occurrences of this kind, I found it good for me to advise poor people to take such goods as were most useful and not costly.

In the time of trading I had an opportunity of seeing that the too liberal use of spirituous liquors and the custom of wearing too costly apparel led some people into great inconveniences. These two things appear to be often connected with each other. By not attending to the use of things that are consistent with universal righteousness, there is an increase of labor that extends beyond what our heavenly Father intends for us. And by great labor (and often by much sweating in the heat) there is a craving of liquors to revive the spirits even among such as are not drunkards. Partly by the luxurious drinking of some and partly by the drinking of others (led to it through immoderate labor), very great quantities of rum are every year expended in our colonies. We should have no need of the greater part if we steadily attended to pure wisdom.

When men take pleasure in feeling their minds elevated with strong drink and so indulge their appetite as to disorder their understandings, they neglect their duty as members of a family or civil society and cast off all regard to religion. Their case is much to be pitied. And where those whose lives are for the most part regular and whose examples have a strong influence on the minds of others adhere to some customs that powerfully draw them to the use of more strong liquor than pure wisdom allows, it hinders the spreading of the spirit of meekness and strengthens the hands of the more excessive drinkers. This is a case to be lamented.

Every degree of luxury has some connection with evil. If those who profess to be disciples of Christ and are looked upon as leaders of the people have the same mind in them that was also in Christ and so stand separate from every wrong way, it is a means of help to the weaker. As I have sometimes been greatly tired in the heat and have taken spirits to revive me, I have found by experience that in such circumstances the mind is not so calm or so fitly disposed for divine meditation as when all such extremes are avoided. I have felt an increasing care to attend to the Holy Spirit that sets right bounds to our desires and leads those who faithfully follow it to apply all the gifts of divine Providence to the purposes for which they were intended. If those who have the care of great estates attended with singleness of heart to this heavenly Instructor that so opens and enlarges the mind as to cause people to love their neighbors as themselves, they would have wisdom given them to manage their concerns without employing some people in providing luxuries of life or others in laboring too hard. But for want of steadily regarding this principle of divine love, a selfish spirit takes place in the minds of people, attended with darkness and manifold confusions in the world.

RECEIVING THE FRUITS OF SLAVERY

From *Journal*, Chapter 4

In May 1757, Woolman and his brother Uriah set off on a journey through Maryland, Virginia, and North Carolina—1,150 miles in two months. In this selection from the beginning, just after entering Maryland, Woolman writes about his struggle over receiving hospitality from slaveholders.

Soon after I entered this province a deep and painful exercise came upon me. I often had some feeling of it, since my mind was drawn toward these parts. I had acquainted my brother with it before we agreed to join as companions. As the people in this and the southern provinces live to a great extent on the labor of slaves, many of whom are used harshly, my concern was that I might listen with singleness of heart to the voice of the True Shepherd and be so supported as to remain unmoved when face-to-face with people.

As it is common for Friends on such a visit to have entertainment free of cost, a difficulty arose in my mind with respect to saving my money by kindness received from what appeared to me to be the gain of oppression. Receiving a gift, considered as a gift, brings the receiver under obligations to the benefactor and has a natural tendency to draw the obliged into siding with the giver. To prevent difficulties of this kind and to preserve the minds of judges from any bias was that divine prohibition: "You shall take no bribe, for a bribe blinds the officials, and subverts the cause of those who are in the right."

Since the disciples were sent forth without any provision for their journey and our Lord said the workman is worthy of his meat, their labor in the gospel was considered a reward for their entertainment and therefore not received as a gift. Yet in regard to my present journey, I could not see my way clear in that respect. The difference appeared thus: the entertainment the disciples met with was from them whose hearts God had opened to receive them, from a love to them and the truth they published. But we, considered as members of the same religious society, look upon it as a piece of civility to receive each other in such visits. Such receptions are, at times, partly in regard to reputation and not from an inward unity of heart and spirit.

Conduct is more convincing than language. Where people manifest by their actions that the slave trade is not so disagreeable to their principles but that it may be encouraged, there is not a sound uniting with some Friends who visit them.

The prospect of so weighty a work and of being so distinguished from many whom I esteemed before myself brought me very low. Such were the conflicts of my soul that I closely sympathized with the prophet when he said in the time of his weakness: "If this is the way you are going to treat me, put me to death at once—if I have found favor in your sight." But I soon saw that this proceeded from the lack of a full resignation to God's will. Many afflictions attended me, and in great abasement, with many tears, my cries were to the Almighty for gracious and fatherly assistance. After a time of deep trial I was favored to understand the state mentioned by the psalmist more clearly than ever I had done before: "My soul within me is like a weaned child." Being thus helped to sink down into resignation, I felt a deliverance from the tempest in which I had been severely exercised. I went forward in calmness of mind, trusting that the Lord Jesus Christ, as I faithfully listened to him, would be a counselor to me in all difficulties. By his strength I should be enabled even to leave money with the members of the Society where I was entertained when I found that omitting it would obstruct that work to which I believed he had called me. As I copy this after my return, I may here add that often I did so under a sense of duty.

This is the way I did it. When I expected soon to leave a Friend's house where I had entertainment and believed that I should not keep clear from the gain of oppression without leaving money, I spoke to one of the heads of the family privately and asked him to accept pieces of silver and give them to such of the Negroes as he believed would make the best use of them. At other times I gave them to the Negroes myself, as the way looked clearest to me. Before I came out, I had provided a large number of small pieces for this purpose. Offering them to some who appeared to be wealthy people was a trial both to me and to them. But the fear of the Lord so covered me at times that my way was made easier than I expected. Few, if any, manifested any resentment at the offer. Most of them, after some conversation, accepted it.

THOUGHTS ON SLAVERY

From *Journal*, Chapter 4

The description of Woolman's 1757 southern journey continues with his description of slavery and a Yearly Meeting in Virginia where Quakers debated how to address the issue of slavery.

From the time of my entering Maryland I have been under much sorrow. Lately it so increased upon me that my mind was almost overwhelmed, and I may say with the psalmist, "In my distress I called upon the LORD; to my God I cried for help." In infinite goodness, God looked upon my affliction and in my private retirement sent the Comforter for my relief. For this I humbly bless God's holy name.

The sense I had of the state of the churches brought a weight of distress upon me. The gold to me appeared dim, and the fine gold changed. Though this is the case too generally, yet the sense of it in these parts has in a particular manner borne heavy upon me. It appeared to me that through the prevailing of the spirit of this world, the minds of many were brought to an inward desolation. Instead of the spirit of meekness, gentleness, and heavenly wisdom that is the necessary companion of the true sheep of Christ, a spirit of fierceness and the love of dominion too generally prevailed. From small beginnings in error great buildings by degrees are raised. From one age to another these errors are more and more strengthened by the general concurrence of the people. As people obtain reputation by their profession of the truth, their virtues are mentioned as arguments in favor of general error. Those of less note, to justify themselves, say that such and such good people did the like. By what other steps could the people of Judah arise to the height in wickedness that gave just ground for the prophet Isaiah to declare in the name of the Lord, "No one brings suit justly, no one goes to law honestly," or for the Almighty to call upon the great city of Jerusalem just before the Babylonian Captivity, "See if you can find one person who acts justly and seeks truth—so that I may pardon Jerusalem"?

The prospect of a way being open to the same degeneracy in some parts of this newly settled land of America in respect to our conduct toward the Negroes has deeply bowed my mind in this journey. Though to relate briefly how these people are treated is no agreeable work, yet after often reading over the notes I made as I traveled, I find my mind engaged to preserve them. Many of the white people in those provinces take little or no care of Negro marriages. When Negroes marry after their own way, some make so little account of those marriages that with views of outward interest, they often part men from their wives by selling them far asunder. This is common when estates are sold by executors. Many whose labor is heavy are followed at their business in the field by a man with a whip, hired for that purpose. They are allowed in common little else but one peck of Indian corn and some salt, for one week, with a few potatoes. (The potatoes they commonly raise by their labor on the first day of the week.)

The correction ensuing on their disobedience to overseers or slothfulness in business is often very severe and sometimes desperate. Many times men and women have scarcely enough clothes to hide their nakedness, and boys and girls ten and twelve years old are often quite naked among their master's children. Some of our Society and some of the society called New Light Presbyterians endeavor to instruct those they have in reading. But commonly this is not only neglected but disapproved. These are the people by whose labor the other inhabitants are in a great measure supported—many of them in the luxuries of life. These are the people who have made no agreement to serve us and who have not forfeited their liberty that we know of. These are the souls for whom Christ died. For our conduct toward them we must answer before God who shows no partiality. Those who know the only true God and Jesus Christ whom God has sent and so are acquainted with the merciful, benevolent, gospel spirit will perceive that the indignation of God is kindled against oppression and cruelty. In beholding the great distress of so numerous a people they will find cause for mourning.

From my lodgings I went to Burleigh Meeting, where I felt my mind drawn into a quiet, resigned state. After a long silence I felt an engagement to stand up, and through the powerful operation of divine love, we were favored with an edifying Meeting. The next Meeting we had was at Black Water and so on to the Yearly Meeting at the Western Branch.

When business began, some queries were produced by some of their members for consideration. If approved, they were to be answered hereafter by their respective Monthly Meetings. They were the Pennsylvania queries and had been examined by a committee of Virginia Yearly Meeting appointed the last year. They made some alterations in them, one of which was in favor of a custom that troubled me. The query was, "Are there any concerned in the importation of Negroes or in buying them after imported?" which was thus altered, "Are there any concerned in the importation of Negroes, or buying them to trade in?" As one query admitted with unanimity was, "Are any concerned in buying or vending goods unlawfully imported or prize goods?" I found my mind engaged to say that as we profess the truth and were there assembled to support the testimony of it, it was necessary for us to dwell deep and act in the wisdom that is pure. Otherwise we could not prosper. I then mentioned their alteration. Referring to the last-mentioned query, I added that since purchasing any merchandise taken by the sword was always allowed to be inconsistent with our principles and since Negroes were captives of war or taken by stealth, it was inconsistent with our testimony to buy them. Their being our fellow creatures and sold as slaves added greatly to the iniquity. Friends appeared attentive to what was said. Some expressed a care and concern about their Negroes. None made any objection in reply to what I said. But the query was admitted as they had altered it.

Since some of their members have heretofore traded in Negroes as in other merchandise, this query will be one step farther than they have hitherto gone. So I did not see it my duty to press for an alteration but felt easy to leave it all to God who alone is able to turn the hearts of the mighty and make way for the spreading of truth on the earth by means agreeable to God's infinite wisdom.

# TAX SCRUPLES

From *Journal*, Chapter 5

The French and Indian War (1754–63) brought new taxes to support the military action. How could Woolman, a servant of the Prince of Peace, pay a war tax? But how could he not pay when other Quakers had no problem with such taxes? Here he struggles with this new scruple.

A few years past, money was made available in our province for carrying on wars and to be repaid by taxes laid on the inhabitants. My mind was often affected with the thoughts of paying such taxes. I believe it right for me to preserve a memorandum concerning it. I was told that Friends in England frequently paid taxes when the money was applied to such purposes. I had conversation with several noted Friends on the subject who all favored the payment of such taxes. Some of them I preferred before myself, and this made me easier for a time. Yet there was in the depth of my mind a scruple that I never could get over. Sometimes I was greatly distressed on that account.

I believed that there were some upright-hearted men who paid such taxes, yet could not see that their example was a sufficient reason for me to do so. I believe that the spirit of truth required of me, as an individual, to suffer patiently the distress of goods rather than pay actively.

To refuse the active payment of a tax that our Society generally paid was exceedingly disagreeable. But to do a thing contrary to my conscience appeared yet more dreadful. When this exercise came upon me, I knew of no one under the same difficulty. In my distress I asked the Lord to enable me to give up all so that I might follow him wherever he was pleased to lead me.

Scrupling to pay a tax on account of the application has seldom been heard of before, even among people of integrity who have steadily borne their testimony against outward wars in their time. I may therefore note some things that have occurred to my mind as I have been inwardly exercised on that account. From the steady opposition that faithful Friends in early times made to wrong things that were then approved, they were hated and persecuted by people living in the spirit of this world. By suffering with firmness, they were made a blessing to the church, and the work prospered. It equally concerns people in every age to take heed to their own spirits. In comparing their situation with ours, it appears to me that there was less danger of their being infected with the spirit of this world through paying such taxes than is the case with us now. They had little or no share in civil government. Many of them declared that they were, through the power of God, separated from the spirit in which wars existed. Since they were afflicted by the rulers on account of their testimony, there was less likelihood of their uniting in spirit with them in things inconsistent with the purity of truth.

We, from the first settlement of this land, have known little or no troubles of that sort. The profession of our predecessors was for a time accounted reproachful. But at length their uprightness was understood by the rulers, and their innocent sufferings moved them. Our way of worship was tolerated, and many of our members in these colonies became active in civil government. Being thus tried with favor and prosperity, this world appeared inviting. Our minds have been turned to the improvement of our country, to merchandise and the sciences, among which are many things that are useful if followed in pure wisdom. But in our present condition I believe it will not be denied that a carnal mind is gaining upon us. Some of our members who are officers in civil government are called upon in their respective stations to assist in things relative to the wars. They are in doubt whether to act or to ask to be excused from their office. But if they see their brothers united in the payment of a tax to carry on the said wars, they may think their case not much different and so might quench the tender movements of the Holy Spirit in their minds. Thus, by small degrees, we might approach so near to fighting that the distinction would be little else than the name of a peaceable people.

It requires great self-denial and resignation of ourselves to God to attain that state in which we can freely cease from fighting when wrongfully invaded if, by our fighting, there were a probability of overcoming the invaders. Whoever rightly attains to it does in some degree feel that spirit in which our Redeemer gave his life for us. Through divine goodness many of our predecessors and many now living have learned this blessed lesson. But many others who have their religion chiefly by education and are not enough acquainted with the cross that crucifies to the world manifest a temper distinguishable from that of an entire trust in God.

SPEAKING OUT

From *Journal*, Chapter 7

In 1760, Woolman went on a four-month trip to New England. In this selection Woolman speaks out publicly during a Yearly Meeting in Newport, Rhode Island, and privately to a group of slave owners.

And now an exercise revived in my mind in relation to lotteries, which were common in those parts. I had mentioned the subject in a former sitting of this Meeting. Then arguments were used in favor of Friends being held excused who were only concerned in such lotteries as were agreeable to law. Now it was opposed as before. But the hearts of some solid Friends appeared to be united to discourage the practice among their members. The matter was zealously handled by some on both sides. In this debate it appeared very clear to me that the spirit of lotteries was a spirit of selfishness and tended to confuse and darken the understanding. Pleading for it in our Meetings, set apart for the Lord's work, was not right. In the heat of zeal, I made reply to what an ancient Friend said. When I sat down, I saw that my words were not enough seasoned with charity. After this I spoke no more on the subject. At length a minute was made, a copy of which was to be sent to their several Quarterly Meetings, inciting Friends to labor to discourage the practice among all professing with us.

Some time after this minute was made I remained uneasy with the manner of my speaking to the ancient Friend. I could not see my way clear to conceal my uneasiness, though I was concerned that I might say nothing to weaken the cause in which I had labored. After some close exercise and hearty repentance for not having attended closely to the safe guide, I stood up. Reciting the passage, I acquainted Friends that though I dared not go from what I had said as to the matter, yet I was uneasy with the manner of my speaking and believed milder language would have been better. As this was uttered in some degree of creaturely abasement after a warm debate, it appeared to have a good savor among us.

Though the Yearly Meeting was now over, there yet remained on my mind a secret though heavy exercise in regard to some leading active members about Newport who were in the practice of keeping slaves. This I mentioned to two ancient Friends who came out of the country and proposed to them to have some conversation with those members if a way opened. One of them and I consulted one of the most noted elders who had slaves. He, in a respectful manner, encouraged me to proceed to clear myself of what lay upon me. Near the beginning of the Yearly Meeting, I had had a private conference with this elder and his wife concerning their slaves. Now the way seemed clear to me to consult with him about the manner of proceeding. I told him I was free to have a conference with them all together in a private house. Or if he thought they would take it unkindly to be asked to come together and to be spoken with in the hearing of one another, I was free to spend some time among them and to visit them all in their own houses. He expressed his liking to the first proposal, not doubting their willingness to come together. As I proposed a visit to only ministers, elders, and overseers, he named some others whom he desired also to be present. Since a caring messenger was needed to acquaint them in a proper manner, he offered to go to all their houses to open the matter to them. About the eighth hour the next morning we met in the meetinghouse chamber, the last-mentioned country Friend, my companion, and John Storer being with us. After a short time of retirement, I acquainted them with the steps I had taken in procuring that Meeting and opened the concern I was under. We then proceeded to a free conference upon the subject. My exercise was heavy, and I was deeply bowed in spirit before the Lord, who was pleased to favor with the seasoning virtue of truth. This created a tenderness among us, and the subject was mutually handled in a calm and peaceable spirit. At length, feeling my mind released from the burden that I had been under, I took my leave of them in a good degree of satisfaction. By the tenderness they manifested in regard to the practice and the concern several of them expressed in relation to the manner of disposing of their Negroes after their deaths, I believed that a good exercise was spreading among them. I am humbly thankful to God, who supported my mind and preserved me in a good degree of resignation through these trials.

DYED CLOTHING

From *Journal*, Chapter 8

In 1761, Woolman continued to brood over the contrasts between rich and poor. He was determined to simplify his life in solidarity with the poor and to avoid all extravagances—things he saw as wasted labor. This led to a new scruple over the use of dyed clothing.

As I have thus considered these things, a question has arisen at times. Do I, in all my proceedings, keep to the use of things that are agreeable to universal righteousness? And then some degree of sadness has at times come over me because I accustomed myself to some things that have occasioned more labor than I believe divine wisdom intended for us.

From my early acquaintance with truth I have often felt an inward distress, occasioned by the striving of a spirit in me against the operation of the heavenly principle. In this state I have been affected with a sense of my own wretchedness. In a mourning condition I have felt earnest longings for the divine help that brings the soul into true liberty. Sometimes, on retiring into private places, the spirit of supplication has been given me. Under a heavenly covering, I have asked my gracious Father to give me a heart resigned in all things to the direction of divine wisdom. In uttering language like this, the thought of my wearing hats and garments dyed with a dye hurtful to them has made a lasting impression on me.

In visiting people of note in the Society who had slaves and laboring with them in brotherly love on that account, I have seen—and the sight has affected me—that a conformity to some customs distinguishable from pure wisdom has entangled many. The desire of gain to support these customs has greatly opposed the work of truth. Sometimes the prospect of the work before me has been such that, bowed down in spirit, I have been drawn into retired places and have besought the Lord with tears that he would take me wholly under his direction and show me the way in which I ought to walk. Then a strong conviction has revived that if I would be God's faithful servant, I must in all things attend to divine wisdom and be teachable. So I must cease from all customs contrary to this wisdom, however common among religious people.

As God is the perfection of power, of wisdom, and of goodness, so I believe God has provided that as much labor shall be necessary for our support in this world as would, if it were rightly divided, be a suitable employment of our time. We cannot go into extravagances or grasp after wealth in a way contrary to God's wisdom without having connection with some degree of oppression and with the spirit that leads to self-exaltation and strife. This spirit frequently brings calamities on countries by parties contending about their claims.

So I was fully convinced and felt an increasing desire to live in the spirit of peace. I have often been sorrowfully affected with thinking on the unquiet spirit in which wars are generally carried on and with the miseries of many of my fellow creatures engaged in them. Some are suddenly destroyed. Some are wounded and after much pain remain disabled. Some are deprived of all their outward substance and reduced to want. And some are carried into captivity. Thinking often on these things, using hats and garments dyed with a dye hurtful to them and wearing more clothes in summer than are useful grew more uneasy to me. I believe them to be customs that do not have their foundation in pure wisdom. The apprehension of being singular from my beloved friends was a constraint upon me, and so I continued in the use of some things contrary to my judgment.

On the thirty-first of Fifth-month, 1761, I was taken ill of a fever. After it had continued nearly a week I was in great bodily distress. One day there was a cry raised in me that I might understand the cause of my affliction and improve under it. Then my conformity to some customs that I believed were not right was brought to my remembrance. In the continuance of this exercise I felt all the powers in me yield themselves up into the hands of the One who gave me being. I was made thankful that God had taken hold of me by these chastisements, since I felt the necessity of further purifying. There was now no desire in me for health until the design of my correction was answered. So I lay abased and broken in spirit. As I felt a sinking down into a calm resignation, so I felt, as in an instant, an inward healing in my nature.

From that time forward I grew better.

Though my mind was thus settled in relation to hurtful dyes, I felt at ease to wear my garments already made and continued to do so about nine months. Then I thought of getting a hat the natural color of the fur. But the apprehension of being looked upon as one affecting singularity felt uneasy to me. Here I had occasion to consider that things, though small in themselves, if they are clearly enjoined by divine authority become great things to us. I trusted that the Lord would support me in the trials that might attend singularity, so long as singularity was only for his sake. On this account I was under close exercise of mind in the time of our General Spring Meeting, 1762. I greatly desired to be rightly directed. When I was deeply bowed in spirit before the Lord, I was made willing to submit to what I apprehended was required of me. When I returned home, I got a hat of the natural color of the fur.

In attending Meetings this singularity was a trial to me—more especially at this time, since white hats were used by some who were fond of following the changeable modes of dress. When some Friends who did not know from what motives I wore it grew shy of me, I felt my way for a time shut up in the exercise of the ministry. In this condition, my mind was turned toward my heavenly Father with fervent cries that I might be preserved to walk before him in the meekness of wisdom. My heart was often tender in Meetings, and I felt an inward consolation that was very precious to me under these difficulties.

VISIT TO THE NATIVE AMERICANS

From *Journal*, Chapter 8

In the summer of 1763, Woolman and Benjamin Parvin set out to visit Native Americans living in Wyalusing, Pennsylvania (about thirty-five miles northwest of present-day Scranton). The area was not yet settled by English colonists. The trip took about three weeks. This selection is from the outward trip, as Woolman considers how the natives were driven back from the coast into the wilderness.

My own will and desires were now very much broken, and my heart was with much earnestness turned to the Lord, to whom alone I looked for help in the dangers before me. I had a prospect of the English along the coast for upward of nine hundred miles where I have traveled. Their favorable situation and the difficulties attending the natives as well as the Negroes in many places were open before me. A weighty and heavenly care came over my mind. Love filled my heart toward all humankind. I felt a strong engagement that we might be obedient to the Lord while in tender mercy he is yet calling to us and that we might so attend to pure universal righteousness as to give no just cause of offense to the Gentiles—those who do not profess Christianity—whether they are the blacks from Africa or the native inhabitants of this continent.

Here I was led into a close and laborious inquiry whether I as an individual kept clear from all things that tended to stir up or were connected with wars either in this land or in Africa. My heart was deeply concerned that in future I might in all things keep steadily to the pure truth and live and walk in the plainness and simplicity of a sincere follower of Christ. In this lonely journey I greatly mourned the spreading of a wrong spirit. I believed that the prosperous, convenient situation of the English would require a constant attention in us to divine love and wisdom, so they could be guided and supported in a way answerable to the will of that good, gracious, and almighty Being, who has an equal regard to all humankind. And here luxury and covetousness with the numerous oppressions and other evils attending them appeared very afflicting to me. I felt in what is immutable that the seeds of great calamity and desolation are sown and growing fast on this continent. I do not have words sufficient to set forth the longing I felt then that we who are placed along the coast and have tasted the love and goodness of God might arise in the strength thereof and like faithful messengers labor to check the growth of these seeds so that they may not ripen to the ruin of our posterity.

On reaching the Indian settlement at Wyoming, we were told that an Indian runner had been at that place a day or two before us and brought news of the Indians having taken an English fort westward and destroyed the people, and that they were endeavoring to take another. Another Indian runner came there about the middle of the previous night from a town about ten miles from Wyalusing and brought the news that some Indian warriors from distant parts came to that town with two English scalps and told the people that it was war with the English.

Our guides took us to the house of a very ancient man. Soon after we had put in our baggage there came a man from another Indian house some distance off. Perceiving there was a man near the door, I went out. The man had a tomahawk wrapped under his match coat out of sight. As I approached him he took it in his hand. I went forward, spoke to him in a friendly way, and perceived that he understood some English. My companion joined me, and we had some talk with him concerning the nature of our visit in these parts. He then went into the house with us and talked with our guides. He soon appeared friendly and sat down and smoked his pipe. Though taking his hatchet in his hand at the instant I drew near to him had a disagreeable appearance, I believe he had no other intent than to be in readiness in case any violence were offered to him.

On hearing the news brought by these Indian runners and being told by the Indians where we lodged that the Indians about Wyoming expected in a few days to move to some larger towns, I thought, to all outward appearance, it would be dangerous traveling at this time. After a hard day's journey I was brought into a painful exercise at night, in which I had to trace back and view the steps I had taken from my first moving in the visit. Though I had to mourn some weakness that at times had attended me, I could not find that I had ever given way to willful disobedience. Believing I had come thus far under a sense of duty, I was now earnest in spirit, beseeching the Lord to show me what I ought to do. In this great distress I grew jealous of myself, lest the desire of reputation as one firmly settled to persevere through dangers or the fear of disgrace from my returning without performing the visit might have some place in me. Full of these thoughts, I lay a great part of the night while my companion slept by me, until the Lord, my gracious Father, who saw the conflicts of my soul, was pleased to give quietness. Then I was again strengthened to commit my life and all things relating to it into God's heavenly hands and got a little sleep toward day.

empathy

From *A Word of Remembrance and Caution to the Rich*, Sections 4 and 6

Sometime in late 1763 or early 1764, Woolman wrote a pamphlet with the title, "A Plea for the Poor." He wrote it in his journal, interrupting the journal entries for forty-six pages. While he was in England, he reworked sections for several essays published there. The whole was not published, however, until 1793, twenty-one years after Woolman's death. The publisher gave it the title above.

Our blessed Redeemer, in directing us how to conduct ourselves one toward another, appeals to our own feelings: "In everything do to others as you would have them do to you." Now, when some who have never experienced hard labor themselves live in fullness on the labor of others, there is often a danger of their not having a right feeling of the laborers' condition. So they are disqualified to judge candidly in their case, since they do not know what they themselves would desire were they to labor hard from one year to another to raise the necessities of life and pay high rent besides. It is good for those who live in fullness to cultivate tenderness of heart and to make the most of every opportunity to be acquainted with the hardships and fatigues of those who labor for their living. So they will seriously ask themselves, *Am I influenced by true charity in fixing all my demands? Have I no desire to support myself in expensive customs because my acquaintances live in such customs?*

A wealthy man, on serious reflection, might find a witness in his own conscience that he indulges himself in some expensive customs that might be omitted consistently with the true design of living and that, were he to change places with those who occupy his estate, he would desire to be discontinued by them. Whoever is thus awakened will necessarily find the injunction binding: "Do to others as you would have them do to you." Divine love imposes no rigorous or unreasonable commands but graciously points out the spirit of brotherhood and the way to happiness, for which we must relinquish all that is selfish.

To pass through a series of hardships and to languish under oppression bring people to a certain knowledge of these things. To enforce the duty of tenderness to the poor, the inspired lawgiver referred the children of Israel to their own experience: "You know the heart of an alien, for you were aliens in the land of Egypt." Whoever has been a stranger among unkind people or under the government of those who were hard-hearted has experienced this feeling. But a person who has never felt the weight of misapplied power does not come to this knowledge except by an inward tenderness in which the heart is prepared to sympathize with others.

Let us reflect on the condition of a poor innocent man on whom the rich man lays heavy burdens, from a desire after wealth and luxuries. When this laborer looks over the cause of his heavy toil and considers that it is laid on him to support what has no foundation in pure wisdom, we may well suppose that an uneasiness arises in his mind toward one who might without any inconvenience deal more favorably with him. He considers that by his industry his fellow creature is benefited and sees that this wealthy man is not satisfied with being supported in a plain way, but to gratify a desire of conforming to wrong customs increases to an extreme the labors of those who occupy his estate. Then we may reasonably judge that he will think himself unkindly used. When he considers that the proceedings of the wealthy are agreeable to the customs of the times and sees no means of redress in this world, how will the sighing of this innocent person ascend to the throne of that great and good Being who created all and who has a constant care over his creatures! Those who toil year after year to furnish others with wealth and extravagances until they are wearied and oppressed by too much labor understand the meaning of that language, "You know the heart of an alien, for you were aliens in the land of Egypt."

Many at this day who do not know the heart of an alien indulge themselves in ways of life that occasion more labor than Infinite Goodness intends for people. And yet they feel compassion for the distresses of those who come directly under their observation. What if they were to change circumstances a while with their laborers and pass regularly through the means of knowing the heart of an alien and come to a feeling knowledge of the constraints and hardships that many poor innocent people pass through in obscure life? What if these who now fare sumptuously every day were to act the other part of the scene until seven times had passed over them and return again to their former states? I believe many of them would embrace a less expensive life and would lighten the heavy burdens of some who now labor out of their sight and pass through tight places with which they are but little acquainted. To see their fellow creatures under difficulties to which they are in no degree accessory tends to awaken tenderness in the minds of all reasonable people. But consider the condition of those who are depressed in answering our demands and labor for us out of our sight while we pass our time in fullness. Consider also that much less than we demand would supply us with things really useful. What heart will not relent? How can reasonable people refrain from easing the suffering of which they themselves are the cause, when they may do so without inconvenience?

THE TYRANNY OF SELF-LOVE

From *A Word of Remembrance and Caution to the Rich*, Section 8

This second selection from Woolman's pamphlet is sections 8 and 9 in the manuscript (of 15). The published edition combined the two sections and renumbered the following sections. The idea of the self as the worst tyrant of all binds together many of Woolman's regular themes: simplicity, pacifism, concern for the poor, and above all faithfulness to God in Christ.

To labor to be established in divine love so that the mind is disentangled from the power of darkness is the great business of human life. Collecting riches, covering the body with finely made, costly apparel, and having magnificent furniture operate against universal love and tend to feed the self. So it is not a property of the children of the light to desire these things. God, who sent ravens to feed Elijah in the wilderness and increased the poor woman's small remains of meal and oil, is now as attentive as ever to the necessities of God's people. When God says to them, "You are my sons and daughters," no greater happiness can be desired by them. For they know how gracious a Father God is.

The greater part of the necessities of life are perishable so that each generation has occasion to labor for them. When we look toward a succeeding age with a mind influenced by universal love, instead of endeavoring to exempt some from those cares that necessarily relate to this life and to give them power to oppress others, we desire that they may all be the Lord's children and live in that humility and order becoming his family. Our hearts, being thus opened and enlarged, will feel content with a state of things as foreign to luxury and grandeur as the pattern our Redeemer laid down.

By desiring wealth for the power and distinction it gives and gathering it on this motive, people may become rich. But since their minds are drawn in a way distinguishable from the drawings of the Father, they cannot be united to the heavenly society where God is the strength of life. "It is easier," says our Savior, "for a camel to go through the eye of a needle than for someone who is rich to enter the kingdom of God." Here our Lord uses an instructive similitude. As a camel while in that form cannot pass through the eye of a needle, so someone who trusts in riches and holds them for the sake of the power and distinction attending them cannot in that spirit enter the kingdom. Now every part of a camel may be so reduced as to pass through a hole as small as the eye of a needle. Yet such is the bulk of the creature and the hardness of its bones and teeth that it could not be so reduced without much labor. People must cease from the spirit that craves riches and be brought into another disposition before they inherit the kingdom, as thoroughly

The Tyranny of Self Love — 61

as a camel must be changed from the form of a camel in passing through the eye of a needle.

When our Savior said to the rich youth, "Go, sell what you own, and give the money to the poor," though undoubtedly it was his duty to have done so, yet to enjoin the selling of all as a duty on every true Christian would be to limit the Holy One. Obedient children who are entrusted with great outward wealth wait for wisdom to dispose of it agreeably to God's will, in whom the orphan finds mercy. It may not be the duty of all to commit at once their substance to other hands but from time to time to look around among the numerous branches of the great family as the stewards of God, who provides for the widows and fatherless. But as disciples of Christ, although entrusted with many goods, they may not conform to sumptuous or luxurious living. For as he lived in perfect plainness and simplicity, the greatest in his family cannot by virtue of their station claim a right to live in worldly grandeur without contradicting him who said, "It is enough for the disciple to be like the teacher."

When our eyes are so single as to discern the selfish spirit clearly, we see that it is the greatest of all tyrants. Many thousand innocent people under some of the Roman emperors were confirmed in the truth of Christ's religion by the powerful effects of his Holy Spirit upon them. They scrupled to conform to heathen rites and were put to death by various kinds of cruel and lingering torments, as is largely set forth by Eusebius.

Now, if we single out Domitian, Nero, or any other of the persecuting emperors, that man, though terrible in his time, will appear as a tyrant of small consequence compared with this selfish spirit. Though his bounds were large, yet a great part of the world was out of his reach. Though he grievously afflicted the bodies of innocent people, yet the minds of many were divinely supported in their greatest agonies. Being faithful unto death, they were delivered from his tyranny. His reign, though cruel for a time, was soon over. And he in his greatest pomp appears to have been a slave to a selfish spirit.

Thus tyranny as applied to a man rises up and soon has an end. But consider the numerous oppressions in many states and the calamities occasioned by contending nations in various countries and ages of the world, and remember that selfishness has been the original cause of them all. Consider that those who are unredeemed from this selfish spirit not only afflict others but are afflicted themselves and have no real quietness in this life or in the future, but, according to the sayings of Christ, have their portion "where their worm never dies, and the fire is never quenched." Consider the havoc that is made in this age and how numbers of people are hurried on, striving to collect treasure to please minds that wander from perfect resignation. In the wisdom that is foolishness with God, they are perverting the true use of things, contending with one another to the point of bloodshed, and exerting their power to support ways of living foreign to the life of one wholly crucified to the world. Consider what great numbers of people are employed in preparing implements of war and the labor and toil of armies set apart for protecting their respective territories from invasion and the extensive miseries that attend their engagements. Meanwhile, those who till the land and are employed in other useful things in order to support not only themselves but those employed in military affairs and also those who own the soil have great hardships to encounter through too much labor. Others, in several kingdoms, are busied in fetching people to help to labor from distant parts of the world, to spend the remainder of their lives in the uncomfortable condition of slaves. Self is the bottom of these proceedings. Amid all this confusion and these scenes of sorrow and distress, can we remember that we are the disciples of the Prince of Peace and the example of humility and plainness that he set for us without feeling an earnest desire to be disentangled from everything connected with selfish customs in food, in clothing, in houses, and in all other things? We are of Christ's family. By walking as he walked, we may stand in that uprightness in which we were first made and have no fellowship with those inventions that people in their fallen wisdom have sought out.

IDENTIFICATION WITH THE POOR

From *Journal*, Chapter 12

In 1772, Woolman went to England to share his concerns about slavery and the poor with Meetings there. Much of this selection, however, deals with a vision Woolman had while sick with pleurisy in January of 1770. This is one of Woolman's last journal entries. He died a month and a half later.

Twenty-third of Eighth-month. — I was this day at Preston Patrick, and had a comfortable Meeting. I have several times been entertained at the houses of Friends who had various things about them that had the appearance of outward greatness. As I have kept inward, way has opened for conversation with such in private in which divine goodness has favored us together with heart-tendering times.

Twenty-sixth of Eighth-month. — Being now at George Crosfield's, in the county of Westmoreland, I feel a concern to commit to writing the following uncommon circumstance.

In a time of sickness with the pleurisy a little more than two years and a half ago, I was brought so near the gates of death that I forgot my name. Being then desirous to know who I was, I saw a mass of matter of a dull, gloomy color between the south and the east. I was informed that this mass was human beings in as great misery as they could be and live. I was mixed with them and henceforth might not consider myself as a distinct or separate being. I remained in this state several hours. I then heard a soft, melodious voice, more pure and harmonious than any I had heard with my ears before. I believed it was the voice of an angel who spoke to the other angels. The words were, "John Woolman is dead." I soon remembered that I was once John Woolman. Since I was sure that I was alive in the body, I greatly wondered what that heavenly voice could mean. I believed beyond doubting that it was the voice of a holy angel. But as yet it was a mystery to me.

I was then carried in spirit to the mines where poor oppressed people were digging rich treasures for those called Christians and heard them blaspheme the name of Christ. I was grieved at this, for his name was precious to me. I was then informed that these heathens were told that those who oppressed them were the followers of Christ, and they said among themselves, "If Christ directed them to use us in this way, then Christ is a cruel tyrant."

All this time the song of the angel remained a mystery. In the morning, when my dear wife and some others came to my bedside, I asked them if they knew who I was. They told me I was John Woolman and thought I was light-headed, for I did not tell them what the angel said. I was not disposed to talk much to anyone, but was very desirous to get so deep that I might understand this mystery.

My tongue was often so dry that I could not speak till I had moved it about and gathered some moisture. As I lay still for a time, I at length felt a divine power prepare my mouth to speak. Then I said, "I have been crucified with Christ; and it is no longer I who live, but it is Christ who lives in me. And the life I now live in the flesh I live by faith in the Son of God, who loved me and gave himself for me." Then the mystery was opened and I perceived there was joy in heaven over a sinner who had repented. The words *John Woolman is dead* meant no more than the death of my own will.

My natural understanding now returned as before. I saw that people setting off their tables with silver vessels when entertaining were often stained with worldly glory and that in the present state of things I should take heed how I fed myself out of such vessels. Going to our Monthly Meeting soon after my recovery, I dined at a Friend's house where drink was brought in silver vessels and not in any other. Since I wanted something to drink, I told him my case with weeping. He ordered some drink for me in another vessel. I afterward went through the same exercise in several Friends' houses in America, as well as in England. I have cause to acknowledge with humble reverence the loving-kindness of my heavenly Father, who has preserved me in such a tender frame of mind that none, I believe, have ever been offended at what I have said on that subject.

After this sickness I did not speak in public Meetings for worship for nearly one year. But my mind was very often in company with the oppressed slaves as I sat in Meetings. Though under God's dispensation I was shut up from speaking, yet the spring of the gospel ministry was many times livingly opened in me. The divine gift operated by abundance of weeping in feeling the oppression of this people. Although it is so long since I passed through this dispensation, the matter remains fresh and lively in my mind, and I believe it safest for me to commit it to writing.

APPENDIX

Reading Spiritual Classics for Personal and Group Formation

Many Christians today are searching for more spiritual depth, for something more than simply being good church members. That quest may send them to the spiritual practices of New Age movements or of Eastern religions such as Zen Buddhism. Christians, though, have their own long spiritual tradition, a tradition rich with wisdom, variety, and depth.

The great spiritual classics testify to that depth. They do not concern themselves with mystical flights for a spiritual elite. Rather, they contain very practical advice and insights that can support and shape the spiritual growth of any Christian. We can all benefit by sitting at the feet of the masters (both male and female) of Christian spirituality.

Reading spiritual classics is different from most of the reading we do. We have learned to read to master a text and extract information from it. We tend to read quickly, to get through a text. And we summarize as we read, seeking the main point. In reading spiritual classics, though, we allow the text to master and form us. Such formative reading goes more slowly, more reflectively, allowing time for God to speak to us through the text. God's word for us may come as easily from a minor point or even an aside as from the major point.

Formative reading requires that you approach the text in humility. Read as a seeker, not an expert. Don't demand that the text meet your expectations for what an "enlightened" author should write. Humility means accepting the author as another imperfect human, a product of his or her own time and situation. Learn to celebrate what is foundational in an author's writing without being overly disturbed by what is peculiar to the author's life and times. Trust the text as a gift from both God and the author, offered to you for your benefit—to help you grow in Christ.

To read formatively, you must also slow down. Feel free to reread a passage that seems to speak specially to you. Stop from time to time to reflect on what you have been reading. Keep a journal for these reflections. Often the act of writing can itself prompt further, deeper reflection. Keep your notebook open and your pencil in hand as you read. You might not get back to that wonderful insight later. Don't worry that you are not getting through an entire passage—or even the first paragraph! Formative reading is about depth rather than breadth, quality rather than quantity. As you read, seek God's direction for your own life. Timeless truths have their place but may not be what is most important for your own formation here and now.

As you read the passage, you might keep some of these questions running through your mind:

- How is what I'm reading true of my own life? Where does it reflect my own *experience*?

- How does this text challenge me? What new *direction* does it offer me?
- What must I change to put what I am reading into practice? How can I *incarnate* it, let this word become flesh in my life?

You might also devote special attention to sections that upset you. What is the source of the disturbance? Do you want to argue theology? Are you turned off by cultural differences? Or have you been skewered by an insight that would turn your life upside down if you took it seriously? Let your journal be a dialogue with the text.

If you find yourself moving from reading the text to chewing over its implications to praying, that's great! Spiritual reading is really the first step in an ancient way of prayer called *lectio divina* or "divine reading." Reading leads naturally into reflection on what you have read (meditation). As you reflect on what the text might mean for your life, you may well want to ask for God's help in living out any new insights or direction you have perceived (prayer). Sometimes such prayer may lead you further into silently abiding in God's presence (contemplation). And, of course, the process is only really completed when it begins to make a difference in the way we live (incarnation).

As good as it is to read spiritual classics in solitude, it is even better to join with others in a small group for mutual formation or "spiritual direction in common." This is *not* the same as a study group that

talks about spiritual classics. A group for mutual formation would have similar goals as for an individual's reading: to allow the text to shine its light on the *experiences* of the group members, to suggest new *directions* for their lives and practical ways of *incarnating* these directions. Such a group might agree to focus on one short passage from a classic at each Meeting (even if members have read more). Discussion usually goes much deeper if all the members have already read and reflected on the passage before the Meeting and bring their journals.

Such groups need to watch for several potential problems. It is easy to go off on a tangent (especially if it takes the focus off the members' own experience and onto generalities). At such times a group leader might bring the group's attention back to the text: "What does our author say about that?" Or, "How do we experience that in our own lives?" When a group member shares a problem, others may be tempted to try to "fix" it. This is much less helpful than sharing similar experiences and how they were handled (for good or ill). "Sharing" someone else's problems (whether that person is in or out of the group) should be strongly discouraged.

One person could be designated as leader, to be responsible for opening and closing prayers; to be the first to share or respond to the text; and to keep notes during the discussion to highlight recurring themes, challenges, directives, or practical steps. These responsibilities could also be shared among several members of the group or rotated.

For further information about formative reading of spiritual classics, try *A Practical Guide to Spiritual Reading* by Susan Annette Muto. *Shaped by the Word* by Robert Mulholland (Upper Room Books®) covers formative reading of the Bible. *Good Things Happen: Experiencing Community in Small Groups* by Dick Westley is an excellent resource on forming small groups of all kinds.

SEEKING A PURER CHRISTIAN LIFE

Sayings and Stories of the
DESERT FATHERS AND MOTHERS

Upper Room Spiritual Classics® — Series 3

Selected, edited, and introduced by
Keith Beasley-Topliffe

**Seeking a Purer Christian Life:
Saying and Stories of the Desert Mothers and Fathers**

Copyright © 2000 by Upper Room Books™
All rights reserved.

No part of this book may be used or reproduced in any manner whatsoever without written permission of the publisher except in the case of brief quotations embodied in critical articles or reviews. For information, write Upper Room Books,™ 1908 Grand Avenue, Nashville, Tennessee 37212.

The Upper Room® Website: http://www.upperroom.org

UPPER ROOM,® UPPER ROOM BOOKS™ and design logos are trademarks owned by the Upper Room,® Nashville, Tennessee. All rights reserved.

Scripture quotations are from the New Revised Standard Version of the Bible Copyright © 1989 by the Division of Christian Education of the National Council of Churches of Christ in the USA. Used by permission. All rights reserved.

Excerpts from *The World of the Desert Fathers* by Columba Stewart OSB, 1986, are printed by permission of SLG Press, Convent of the Incarnation. Fairacres, Oxford, England. Sisters of the Love of God.

Excerpts from *Harlots of the Desert* by Benedicta Ward SLG, 1987. Published by Cistercian Publications, Kalamazoo, Michigan 49008.

Cover design: Gore Studio, Inc.
Interior design and layout: Nancy J. Cole

First printing: 2000

Library of Congress Cataloging-in-Publication Data

Seeking a purer Christian life : sayings and stories of the Desert
　　Fathers and Mothers / selected, edited, and introduced by Keith
　　Beasley-Topliffe.
　　　　　p. cm. — (Upper Room spiritual classics. Series 3)
　　ISBN 0-8358-0902-1
　　1. Desert Fathers Quotations. 2. Spiritual life—Christianity
Quotations, maxims, etc. I. Beasley-Topliffe, Keith. II. Series.
BR63.S44 2000
270.2—dc21　　　　　　　　　　　　　　　　　　　　　　99-37907
　　　　　　　　　　　　　　　　　　　　　　　　　　　　　　CIP

Printed in the United States of America

TABLE OF CONTENTS

Introduction	5
Anthony's Beginnings in Discipline	12
Anthony's Struggle	16
Anthony's Testimony	19
Anthony's Advice	23
Maria and Abraham	27
Two Wise Women	33
Maria the Monk	37
Spiritual Direction	41
Abba Apollo on Hospitality	44
Abba Patermuthius	48
Abba Paphnutius	52
Sayings on Prayer	56
Sayings on Judging Others	61
Sayings on the Goal of Discipline	65
Appendix: Reading Spiritual Classics for Personal and Group Formation	69

INTRODUCTION

What does it take to lead a Christian life? Would a simpler lifestyle help us learn detachment from the things of this world? Would getting away from the distractions of our lives make us holier?

In the third, fourth, and fifth centuries, thousands of men and women abandoned the cities of the eastern Mediterranean to seek simplicity, solitude, and Christian community in the deserts of Egypt and Syria. Some lived alone, seeing others only at daily or weekly services of worship. Some lived in communities of thousands, working and worshiping together. They learned that fleeing external distractions only brought them face-to-face with the root of temptation in their own thoughts—the demons of lust, greed, pride, and envy were still with them. They also learned about the depths of God's mercy and forgiveness and the power of the Holy Spirit to overcome every other spirit and cleanse the soul.

Though the desert dwellers rarely wrote anything, others began to tell stories about them: how they came to repentance, how they fought against temptation, how they lived in community. They also wrote the teachings of the desert mothers and fathers, sometimes arranged in long speeches, sometimes only a few words of wisdom. Through these writings, desert teachings about prayer, spiritual disciplines, and living together spread throughout the Christian world and became the foundation of monasticism in

Western Europe as well as in the Eastern Church. The following selections include both stories and sayings illustrating the wisdom of the desert.

The World of the Desert

When Anthony, the first of the desert fathers, journeyed into the desert around A.D. 285, the Roman Empire still controlled all the area around the Mediterranean Sea. Though frequently torn by war between rival emperors, the empire provided a common culture in which Christianity grew despite persecution. By the late third century, Christianity was often tolerated even though officially illegal. Christians were able to build large churches in many cities. In 303, however, Emperor Diocletian attempted to restore Rome's power through strict adherence to the Roman gods. Many Christians were imprisoned or killed. Others denied Christ and sacrificed to the gods of Rome.

After Diocletian's death, one of the rivals competing for power became a Christian. Constantine saw in a dream that he could win if his banners displayed the sign of the cross. After his victory, he first declared toleration for all religions, then made Christianity the official religion of the empire. Suddenly bishops had secular as well as spiritual power, and only Christians could hope for advancement in government service.

Constantine soon discovered that the faith he had embraced and promoted was split in many factions. Debate raged over doctrinal issues such as the nature of Christ and his relation to God the Father and over practical questions such as what to do about Christians who had fallen away during persecution and now wished to return. Convinced that only a united church could unite the empire, he called a council in Niceaa (325) to decide these matters, and he offered the might of the empire to enforce its decisions.

These changes in the church and the world provided several motives for men and women to go into the desert. Some may have become disgusted with the secularization of Christianity, believing that it had become so easy to be a Christian that few took spiritual disciplines seriously. Others may have sought a refuge from the controversies, a place where living a Christian life was more important than debating fine points of doctrine. The desert offered opportunities for harsh discipline and hard work, solitude for prayer, space to form new kinds of communities dedicated to Christian living.

Life in the Desert

Anthony, first of the fathers, was born about 251 in Egypt in a Christian family. His parents died when he was about eighteen. He then sold his estate, placed his sister with a community of women, and began to seek spiritual guidance from older men in the area. He lived outside his home village for some time, then (about 285) lived alone in an abandoned fort in the mountains just east of the Nile for about twenty years. Many people came to seek his wisdom and some stayed nearby as disciples. He returned to Alexandria briefly during the Diocletian persecution, then returned to the desert to organize his followers into a slightly more structured community. About 313 he went farther into the desert to a mountain near the Red Sea. He lived there until his death in 356 at the age of 105. His friend Athanasius, bishop of Alexandria, wrote a book of Anthony's life the next year. It was quickly translated into several languages and spread throughout the empire. Reading the *Life of Anthony* was a key ingredient in the conversion of Augustine ten years later.

Meanwhile, many others had followed Anthony into the desert on both sides of the Nile in central Egypt (the Thebaid). About 320, Pachomius founded a community in Tabennisi in Upper Egypt (that is, upstream farther south). His leadership was chronicled in the *Rule of Pachomius*. Other communities grew in the salt marshes of the Nile Delta and in the desert east of Jerusalem in Syria.

Soon there were three basic forms of desert life. A few were solitaries like Anthony, though their solitude was often interrupted by visitors or ended as communities of disciples grew up around them. Some lived in clusters of separate huts or cells, close enough to permit worship and guidance in common while still preserving solitude most of the time. Most (including almost all the women) lived in highly structured communities like that of Pachomius. Thousands resided in some of these communities.

The primary work of these desert dwellers was prayer. Prayer was supposed to be constant, whatever else the monk or nun might be doing. Some monks made baskets or ropes to support themselves. Others hired out as farm laborers. Some, who carried on ministries of spiritual direction (including leadership of communities), were given the title Amma (Mother) or Abba (Father).

By the end of the fourth century the desert was filled with tens of thousands of men and women. People came from long distances to learn from the wisest. Palladius visited Egypt in 388 and wrote a history of the monks for his friend Lausus (and so called the *Lausiac History*) thirty years later. In 385 their monastery in Jerusalem sent John Cassian and his companion to visit the most famous fathers and bring back a report. Much later Cassian moved to southern France where he wrote *Institutes* and *Conferences*, interpreting the desert life for monastic communities in Western Europe. In 394, another group of tourist monks from Jerusalem visited Egypt. Ten years later one of them wrote *History of the Monks in Egypt*, an account of the trip. Meanwhile collections of sayings of various fathers (and some mothers too) were written down and collected. Many sayings include a brief story to provide context.

By the beginning of the fifth century, with Roman power declining, the desert became unsafe. Bands of raiders swept in from the desert to devastate monasteries and other communities. Many monks moved to safer areas. Others stayed and were killed. The era of Egyptian monasticism was over.

FURTHER READING

There have been several modern translations of the sayings and stories of the desert. Most notable is a series of translations by Benedicta Ward and various collaborators. These include *The Sayings of the Desert Fathers*, *The Lives of the Desert Fathers* (a translation of *History of the Monks in Egypt*), and *Harlots of the Desert*—all available from Cistercian Publications—as well as *The World of the Desert Fathers* and *The Wisdom of the Desert Fathers* from SLG Press. All of them are very readable and contain excellent introductions. A few of the sayings were translated and introduced by Thomas Merton in *The Wisdom of the Desert* (New Directions). Paulist Press has published selections from John Cassian's *Conferences* as well as a translation of the *Life of Anthony* by Athanasius. Modern translations of the *Lausiac History* and *Rule of Pachomius* are less readily available.

The traditions of desert spirituality were carried forward in the Eastern Church by many writers. Much of their wisdom is anthologized in the *Philokalia*, available in English translation in several volumes from Faber and Faber. In the Western Church, the *Rule of St. Benedict* (available in many translations) set the standard for Western monasticism.

NOTE ON THE TEXT

Selections from the *Life of Anthony* are from the translation in the *Nicene and Post-Nicene Fathers*, Series 2. The story of Maria and Abraham is from Benedicta Ward's translation of an early Latin version in *Harlots of the Desert*. Selections from the *Lausiac History* and *History of the Monks in Egypt* are from Ernest A. Wallis Budge's translation of a Syriac anthology of monastic sources called *The Paradise of the Fathers*. Selections from *Sayings of the Fathers* are from Benedicta Ward's translation of the "alphabetical collection" in *The Sayings of the Desert Fathers* except for the stories of the two wise women from *The World of the Desert Fathers*, translated by Columba Stewart.

All selections have been edited for length and inclusive language. Grammar, punctuation, and spelling have been modernized and Americanized. The older translations have required more extensive modernization. Where possible, scriptural quotes have been conformed to the New Revised Standard Version.

ANTHONY'S BEGINNINGS IN DISCIPLINE

From *Life of Anthony*, Chapters 1–4

Athanasius, bishop of Alexandria wrote The Life of Anthony in 357, the year after Anthony's death. He knew Anthony personally and received the testimony of others. This selection begins the story.

You should know that Anthony was an Egyptian by descent. His parents were of good family and possessed considerable wealth. Since they were Christians, he also was reared in that faith. In infancy he was brought up with his parents, knowing nothing else but them and his home. But when he was grown to boyhood and was advancing in years, he could not stand to learn letters or to associate with other boys. All his desire was, as it is written of Jacob, to live as "a quiet man" at home. He used to attend the Lord's house with his parents. He was not idle as a child nor did he despise his parents when older. He was obedient to his father and mother and attentive to what was read, keeping in his heart what was profitable in what he heard. Though as a child he was brought up in moderate affluence, he did not trouble his parents for varied or luxurious fare, nor was this a source of pleasure to him. He was content simply with what he found and did not seek anything further.

Anthony's Beginnings in Discipline — 13

After the deaths of his father and mother he was left alone with one little sister. He was about eighteen or twenty, and the care of both home and sister rested on him. Not six months after the deaths of his parents, he went according to custom into the Lord's house. As he walked, he communed with himself and reflected how the apostles left all and followed the Savior, and how, in Acts, people sold their possessions and brought and laid them at the apostles' feet for distribution to the needy, and how great a hope was laid up for them in heaven. Pondering these things, he entered the church. It happened that the Gospel was being read, and he heard the Lord saying to the rich man, "If you wish to be perfect, go, sell your possessions, and give the money to the poor, and you will have treasure in heaven; then come, follow me." Anthony went out immediately from the church, as though God had put him in mind of the saints and the passage had been read on his account. He gave the possessions of his ancestors to the villagers—they were three hundred acres, productive and very fair—that they should be no more a clog upon himself and his sister. All the rest that was movable he sold. Having got together much money, he gave it to the poor, reserving just a little for his sister's sake.

He went again into the church and heard the Lord say in the Gospel, "Do not worry about tomorrow." He could stay no longer but went out and gave those things also to the poor. He committed his sister to known and faithful virgins and put her into a convent to be brought up. From then on, he devoted himself outside his house to discipline, watching over himself and training himself with patience. There were not yet many monasteries in Egypt, and no monk at all knew of the distant desert. All who wished to watch over themselves practiced the discipline in solitude near their own villages.

There was an old man then in the next village who had lived the life of a hermit from his youth. After he had seen this man, Anthony imitated him in piety. At first he lived in places outside the village. Then if he heard of a good man anywhere, he went forth like the prudent bee and sought him, not returning to his own place until he had seen him and gotten from the good man supplies for his journey in the way of virtue. So by dwelling there at first, he confirmed his purpose not to return to his ancestral home or to the remembrance of his kinsfolk.

Anthony kept all his desire and energy for perfecting his discipline. He worked with his hands since he had heard, "Anyone unwilling to work should not eat." He spent part on bread and gave part to the needy. He was constant in prayer, knowing that people ought to pray in secret unceasingly. He paid such attention to what was read that none of the things that were written fell from him to the ground. He remembered all, and afterward his memory served him for books.

While he lived in that way, Anthony was loved by all. He subjected himself in sincerity to the good men whom he visited and learned thoroughly where each surpassed him in zeal and discipline. He observed the graciousness of one and the unceasing prayer of another. He learned from another's freedom from anger and another's loving-kindness. He paid attention to one as he watched and to another as he studied. He admired one for his endurance and another for his fasting and sleeping on the ground. He watched carefully the meekness of one and the long-suffering of another and noted the piety toward Christ and the mutual love that animated all. He returned to his own place of discipline filled with these things and then strove to unite the qualities of each. He was eager to show in himself the virtues of all. He had no rivalry with others of the same age except this: that he should not be second to them in higher things. He did this in a way that hurt nobody's feelings, but made them rejoice over him. So all the people of that village and the good men he spoke with intimately, when they saw that he was a man of this sort, would call him God-beloved. Some welcomed him as a son, others as a brother.

 ANTHONY'S STRUGGLE

From *Life of Anthony*, Chapters 12–14

After several years of disciplined living near his home, Anthony wanted more solitude. He went south into the desert between the Nile and the Red Sea. He was about thirty-five years old.

More and more confirmed in his purpose, Anthony hurried to the mountain. He found a fort, so long deserted that it was full of creeping things, on the other side of the river. He crossed over to it and dwelled there. The reptiles immediately left the place, as though someone were chasing them. He sealed up the entrance completely, having stored up loaves for six months—it is a custom of the Thebans, and the loaves often remain fresh a whole year. Since he found water inside, he could stay inside by himself, never going out or looking at anyone who came. Thus he spent a long time training himself, and received loaves, let down from above, twice a year.

But those of his acquaintances who came often used to spend days and nights outside since he did not permit them to enter. They heard something like crowds inside, making noises and crying with piteous voices, "Go from what is ours. What are you doing in the desert? You cannot withstand our attack." So at first those outside thought that there were some men fighting with him, and that they had entered by ladders. But when they stooped down, they saw through a hole there was nobody. They were afraid, figuring it was demons, and they called on Anthony. He heard them quickly, though he had not given a thought to the demons. Coming to the door, he asked them to leave and not to be afraid, He said, "The demons seem to make attacks against those who are cowardly. Sign yourselves therefore with the cross and depart boldly. Let them make sport for themselves." So they departed fortified with the sign of the cross.

But Anthony remained completely unharmed by the evil spirits. Nor was he wearied with the contest, for visions from above came to his aid, and the weakness of the foe relieved him of much trouble and armed him with greater zeal. His acquaintances would often come expecting to find him dead and would hear him singing, "Let God rise up. Let his enemies be scattered; let those who hate him flee before him. As smoke is driven away, so drive them away; as wax melts before the fire, let the wicked perish before God." And again, "All nations surrounded me; in the name of the Lord I cut them off!"

And so for nearly twenty years, he continued training himself in solitude, never going forth, and but seldom seen by any. After this many eagerly wanted to imitate his discipline, and his acquaintances came and began to cast down and wrench off the door by force. Anthony, as from a shrine, came forth initiated in the mysteries and filled with the Spirit of God.

Then for the first time he was seen outside the fort by those who came to see him. When they saw him, they wondered at the sight, for his body was in the same shape as before and was neither fat like a man without exercise nor lean from fasting and striving with the demons. He was just the same as they had known him before his retirement. His soul was still free from blemish, neither contracted as if by grief nor relaxed by pleasure nor possessed by laughter or dejection, for he was not troubled when he beheld the crowd or overjoyed at being saluted by so many.

Through him the Lord healed the bodily illnesses of many present and cleansed others from evil spirits. God gave grace to Anthony in speaking so that he consoled many who were sorrowful and united those who had differences, exhorting all to prefer the love of Christ before all that is in the world. And while he exhorted and advised them to remember the good things to come and the loving-kindness toward us of God, "who did not withhold his own Son, but gave him up for all of us," he persuaded many to embrace the solitary life. And so it happened in the end that cells arose even in the mountains, and the desert was colonized by monks who came forth from their own people and enrolled themselves for citizenship in the heavens.

ANTHONY'S TESTIMONY

From *Life of Anthony*, Chapters 39–42

After coming out from his cell, Anthony began to speak about struggling against temptations and demonic attacks. In this selection he concludes the discourse with some of his experiences.

How often have the evil spirits called me blessed, and I have cursed them in the name of the Lord! How often have they predicted the rising of the river, and I answered them, "What have you to do with it?" Once they came threatening and surrounded me like soldiers in full armor. At another time they filled the house with horses, wild beasts, and creeping things. But I sang, "Some take pride in chariots, and some in horses, but our pride is in the name of the Lord our God," and they were turned to flight by the Lord. Once they came in darkness, bearing the appearance of a light, and said, "We came to give you a light, Anthony." But I closed my eyes and prayed. Immediately the light of the wicked ones was quenched. A few months later they came as though singing psalms and babbling the words of Scripture. "But I am like the deaf. I do not hear." Once they shook the cell with an earthquake, but I continued praying with unshaken heart. And after that, they came again making noises, whistling, and dancing. But as I prayed and lay singing psalms to myself, they immediately began to lament and weep as if their strength had failed them. But I gave glory to the Lord who had brought them down and made an example of their daring and madness.

Once a very tall demon appeared with pomp and dared to say, "I am the power of God and I am Providence. What do you want me to give you?" But I then breathed on him and spoke the name of Christ and prepared to hit him. And I seemed to have hit him, and at once, big as he was, he and all his demons disappeared at the name of Christ. At another time while I was fasting, he came full of craft, under the semblance of a monk with what seemed to be loaves and advised me, "Eat and cease from all your labors. You also are a man and likely to fall sick." But I, perceiving his trick, rose up to pray. He could not endure it, for he departed and seemed to go through the door like smoke. Often they would beat me, and I repeated again and again, "Nothing shall separate me from the love of Christ." At that they fell to beating one another. But it was not I who stopped them and destroyed their power: it was the Lord, who said, "I watched Satan fall from heaven like a flash of lightning." But, children, in the Apostle's words, "I have applied all this to myself," that you might learn not to faint in discipline or to fear the devil or the delusions of the demons.

And since I have become a fool in describing these things, receive this also as an aid to your safety and fearlessness. Believe me, for I do not lie. Once someone knocked at the door of my cell. When I went out, I saw one who seemed of great size and tall. Then when I asked, "Who are you?" he said, "I am Satan." Then when I said, "Why are you here?" he answered, "Why do the monks and all other Christians blame me undeservedly? Why do they curse me hourly?" Then I answered, "Why do you trouble them?" He said, "I am not the one who troubles them. They trouble themselves, for I have become weak. Have they not read, 'The enemies have vanished in everlasting ruins; their cities you have rooted out'? I no longer have a place, a weapon, a city. The Christians are spread everywhere, and at length even the desert is filled with monks. They should look after themselves and not curse me unreservedly." Then I marveled at the grace of the Lord and said to him: "You are always a liar and never speak the truth. But at least you have spoken this truly, even if against your will, for the coming of Christ has made you weak. He has cast you down and stripped you." But when he heard the Savior's name, he could not bear the burning from it and vanished.

If, therefore, the devil himself confesses that his power is gone, we ought utterly to despise both him and his demons. Since the enemy with his hounds has tricks only of this sort, we—now that we know their weakness—are able to despise them. So let us not despair or have a thought of cowardice in our hearts or frame fears for ourselves, saying, I am afraid a demon might come and overthrow me or lift me up and cast me down or confound me by rising against me suddenly. Let us not have such thoughts in mind at all or be sorrowful as though we were perishing. Rather let us be courageous and rejoice always, believing that we are safe. Let us consider in our souls that the Lord who is with us put the evil spirits to flight and broke their power. Let us consider and take to heart that while the Lord is with us, our foes can do us no harm. For when they come, they approach us in a form corresponding to the state in which they discover us and adapt their delusions to the condition of mind in which they find us. If, therefore, they find us timid and confused, they at once attack like robbers, having found our minds unguarded. Whatever we are thinking about, they do—and more also. For if they find us fainthearted and cowardly, they greatly increase our terror by their delusions and threats. But if they see us rejoicing in the Lord, contemplating the bliss of the future, mindful of the Lord, considering that all things are in God's hand and that no evil spirit has any strength against the Christian or any power at all over anyone—if they behold the soul fortified with these thoughts—they are baffled and turned backward.

ANTHONY'S ADVICE

From *Life of Anthony*, Chapters 55–56, 58

After a brief return to the city to encourage Christians suffering persecution, Anthony returned to the desert, going even father into the wilderness. Even there people followed him, some building cells near his, others simply asking advice. Here is some of the guidance he offered.

"Believe in the Lord and love him. Keep yourselves from impure thoughts and fleshly pleasures. Pray continually. Avoid vanity. Sing psalms before sleep and on awaking. Hold in your heart the commandments of Scripture. Be mindful of the works of the saints so that your souls, being put in remembrance of the commandments, may be brought into harmony with the zeal of the saints."

He especially counseled them to meditate continually on the Apostle's word, "Do not let the sun go down on your anger." He considered this was spoken of all commandments in common and that not on anger alone, but not on any other sin of ours ought the sun to go down. He said, "It is good and needful that neither should the sun condemn us for an evil by day nor the moon for a sin by night or even for an evil thought. So that this state may be preserved in us, it is good to hear the Apostle and keep his words, for he says, 'Examine yourselves and test yourselves.' Daily, therefore, let all take an account of their actions both by day and by night. And if they have sinned, let them cease from it. If they have not, let them not be boastful but abide in what is good without being negligent or condemning their neighbors or justifying themselves, 'until the Lord comes, who will bring to light the things now hidden,' as the blessed apostle Paul says. For often we do things unawares that we do not know. But the Lord sees all things. So let us have sympathy for one another and commit the judgment to God. Let us bear one another's burdens. But let us examine ourselves and hasten to fill up whatever is lacking. As a safeguard against sin, let the following be observed. Let us each one note and write down our actions and the impulses of our soul as though we were going to relate them to one another. Be assured that if we would be utterly ashamed to have them known, we will abstain from sin and harbor no base thoughts in our minds. For who wishes to be seen while sinning? Who will not lie after the commission of a sin, through the wish to escape notice? As we would not commit carnal sin while we are looking at one another, so if we record our thoughts as though about to tell them to one another, we shall more easily keep ourselves free from vile thoughts through shame. So let what we write take the place of the eyes of our fellow hermits. Then blushing as much to write as if we had been caught, we may never think of what is unseemly. Thus forming ourselves, we shall be able to keep the body in subjection, to please the Lord, and to trample on the tricks of the enemy."

This was the advice he gave to those who came to him. And with those who suffered he sympathized and prayed. And often the Lord heard him on behalf of many. Yet he did not boast because he was heard or complain if not. But always he gave the Lord thanks and asked the sufferer to be patient and know that healing belonged neither to him nor to any human, but only to the Lord, who does good when and to whom he will. The sufferers therefore used to receive the words of the old man as though they were a cure, learning not to be downhearted but to endure patiently. And those who were healed were taught to give thanks to not Anthony but to God alone.

There was also a maiden from Busiris Tripolitana, who had a terrible and very hideous disorder. For what ran from her eyes, nose, and ears fell to the ground and immediately became worms. She was paralyzed also and squinted. Her parents had heard of monks going to Anthony and believed in the Lord who healed the woman with the issue of blood. So they asked to be allowed, together with their daughter, to journey with them. And when they let them, the parents and the girl remained outside the mountain with Paphnutius, the confessor and monk. But the monks went in to Anthony. And when they were almost ready to tell about the damsel, he anticipated them and detailed the sufferings of the child and how she journeyed with them. Then they asked that she should be admitted. Anthony did not allow it, but said, "Go, and if she is not dead, you will find her healed. For the accomplishment of this is not mine, that she should come to me, wretched man that I am, but her healing is the work of the Savior, who in every place shows pity to those who call upon him. So the Lord has inclined to her as she prayed, and his loving-kindness has declared to me that he will heal the child where she now is." So the wonder took place. When the monks went out, they found the parents rejoicing and the girl whole.

MARIA AND ABRAHAM

From *Life of Maria the Harlot* by Archdeacon Ephraim

Stories of repentance were popular among the desert monks, especially repentance of flagrant sinners such as murderers, thieves, and prostitutes. This story was written down by Ephraim, a disciple of Abraham and so personally acquainted with the details. Maria was an orphan whose uncle Abraham took her to the desert to live in a small room built onto his own hut. There she grew up, praying and learning the Scriptures. When she was seduced by a monk, she felt she was ruined and ran to the city to become a prostitute. It took Abraham two years to learn where she was.

Abraham put on the dress of a soldier and put a large hat on his head so that it hid his face, and he opened the door of his cell. He took with him a pound's weight in coins, and getting on the horse, he hastened away. He went through the countryside to the city, adopting the customs of the inhabitants so that he might not be recognized. Thus blessed Abraham made use of an alien dress that he might turn her back from her flight. Let us marvel at this second Abraham, for as the first Abraham went into battle with the kings and brought out his nephew, Lot, so this second Abraham went to war with the devil so that he might overcome him and bring back his niece with even more triumph.

When he reached the place, he wanted to arrange to see her with the least possible interruption, so he went up to the brothel-keeper and smiled, saying, "My friend, I hear that you have a very good girl indeed here. If I may, I would very much like to have her." The brothel-keeper said, "As you say, I have one who is beautiful beyond the usual run. Her beauty excels everything that nature can create." The old man then asked her name, and she replied that she was called Maria. Smiling with joy, Abraham then said, "I beg you to take me into her presence so that I may enjoy her today, for I have heard this girl praised by many." When the brothel-keeper heard this, she summoned Maria. When her uncle saw her in the dress of a harlot, he was almost overcome by grief. He had to hold back his tears by force, lest the brothel-keeper should know him and make him leave the courtyard.

When they had rested and drunk a little, this amazing man began to fondle her. He got up and put his arm around her neck and stroked it with his lips. When his lips touched her, Maria smelled the sweet smell of asceticism coming from his body, and she remembered the days when she, too, had lived as an ascetic. As if pierced by a spear, she cried out from her heart and burst into tears, unable to bear it; and she said as if to herself, "Alas, alas, how desolate I am!" The brothel-keeper was angry when she noticed this and said in surprise, "Whatever is the matter with you, Mistress Maria? You have been here for two years and never before have I had word of complaint from you." Maria said to her, "It would be better for me if I could die before the third year has passed." At that, the blessed old man was afraid she would recognize him, so he said soothingly to her, "If you go on thinking about your sins, how can we expect to enjoy ourselves?"

Then the holy man offered the brothel-keeper the money he had brought and said to her, "My friend, I want you to make us a very good meal so that I may have this girl now. I have come a very long way out of love for her." Forty years of abstinence when he tasted nothing but bread, and now without hesitation he chewed meat to save a soul from hell! The choir of holy angels rejoiced and was amazed at his discretion, for without hesitation he ate and drank in order that he might draw a soul out of the mire! Wisdom of wisdom, how this man, wise, discreet and prudent, seemed a fool and indiscreet so that he might snatch from the mouth of the lion the soul it had eaten and set free from the darkness and bonds of sin the soul that had been taken and bound!

When they had eaten, the girl drew Abraham to the bed to lie down and took him toward the inner chamber, and he said, "Let us go in." When he got inside, he saw the bed set on a platform, and he seated himself on it, as if eagerly. (What shall I say of you, athlete of Christ? After forty years of conversion, you lie down on a prostitute's bed and wait for her to come to you! All this you did for the praise and glory of Christ in order to save that lost soul.)

When he had seated himself on the bed, Maria said to him, "Come, sir, let me unfasten your trousers for you." And he said, "First close the door carefully and lock it." When she had locked the door, she came toward him, and the old man said to her, "Mistress Maria, come close to me." And when she had come close, he held her firmly with one hand, as if about to kiss her, but snatching the hat from his head, in a voice breaking with tears, he said to her, "Don't you know me, Maria, my child? Dear heart, am I not he who took care of you? Who hurt you, my daughter? What has become of your virginity, your tears, your vigils, all your prayers? From what a height you have fallen, my child, into such a pit as this! Why, when you sinned, did you not tell me? Why could you not come and speak of it with me? For of course I would have done penance for you. Why instead did you hurt me and give me this unbearable weight of grief? For who is without sin, save God alone?" While he was saying this and much besides, Maria sat like a stone between his hands, overcome both by shame and by fear. In tears, the old man said to her, "Why do you not speak to me, my heart? Have I not come to take you home, my child?" And so until the middle of the night Abraham consoled Maria with words of this kind and covered her with tears. After a while she plucked up courage, and weeping, she said to him, "I could not come to you; I was so very much ashamed. How can I pray again to God when I am defiled with sin as filthy as this?" The holy man said to her, "Upon me be your sin, Maria, and let God lay it to my account. Only listen to me and come, let us go back where we belong. My dear, do not draw back from the mercy of God. To you, your sins seem like mountains, but God has spread mercy over all that God has made. So we once read together how an unclean woman came to the Lord, and he did not send her away but cleansed her. And she washed his feet with her tears and wiped them with the hairs of her head. If spark could set fire to the ocean, then indeed your sins could defile the purity of God! It is not new to fall, my daughter. What is wrong is to lie down when you have fallen. Remember where you stood before you fell. The devil once mocked you, but now he will know that you can rise more strong than ever before. I beg you, take pity on my old age, and do not make me grieve any more. Get up, and come with me to our cell. Do not be afraid. Sin is only part of being human. It happened to you very quickly, and now by the help of God you are coming out of it even more quickly, for God does not will the death of sinners, but that they may live." Then she said to him, "If you know of any penance I can do that God will receive from me, command me and I will do it." So she laid her head on his feet and wept away the rest of the night, saying, "What shall I return to the Lord for all his bounty to me?"

When morning came, blessed Abraham said to her, "Get up, my daughter, and let us go home." She said to him, "I have this small amount of gold and these clothes. What do you want me to do with them?" And Abraham said, "Leave it all here, Maria, for it came from evil." So they got up and went out. He placed her on the horse, and he went first leading it, like a shepherd with the lost sheep he had found, bearing it home upon his shoulders with joy.

 TWO WISE WOMEN

From *The Sayings of the Fathers*

For many monks, the strongest temptations for breaking their vows and leaving the desert were sexual. Here are two stories of women who, by refusing lustful men, helped them to overcome temptation and live holy lives.

A brother was sent on an errand by his abbot. Arriving at a place that had water, he found a woman there washing clothes. Overcome, he asked her if he might sleep with her. She said to him, "Listening to you is easy, but I could be the cause of great suffering for you." He said to her, "How?" She answered, "After committing the deed, your conscience will strike you, and either you will give up on yourself, or it will require great effort for you to reach the state that is yours now. Therefore, before you experience that hurt, go on your way in peace." When he heard this, he was struck with contrition and thanked both God and her wisdom. He went to his abbot, informed him of the event, and he, too, marveled. And the brother urged the rest not to go out of the monastery, and so he himself remained in the monastery, not going out until death.

—

There were two traders from Apamea in Syria who were friends and who traded abroad. One was wealthy, and the other was of moderate fortune. The wealthy man had a wife who was beautiful and also chaste, as events would prove. For when her husband died and the other man saw her worthiness, he wanted to take her to himself as his wife. But he was hesitant to speak to her, for fear that she would not accept. She was wise and knew what was going on and said to him, "Master Simeon"—for this was his name—"I see that you are thinking about something. Tell me what you feel and I will reassure you." At first he was hesitant to speak, but later he confessed to her and pleaded with her to become his wife. She said to him, "If you do what I command you, I will accept." He said to her, "Whatever you command me, I will do." She said to him, "Go into your workshop and fast until I summon you, and in truth I will not eat anything until I call for you." He agreed, but she did not tell him a specific time when she would call for him.

He went off for one day, then a second, then a third, and still she did not call for him. But he persevered, either because of love for her or because God had arranged matters and provided him with endurance, having seen where God was going to call him—for after all this he became a vessel of election. On the fourth day, she sent for him. He had little strength. Being unable to come on foot due to his suffering, he had to be carried. She for her part prepared a table and a bed and said to him, "Look, here is a table and there is a bed. Where do you wish to begin?" He said to her, "I implore you, have mercy on me and give me a bit to eat because I am weak. For if it were to be a woman first, I would not be capable of it due to the feebleness afflicting me." Then she said to him, "See you when you were hungry you preferred food to me, to every woman, and to pleasure? Therefore, whenever you have such thoughts, make use of this medicine and be free from every foul thought. For you have convinced me that after my husband, I shall marry neither you nor any other. But under the protection of Christ I hope to remain as I am, a widow." Then struck with contrition and marveling at her wisdom and self-restraint, he said to her, "Since the Lord has seen fit to oversee my salvation by means of your wisdom, what do you advise me to do?" She, moved by his youth and beauty, and being careful lest at that moment she also might suffer such a temptation, said to him, "By God, I believe that you love no one more than me." He said to her, "It is so." She said to him, "I, and this is God's truth, also love you, but since it is the voice of the Lord that says, 'Whoever comes to me and does not hate father and mother, wife and children, brothers and sisters, yes, and even life itself, cannot be my disciple,' let us part from each other because of God, so that the Lord might consider you to have renounced your wife because of God, and me to have renounced my husband. For there is a monastery of hermits in our region at Apamea, and if you are fully intending to be saved, become a monk there and you will truly please God." Immediately he gave up his trade, hastened to that monastery, and remained there until the time of his death. And he was esteemed, for he had a clean mind. He saw things in a suitable manner and regarded them spiritually.

MARIA THE MONK

From the *Lausiac History of Palladius*

About 420, Palladius wrote a collection of stories about the desert for his patron, Lausus. Palladius may have titled the book Paradise, but it has come to be known as the Lausiac History. The monks believed that it was better to suffer false accusations and attacks in silence rather than accuse another of lying. Here a very unusual monk carries such patience to an amazing extreme.

There was a certain worldly man who wished to become a monk. He had a little daughter who asked him to take her with him to the monastery. He said, "If you wish to become a nun, let me take you to a house for virgins." But she said to him, "I cannot be separated from you." Her father was greatly distressed because she wept night and day and begged not to be separated from him. He made up his mind to take her with him and changed her name from Maria to Maryana as if she had been a boy. Then he committed the matter to God and took her into a monastery without anyone perceiving that Maryana was a girl. After several years Maryana's father died performing the excellent works of the monastic life. The abbot saw that Maryana was working hard and excelling spiritually and rejoiced in him (not knowing he was not a boy). He commanded that he should not be sent out on the highways to beg because he was a child.

When the abbot saw that the brothers envied Maryana because he did not go out, he called Maryana and said to him, "Since the brothers envy you because you do not do the work as they do, I command you to do it." Then Maryana fell down before the abbot and said, "Whatever you command me to do I will do gladly, O Father." Whenever the brothers went out, they visited a certain believer in order to rest a little and refresh themselves. So when Maryana went out, this believer saw him in the evening and brought him to his house to rest there for the night. The believer had a daughter, and on the night Maryana stayed with him someone seduced her and said, "If your father asks you who seduced you, tell him it was Maryana the monk." As soon as Maryana had departed, the father knew that his daughter had been seduced and asked, "Who has seduced you?" She said, "Maryana, the monk." Then the father immediately went to the monastery and spoke with tears before the abbot and all the brothers, "What offense have I committed against you that you should seduce my daughter?" When the abbot heard this, he was greatly moved and said, "What do you say? Who seduced your daughter? Tell me who it is and I will expel him from the monastery at once." And the man said, "It is Maryana." Then the abbot called for Maryana, but he could not be found. Then they knew that he was out on a journey. The abbot told the father, "There is nothing further I can do but this: when Maryana returns from the highway, I will not allow him to enter."

When Maryana came back from the road, they would not allow him to enter the monastery, and he wept at the door and said, "What is my offense that I am not permitted to enter?" Then the doorkeeper said, "You have seduced the daughter of the believer whom the monks visit." Maryana begged the doorkeeper, "For the Lord's sake go in and persuade the abbot to let me enter the monastery. Whatever he orders because of my fall I will do." So the doorkeeper went in, and the abbot said, "Go tell Maryana, 'Because you have done this, you will never see my face again. Go away wherever you please.'" When Maryana heard that, he was greatly afflicted and sat by the door night and day and wept because of what had happened to him.

After the maiden (through whom Maryana had been trodden in the dust) had given birth to her child, her father took the boy and brought it to Maryana, saying, "Look, here is your son. Take him and raise him." Maryana took the child, saying, "Glory to God who can bear with sinners like myself." Each day he took the child and went up the mountain to the goats of the monastery, and the child nursed on goats' milk. Then Maryana returned to the door of the monastery. He never left the door except when he went to give the child milk. He asked those who went in or out, with tears, to join him in praying God to forgive his sin. He sat there for four years, and tears were never absent from his eyes by night or day. Everyone who heard him weeping was grieved for his sake. For four years Maryana suffered affliction by the door and showed the child to everyone, saying, "Pray for me, for I fell into fornication, and this child is the result of it." Then God moved the abbot's mind to bring Maryana into the monastery.

As soon as Maryana heard this, he fell down before the Lord and said, "Glory to you, O Lord, who have not been unmindful of such a sinner as I am! I thank you for all the goodness you have shown me. What can I give you in return? For you have brought me into the monastery when I thought I must die by the door." Maryana, who was carrying the child and weeping and sighing and groaning, fell down before the abbot and the whole brotherhood and said, "Forgive me, masters and fathers, for I have angered God with evil works and greatly afflicted you. Pray for me, that God may forgive my fall."

After many years Maryana, having prevailed mightily in the great labors of spiritual excellence, delivered his soul to our Lord. When he was dead, the brothers came to anoint him with oil and saw that Maryana was a woman. They ran quickly and called the man who had made the accusation against Maryana. When he came and saw her, great wonder laid hold of him. He begged God to forgive him the great sin and wrong he had done to Maryana.

SPIRITUAL DIRECTION

From the *Lausiac History of Palladius*

Many people came to the desert fathers seeking a word of direction. In this selection, Macarius, a disciple of Anthony, takes a word to a monk who needs special care.

Abba Macarius used to dwell by himself in the desert. Below him was another desert where many lived. The old man was watching the road one day and saw Satan traveling on it in the form of a man. He was wearing a garment full of holes, and various fruits were hanging about him. The old man Macarius said to him, "Where are you going?" He said, "I am going to visit the brothers and to make them mindful of their work." The old man said, "Why do you need those various fruits?" Satan answered, "I am carrying them to the brothers for food." The old man said, "All these?" And Satan said, "Yes. If one doesn't please a brother, I hand him another. If that doesn't please him, I give him another. One or the other of these must certainly please him." Having said these things, Satan went on his way.

Then the old man kept watching the road until Satan came along to return. When he saw him, he asked, "Have you been successful?" And Satan said, "Where can I get help?" The old man said, "For what purpose?" Satan said, "They have all forsaken me and rebelled against me. Not one of them will allow himself to be persuaded by me." The old man said, "Don't you have even one friend left there?" And Satan said, "Yes, I have one brother, but only one, who will be persuaded by me, even though whenever he sees me, he turns away his face as if from an enemy." The old man said to him, "What is the name of this brother?" And Satan said, "Theopemptus." Then he departed and went on his way.

Abba Macarius rose up and went down to the lower desert. The brothers heard and brought palm leaves and went out to meet him. Every monk prepared his cell, thinking that he would stay there. But the old man asked for the brother named Theopemptus, who received him joyfully. When the brothers began to speak among themselves, the old man said to him, "What do you have to say, my brother? How are your affairs?" And Theopemptus said, "At the present moment matters are well with me," for he was ashamed to speak. The old man said, "Look, I have lived a life of stern discipline for many years and am held in honor by everyone. Nevertheless, even though I am an old man, the spirit of fornication disturbs me." And Theopemptus answered, "Believe me, father, it disturbs me also." And the old man, like one who was bothered by many thoughts, made a reason for talking. At length he led the brother to confess the matter. Afterward, he said to him, "How long do you fast?" The brother said, "Until the ninth hour." The old man said, "Fast until evening and continue to do so. Repeat passages from the book of the Gospels and from the other scriptures. If a thought rises in your mind, don't look downward but always upward, and the Lord will help you." And so, having made the brother reveal his thought and having given him encouragement, he departed to go to his own desert. As he traveled along the road, he watched according to his custom.

He saw the devil again and said to him, "Where are you going?" He answered, "I go to remind the brothers of their work." When he came back again, the holy man said to him, "How are the brothers?" The devil said, "They are in an evil case." And the old man said, "Why?" The devil said, "They are all like savage animals and rebellious. But the worst thing of all is that even the one brother who used to be obedient to me has turned, I know not why. He will not be persuaded by me in any way and is the most savage of them all against me. On account of this, I have taken an oath never again to go to that place or at least only after a very long time."

ABBA APOLLO ON HOSPITALITY

From *History of the Monks in Egypt*

In 394–95, a group of monks from Jerusalem visited Egypt to learn from the desert fathers. One of the party wrote History of the Monks in Egypt, *describing the journey and what they had heard from those they met. In this selection the author tells of the group's reception by Abba Apollo, the leader of a community of five hundred monks.*

When three of us went to visit the blessed Apollo, the brothers with him saw us and recognized us by the descriptions they had heard from him of our journey. They met us with gladness and sang songs of praise, for this is the custom with all the brothers. They bowed down with their faces to the ground, then rose up and gave us the salutation of peace and said to their companions, "Behold, the brothers of whom our abba spoke to us three days ago have come to us." For he had said, "Behold, after three days three brothers will come to you from Jerusalem." Some of the brothers went before us, rejoicing and singing psalms, and some followed behind answering them until we arrived at the place where the blessed man was. When our father Apollo heard the sound of their singing, he also came forth to meet us, according to the custom of the brothers. When he saw us, he was the first to bow low to the ground. Then he stretched out his hand and rose up and kissed us and led us in and prayed and washed our feet with his own hands. He urged us to rest ourselves and eat, for it was his custom to do this to all the brothers who came to visit him.

Now the brothers who were with him did not go straight to their meal, but first received the Eucharist of Christ together. They did this daily at the ninth hour and then ate their meal. While they were eating they learned his commandments until the time for sleep. Then some of them went into the desert and repeated the Scriptures by heart the whole night long. Others stayed with him to glorify God until the morning. Many of them used to come down at the ninth hour and receive the Eucharist and then return to their places. The spiritual food alone would be sufficient for them till the ninth hour on the next day. Many of them would remain without ordinary food for several days at a time: from one Sunday to another. We observed their joy in the desert, with which nothing on the earth—no bodily delight—can be compared. Among them no one was sorry or afflicted with grief. But if anyone was found to be in affliction, our father Apollo knew the cause and was able to tell him the secret thoughts of his mind. He would say, "It is not proper for us to be afflicted at our redemption, for we are those who are about to inherit the kingdom of heaven. Let evil people be in mourning, and let the righteous rejoice. For they have their happiness in earthly things and cultivate them. Why shouldn't we, who are worthy of the blessed hope, rejoice always, according to the encouraging words of the blessed Apostle Paul, 'Rejoice always, pray without ceasing, give thanks in all circumstances'?"

What shall I say concerning the grace in the words of the blessed Apollo? He discussed many things concerning rigorous discipline and exhorted us how to receive the brothers. He told us that when brothers came to visit us, it was proper to bow low before them. "Not," he said, "that we bow down before them, but before God who is in them. When you see your brother, you see Christ. We have derived the custom of urging brothers from time to time to come in and rest and refresh themselves from Abraham and also from Lot, who urged the angels to stay with him.

"If possible, monks should partake of the mysteries of Christ each day. For whoever keeps away from them keeps away from God. For the voice of our Life Giver says, 'Those who eat my flesh and drink my blood abide in me, and I in them.' It is very helpful for monks to remember the passion of our Redeemer at all times because by this remembrance we become worthy of the forgiveness of our sins always. So it is right that we should always make ourselves worthy to receive the holy mysteries of our Redeemer.

"Let no one break the established fasts unless it would cause great suffering. We keep the fast on

Wednesday because on that day the Jews plotted to betray our Lord and on Friday because on that day he was crucified. So whoever breaks these becomes one of the betrayers. But if your brother comes to you during a period of fasting and is in need of refreshment—even at the wrong time—set the table for him by himself. If he does not want to eat, do not force him. This is a universal tradition of hospitality."

On several occasions we conversed together the whole Sabbath. When he was escorting us on our way back, he said to us, "Have peace with one another and let no one separate himself from his companion on the way." Then he said to the brothers who were with him, "Who among you is willing to go and escort these brothers on the way to the other fathers?" With very few exceptions, all the brothers sought anxiously to go with us and to escort us on our way. But the holy man Apollo selected three of them who were mighty in their disciplined work and understanding in their speech. He commanded them not to leave us until we had seen all the fathers whom we wished to see and had rejoiced in conversing with them. Then he blessed us and sent us away, saying, "The Lord bless you from Zion. May you see the prosperity of Jerusalem all the days of your life."

ABBA PATERMUTHIUS

From *History of the Monks in Egypt*

When the monks visited Abba Copres, he told amazing stories about an earlier monk named Patermuthius.

Patermuthius was first and foremost of all the monks who lived here. He first wore this clothing—he invented it. Formerly he was a thief who plundered the pagan tombs. He had a great reputation for committing wickedness of every kind. He once went to rob the religious house of a certain blessed woman. Without knowing it he found himself on the roof of her house. But he was unable to go into her house and plunder it because the roofs of the house were as flat as the ground and had no rain pipes (there is no rain in Thebaid) and there was no place on the roof to enter the house. So he was neither able to descend nor to escape from it and had to stay there until morning. He wondered meanwhile what to do until daylight came. While he was there he sank into a light sleep and saw an angel who said to him, "Do not devote such close attention and diligence and watching to your life of thievery. If you wish to change your wickedness into a life of good deeds, you must join the army of angels before Christ the King, and you shall receive from him this power and authority." And as soon as he had heard these things, he received them gladly. And the angel showed him a company of monks and commanded that he should lead them.

When he woke up from his slumber, he saw the nun standing before him, saying to him, "O man, what are you doing here? Who are you?" He said, "I do not know, but I beg you to show me the church." When she had shown him the church, he went and fell down before the feet of the elders and entreated them to let him become a Christian so that he might repent. Now when the elders knew who he was, they marveled at him and began to warn him that he must stop being a murderer. He begged them to teach him the Psalms. When he had learned three verses of the first psalm, he said, "These are enough for me to learn." He stayed there three days and then departed into the desert. Patermuthius lived there for three years in prayer and tears and fed himself on the roots in the desert and wandered about eating them.

After three years he returned to the church and repeated before the fathers the belief and all the doctrine of the church. Although he had never learned letters, he could repeat the Scriptures by heart. Then the elders marveled at him and wondered how a man of his kind could have attained such a degree of learning and discipline. When they had baptized him, they entreated him to remain with them. He stayed with them for seven more days, then departed to the desert, where he lived for another seven years. Every

Sunday he found bread in his pillowcloth. When he had prayed and given thanks, he would eat it and then fast again until the following Sunday without any suffering.

He came back again from that wilderness with works of spiritual excellence and demonstrated his rule of abstinence and self-denial and incited many to follow after him. A certain young man asked to become his disciple. Patermuthius received him and dressed him in the way he was dressed: he wore a shirt with short sleeves and an outer garment, and he placed a cowl upon his head and tied a napkin about his loins. He showed him the way and the rules of a life of mourning and trained him and placed a cape on his shoulders.

Now the custom of the blessed man was that when a Christian died, he remained with him the whole night long in vigil and prayer and reverently dressed him and buried him. When that disciple saw him dressing the Christians who died in this way, he said to him, "Will you also dress me in this manner when I die, master?" And he said unto him, "I will dress you in this fashion and wrap you in a shroud until you say to me, 'I have enough.'" Now after no great length of time that disciple died, and the words of his master were indeed fulfilled. Patermuthius dressed him reverently in the fear of God, as was right, and he said in a loud voice before all those who were standing there, "Have I dressed you well, O my son, or do you still lack anything?" And the dead man sent forth a voice, and they all heard it, saying, "You have dressed me, O my father. You have fulfilled your promise and completed your undertaking." Wonder laid hold upon all those who were standing there, and they glorified God. Then the blessed man departed into the desert according to his custom and occupied himself in his daily round of devotion.

ABBA PAPHNUTIUS

From *History of the Monks in Egypt*

As the monks continued their tour, they were shown the cell of Abba Paphnutius, who had recently died, and learned his story.

After Paphnutius had performed great spiritual deeds, he asked God which of the saints whose lives had been pleasing to God he resembled. An angel appeared to him and said, "You are like a singer who lives in such and such a city." The blessed man made his way to the singer. Having found him, he asked him about his life. The singer answered, "I am a sinner and a miserable wretch and a fornicator. Only a short time ago I gave up a life of theft and became as I am." Paphnutius asked him, "What good have you done?" He answered, "I did not know that I had ever done anything good except once. When I was a thief, I saw a certain holy virgin being forced by thieves. She was nearly raped, but I rescued her from them and took her by night to the city. And on another occasion I found a beautiful woman wandering about in the desert. She had fled from the agents of the general and counselor because of her husband's tax debts. She was crying to herself because of her troubles and because she had to roam about and wander in the desert. When I saw her, I asked her the cause of her weeping. She answered me, 'My lord, ask no questions about a miserable woman like myself. Take me as your slave and carry me wherever you want. My husband owes a debt of three hundred gold coins for taxes to the governor. For the past two years he has been scourged and kept in prison. My three beloved children have been sold into slavery, and I myself have been seized on several occasions and carried off and beaten cruelly. Finally I escaped and fled from place to place. And now I am here wandering about in this desert. For the last three days I have eaten nothing at all.' Then I had compassion on her and took her to my cave and gave her three hundred gold coins. Then I took her to the city so she could free herself and redeem her children and husband."

Then Paphnutius said, "I do not know that I have done anything like this, but you must have heard of my efforts. Now God revealed to me that you were not inferior to me in your works. Since God's care for you is not small, as God has shown me, brother, do not neglect yourself as if you were of no account." And immediately the singer threw away the reed pipe he was holding and abandoned the songs he used to sing to cheer the workers and turned to the sweet words of the Holy Spirit and clung to Paphnutius and departed to the desert. Having passed three years in hard work there, he ended his life with praises and prayers and other works of discipline.

Then he traveled the road of the heavenly beings and was numbered among the company of the holy ones and among the army of the righteous and went to his rest.

Paphnutius asked God again which of the saints he resembled. And again a divine voice came to him: "You are like the chief of a village near you." At once Paphnutius went down there. When he had knocked at the door, the master of the house came, as was his custom, to receive strangers. He opened the door and brought him inside and washed his feet and set a table before him and asked him to eat. The blessed man asked him, "Tell me what good deeds you do, for, according to what God has told me, you are more excellent than many monks." Then the man said, "I am a sinner and not worthy to be compared to monks." The blessed man kept asking him, and the man answered, "I do not feel any urgency to tell you my deeds. But since you have said you were sent by God, I will show you what I have done. For the last thirty years I have kept myself away from my wife and have had intercourse with her only three times. I have three children by her, and they take care of my business. But to this very day I have never stopped receiving strangers. No one in my village can boast of excelling me in hospitality to strangers. No poor person or stranger has ever departed from me with an empty hand or without suitable provisions for the way. I have never neglected to comfort with my gifts the poor person who has been brought low. No strife has ever taken place near me that I have not ended peacefully. The members of my house have never been blamed for committing abominable deeds. I have set my fields aside for everyone's pleasure, and I have gathered in what was left over. I have never allowed the rich to carry away the poor by force. I have never caused anyone to grieve in all my life. I have never passed a bad judgment on anyone. According to the will of God, I know in myself that I have done these things."

When Paphnutius heard the glorious character of the man's life and works, he kissed him on the head and said, "The Lord bless you from Zion. May you see the prosperity of Jerusalem all the days of your life. You have performed these things well, but you are lacking one of the prime virtues: the knowledge of the wisdom of God. You will not be able to acquire that without labor, for you must deny the world and yourself and take up the cross of our Lord and follow him." When that man had heard these things, at once, without consulting his children, he clung to the blessed man and went with him to the mountain.

After three years, Paphnutius saw angels carrying the soul of that man up to heaven and praising God and saying, "Happy are those whom you choose and bring near to live in your courts." And the righteous answered, "Great peace have those who love your law." And Paphnutius knew that that man had filled full his measure.

SAYINGS ON PRAYER

From The Sayings of the Fathers

The wisdom of the desert is preserved in brief stories and sayings as well as longer stories, discourses, and travelers' reports. The Sayings of the Fathers is the greatest collection of these short sayings. Here are several on the general topic of prayer, especially as summarized in the prayer of the tax collector (publican) in Luke 18:13: "God, be merciful to me, a sinner!"

Abba Evagrius said, "Sit in your cell, collecting your thoughts. Remember the day of your death. See then what the death of your body will be; let your spirit be heavy, take pains, condemn the vanity of the world, so as to be able to live always in the peace you have in view without weakening. Remember also what happens in hell and think about the state of the souls down there, their painful silence, their most bitter groanings, their fear, their strife, their waiting. Think of their grief without end and the tears their souls shed eternally. But keep the day of resurrection and of presentation to God in remembrance also. Imagine the fearful and terrible judgment. Consider the fate kept for sinners, their shame before the face of God and the angels and archangels and all people, that is to say, the punishments, the eternal fire, worms that rest not, the darkness, gnashing of teeth, fear, and supplications. Consider also the good things in store for the righteous: confidence in the face of God the Father and God's Son, the angels and archangels and all the people of the saints, the kingdom of heaven, and the gifts of that realm, joy and beatitude.

"Keep in mind the remembrance of these two realities. Weep for the judgment of sinners; afflict yourself for fear lest you too feel those pains. But rejoice and be glad at the lot of the righteous. Strive to obtain those joys but be a stranger to those pains. Whether you be inside or outside your cell, be careful that the remembrance of these things never leaves you so that, thanks to their remembrance, you may at least flee wrong and harmful thoughts."

—

Amma Syncletica said, "Imitate the publican, and you will not be condemned with the Pharisee. Choose the meekness of Moses, and you will find your heart that is a rock changed into a spring of water."

—

Abba Macarius was asked, "How should one pray?" The old man said, "There is no need at all to make long discourses; it is enough to stretch out one's hands and say, 'Lord, as you will, and as you know, have mercy.' And if the conflict grows fiercer, say, 'Lord, help!' God knows very well what we need and shows us mercy."

—

A soldier asked Abba Mius if God accepted repentance. After the old man had taught him many things, he said, "Tell me, my dear, if your cloak is torn, do you throw it away?" He replied, "No, I mend it and use it again." The old man said to him, "If you are so careful about your cloak, will not God be equally careful about God's creature?

—

Amma Sarah said, "If I prayed God that all people should approve of my conduct, I should find myself a penitent at the door of each one, but I shall rather pray that my heart may be pure toward all."

—

Abba Nilus said, "Do not always want everything to turn out as you think it should, but rather as God pleases. Then you will be undisturbed and thankful in your prayer."

—

The blessed Epiphanius, bishop of Cyprus, was told this by the abbot of a monastery that he had in Palestine, "By your prayers we do not neglect our appointed round of psalmody, but we are very careful to recite Terce, Sext, and None." Then Epiphanius corrected them with the following comment, "It is clear that you do not trouble about the other hours of the day, if you cease from prayer. The true monk should have prayer and psalmody continually in his heart."

—

Amma Theodora said, "It is good to live in peace, for the wise person practices perpetual prayer. It is truly a great thing for a virgin or a monk to live in peace, especially for the younger ones. However, you should realize that as soon as you intend to live in peace, at once evil comes and weighs down your soul through depression, faintheartedness, and evil thoughts. It also attacks your body through sickness, debility, weakening of the knees, and all the members. It dissipates the strength of soul and body so that one believes one is ill and no longer able to pray. But if we are vigilant, all these temptations fall away. There was, in fact, a monk who was seized by cold and fever every time he began to pray, and he suffered from headaches too. In this condition, he said to himself, I am ill, and near to death; so now I will get up before I die and pray. By reasoning in this way, he did violence to himself and prayed. When he had finished, the fever abated also. So, by reasoning in this way, the brother resisted and prayed and was able to conquer his thoughts."

—

A brother asked Abba Rufus, "What is interior peace, and what use is it?" The old man said, "Interior peace means to remain sitting in one's cell with fear and knowledge of God, holding far off the remembrance of wrongs suffered and pride of spirit. Such interior peace brings forth all the virtues, preserves the monk from the burning darts of the enemy, and does not allow him to be wounded by them. Yes, brother, acquire it. Keep in mind your future death, remembering that you do not know at what hour the thief will come. Likewise be watchful over your soul."

—

Abba Zeno said, "If a man wants God to hear his prayer quickly, then before he prays for anything else, even his own soul, when he stands and stretches out his hands toward God, he must pray with all his heart for his enemies. Through this action God will hear everything that he asks."

SAYINGS ON JUDGING OTHERS

From *The Sayings of the Fathers*

It was a constant temptation for those striving to excel in the spiritual life to compare themselves to others. Here are some cautions against passing judgment.

One day Abba Isaac went to a monastery. He saw a brother committing a sin and he condemned him. When he returned to the desert, an angel of the Lord came and stood in front of the door of his cell and said, "I will not let you enter." But he persisted, saying, "What is the matter?" and the angel replied, "God has sent me to ask you where you want to throw the guilty brother whom you have condemned." Immediately he repented and said, "I have sinned; forgive me." Then the angel said, "Get up. God has forgiven you. But from now on, be careful not to judge someone before God has done so."

—

Abba Macarius said, "If you reprove someone, you yourself get carried away by anger and you are satisfying your own passion; do not lose yourself, therefore, in order to save another."

—

A brother at Scetis committed a fault. A council was called to which Abba Moses was invited, but he refused to go to it. Then the priest sent someone to say to him, "Come, for everyone is waiting for you." So he got up and went. He took a leaking jug, filled it with water, and carried it with him. The others came out to meet him and said to him, "What is this, Father?" The old man said to them, "My sins run out behind me, and I do not see them, and today I am coming to judge the errors of another." When they heard that, they said no more to the brother but forgave him.

—

Whenever Abba Agathon's thoughts urged him to pass judgment on something that he saw, he would say to himself, *Agathon, it is not your business to do that.* Thus his spirit was always recollected.

—

Abba Moses said, "If the monk does not think in his heart that he is a sinner, God will not hear him." The brother said, "What does that mean, to think in his heart that he is a sinner?" Then the old man said, "When someone is occupied with his own faults, he does not see those of his neighbor."

—

Abba Nilus said, "Everything you do in revenge against a brother who has harmed you will come back to your mind at the time of prayer."

—

It was said of Abba John that when he went to church at Scetis, he heard some brothers arguing, so he returned to his cell. He went round it three times and then went in. Some brothers who had seen him wondered why he had done this, and they went to ask him. He said to them, "My ears were full of that argument, so I circled round in order to purify them, and thus I entered my cell with my mind at rest."

—

A brother asked Abba Poemen, "Is it better to speak or to be silent?" The old man said to him, "One who speaks for God's sake does well; but one who is silent for God's sake also does well."

—

Abba Poemen said, "A man may seem to be silent, but if his heart is condemning others, he is babbling ceaselessly. But there may be another who talks from morning till night and yet he is truly silent. That is, he says nothing that is not profitable."

—

A brother questioned Abba Poemen, saying, "I have found a place where peace is not disturbed by the brothers; do you advise me to live there?" The old man said to him, "The place for you is where you will not harm your brother."

—

Amma Syncletica said, "If you find yourself in a monastery, do not go to another place, for that will harm you a great deal. Just as the bird who abandons the eggs she was sitting on prevents them from hatching, so monks or nuns grow cold and their faith dies when they go from one place to another."

—

A brother asked Abba Poemen, "Some brothers live with me; do you want me to be in charge of them?" The old man said to him, "No, just work first and foremost, and if they want to live like you, they will see to it themselves." The brother said to him, "But it is they themselves, Father, who want me to be in charge of them." The old man said to him, "No, be their example, not their legislator."

SAYINGS ON THE GOAL OF DISCIPLINE

From *The Sayings of the Fathers*

In many ways, the men and women of the desert were asked, "What should I do?" or "What is this life really about?" Here are some of the answers.

Abba John said, "I think it best that a person should have a little bit of all the virtues. Therefore, get up early every day and acquire the beginning of every virtue and every commandment of God. Use great patience, with fear and long-suffering, in the love of God, with all the fervor of your soul and body. Exercise great humility; bear with interior distress; be vigilant and pray often with reverence and groaning, with purity of speech and control of your eyes. When you are despised, do not get angry; be at peace, and do not render evil for evil. Do not pay attention to the faults of others, and do not try to compare yourself with others, knowing you are less than every created thing. Renounce everything material and what is of the flesh. Live by the Cross, in warfare, in poverty of spirit, in voluntary spiritual asceticism, in fasting, penitence, and tears, in discernment, in purity of soul, taking hold of what is good. Do your work in peace. Persevere in keeping vigil, in hunger and thirst, in cold and nakedness, and in sufferings. Shut yourself in a tomb as though you were already dead so that at all times you will think death is near."

—

A brother questioned an old man, saying, "What good work should I do so that I may live?" The old man said, "God knows what is good. I have heard it said that one of the fathers asked Abba Nisterus the Great, the friend of Abba Anthony, and said to him, 'What good work is there that I could do?' He said to him, 'Are not all actions equal? Scripture says that Abraham was hospitable and God was with him. David was humble, and God was with him. Elias loved interior peace, and God was with him. So, do whatever you see your soul desires according to God and guard your heart.'"

—

A brother asked Abba Poemen what he should do about his sins. The old man said to him, "Those who wish to purify their faults purify them with tears, and those who wish to acquire virtues acquire them with tears. For weeping is the way the Scriptures and our fathers give us when they say 'Weep!' Truly, there is no other way than this."

—

A brother questioned Abba Matoes, saying, "Give me a word." He said to him, "Go, and pray God to put compunction in your heart and give you humility; be aware of your faults; do not judge others but put yourself below everyone; do not be friendly with a boy or with a heretical friend; put freedom of speech far from you; control your tongue and your belly; drink only a small quantity of wine; and if someone speaks about some topic, do not argue with him, but if he is right, say, 'Yes'; if he is wrong, say, 'You know what you are saying,' and do not argue with him about what he has said. That is humility."

—

Abba Poemen said, "To throw yourself before God, not to measure your progress, to leave behind all self-will—these are the instruments for the work of the soul."

—

Abba Poemen said, "If three people meet, of whom the first fully preserves interior peace, and the second gives thanks to God in illness, and the third serves with a pure mind, these three are doing the same work."

—

Someone asked Abba Anthony, "What must one do in order to please God?" The old man replied, "Pay attention to what I tell you: whoever you may be, always have God before your eyes; whatever you do, do it according to the testimony of the Holy Scriptures; in whatever place you live, do not easily leave it. Keep these three precepts and you will be saved."

—

Abba Poemen said that Abba John said that the saints are like a group of trees, each bearing different fruit, but watered from the same source. The practices of one saint differ from those of another, but the same Spirit works in all of them.

—

Amma Syncletica said, "In the beginning there are a great many battles and a good deal of suffering for those who are advancing toward God and afterward, ineffable joy. It is like those who wish to light a fire; at first they are choked by the smoke and cry, and by this means obtain what they seek (as it is said: 'Our God is a consuming fire'): so we also must kindle the divine fire in ourselves through tears and hard work."

—

Abba Amoun of Nitria came to see Abba Anthony and said to him, "Since my rule is stricter than yours, how is it that your name is better known among people than mine is?" Abba Anthony answered, "It is because I love God more than you."

—

Abba Lot went to see Abba Joseph and said to him, "Abba, as far as I can, I say my little office; I fast a little; I pray and meditate; I live in peace; and as far as I can, I purify my thoughts. What else can I do?" Then the old man stood up and stretched his hands toward heaven. His fingers became like ten lamps of fire, and he said to him, "If you will, you can become all flame."

APPENDIX

Reading Spiritual Classics for Personal and Group Formation

Many Christians today are searching for more spiritual depth, for something more than simply being good church members. That quest may send them to the spiritual practices of New Age movements or of Eastern religions such as Zen Buddhism. Christians, though, have their own long spiritual tradition, a tradition rich with wisdom, variety, and depth.

The great spiritual classics testify to that depth. They do not concern themselves with mystical flights for a spiritual elite. Rather, they contain very practical advice and insights that can support and shape the spiritual growth of any Christian. We can all benefit by sitting at the feet of the masters (both male and female) of Christian spirituality.

Reading spiritual classics is different from most of the reading we do. We have learned to read to master a text and extract information from it. We tend to read quickly, to get through a text. And we summarize as we read, seeking the main point. In reading spiritual classics, though, we allow the text to master and form us. Such formative reading goes more slowly, more reflectively, allowing time for God to speak to us through the text. God's word for us may come as easily from a minor point or even an aside as from the major point.

Formative reading requires that you approach the text in humility. Read as a seeker, not an expert. Don't demand that the text meet your expectations for what an "enlightened" author should write. Humility means accepting the author as another imperfect human, a product of his or her own time and situation. Learn to celebrate what is foundational in an author's writing without being overly disturbed by what is peculiar to the author's life and times. Trust the text as a gift from both God and the author, offered to you for your benefit—to help you grow in Christ.

To read formatively, you must also slow down. Feel free to reread a passage that seems to speak specially to you. Stop from time to time to reflect on what you have been reading. Keep a journal for these reflections. Often the act of writing can itself prompt further, deeper reflection. Keep your notebook open and your pencil in hand as you read. You might not get back to that wonderful insight later. Don't worry that you are not getting through an entire passage—or even the first paragraph! Formative reading is about depth rather than breadth, quality rather than quantity. As you read, seek God's direction for your own life. Timeless truths have their place but may not be what is most important for your own formation here and now.

As you read the passage, you might keep some of these questions running through your mind:

- How is what I'm reading true of my own life? Where does it reflect my own *experience*?

- How does this text challenge me? What new *direction* does it offer me?
- What must I change to put what I am reading into practice? How can I *incarnate* it, let this word become flesh in my life?

You might also devote special attention to sections that upset you. What is the source of the disturbance? Do you want to argue theology? Are you turned off by cultural differences? Or have you been skewered by an insight that would turn your life upside down if you took it seriously? Let your journal be a dialogue with the text.

If you find yourself moving from reading the text to chewing over its implications to praying, that's great! Spiritual reading is really the first step in an ancient way of prayer called *lectio divina* or "divine reading." Reading leads naturally into reflection on what you have read (meditation). As you reflect on what the text might mean for your life, you may well want to ask for God's help in living out any new insights or direction you have perceived (prayer). Sometimes such prayer may lead you further into silently abiding in God's presence (contemplation). And, of course, the process is only really completed when it begins to make a difference in the way we live (incarnation).

As good as it is to read spiritual classics in solitude, it is even better to join with others in a small group for mutual formation or "spiritual direction in common." This is *not* the same as a study group that

talks about spiritual classics. A group for mutual formation would have similar goals as for an individual's reading: to allow the text to shine its light on the *experiences* of the group members, to suggest new *directions* for their lives and practical ways of *incarnating* these directions. Such a group might agree to focus on one short passage from a classic at each meeting (even if members have read more). Discussion usually goes much deeper if all the members have already read and reflected on the passage before the meeting and bring their journals.

Such groups need to watch for several potential problems. It is easy to go off on a tangent (especially if it takes the focus off the members' own experience and onto generalities). At such times a group leader might bring the group's attention back to the text: "What does our author say about that?" Or, "How do we experience that in our own lives?" When a group member shares a problem, others may be tempted to try to "fix" it. This is much less helpful than sharing similar experiences and how they were handled (for good or ill). "Sharing" someone else's problems (whether that person is in or out of the group) should be strongly discouraged.

One person could be designated as leader, to be responsible for opening and closing prayers; to be the first to share or respond to the text; and to keep notes during the discussion to highlight recurring themes, challenges, directives, or practical steps. These responsibilities could also be shared among several members of the group or rotated.

For further information about formative reading of spiritual classics, try *A Practical Guide to Spiritual Reading* by Susan Annette Muto. *Shaped by the Word* by Robert Mulholland (Upper Room Books®) covers formative reading of the Bible. *Good Things Happen: Experiencing Community in Small Groups* by Dick Westley is an excellent resource on forming small groups of all kinds.

TOTAL DEVOTION TO GOD

Selected Writings of
WILLIAM LAW

Upper Room Spiritual Classics® — Series 3

Selected, edited, and introduced by
Keith Beasley-Topliffe

**Total Devotion to God:
Selected Writings of William Law**

Copyright © 2000 by Upper Room Books™
All rights reserved.

No part of this book may be used or reproduced in any manner whatsoever without written permission of the publisher except in the case of brief quotations embodied in critical articles or reviews. For information, write Upper Room Books,™ 1908 Grand Avenue, Nashville, Tennessee 37212.

The Upper Room® Website: http://www.upperroom.org

UPPER ROOM,® UPPER ROOM BOOKS™ and design logos are trademarks owned by the Upper Room,® Nashville, Tennessee. All rights reserved.

Scripture quotations are from the New Revised Standard Version of the Bible Copyright © 1989 by the Division of Christian Education of the National Council of Churches of Christ in the USA. Used by permission. All rights reserved.

Cover design: Gore Studio, Inc.
Interior design and layout: Nancy J. Cole

First printing: 2000

Library of Congress Cataloging-in-Publication Data

Law, William, 1686–1761..
    Total devotion to God : selected writings of William Law / selected, edited, and introduced by Keith Beasley-Topliffe.
      p. cm. — (Upper Room spiritual classics. Series 3)
      ISBN 0-8358-0901-3
    1. Christian life—Anglican authors. I. Beasley-Topliffe, Keith.
II. Title. III. Series.
BV4501.2.L3583 2000   99-37905
248.4'83—dc21   CIP

Printed in the United States of America

TABLE OF CONTENTS

Introduction	5
Devout Life	12
Seeking Perfection	16
Business	20
Miranda's Life	23
Miranda's Charity	28
Prayer and Devotion	32
Discipline	36
Seeing Clearly	40
Negotius	44
Soul and Body	49
Humility and Pride	53
Intercession	57
Resignation to God's Will	62
Confession	66
Appendix: Reading Spiritual Classics for Personal and Group Formation	72

INTRODUCTION

For many Christians today, it is enough to be lukewarm in their devotion, as good a Christian as the next person. Anything more seems excessive, maybe even fanatical. We can become much more concerned with being saved than with figuring out what to do with the rest of our lives that Christ has redeemed.

William Law speaks against such an attitude in our day as he did in his own, two and a half centuries ago. Calmly, reasonably, he argues that only total devotion to God, dedication to holy living, is a proper response to God's love. If it is good to be good Christians, then surely it is excellent (not fanatical) to be excellent Christians. If we claim to follow Christ, why not follow him as well as we can?

In the following selections, taken from *A Serious Call to a Devout and Holy Life*, Law shows the importance of devotion. He argues that a disciplined life is by no means a dull or narrow one. He offers extensive suggestions for daily prayer that can shape the rest of one's life into one of praise for God and love for neighbor. Above all, he calls for religion that goes beyond duty to the outpouring of a God-filled heart.

LAW'S WORLD

In the century and a half before Law's birth, England went through a great deal of political and religious conflict. King Henry VIII broke with Rome in 1532. However, his daughter Mary restored Catholicism in 1553 and executed many leaders of the English

Reformation. Five years later her sister Elizabeth became queen, and England was again Protestant. During Elizabeth's forty-four-year reign, the Church of England became firmly entrenched.

When Elizabeth died in 1603, she was succeeded by her cousin James I, who was already king of Scotland. During his rule he authorized the translation of the Bible (1611) that commonly bears his name. He and his son, Charles I (reigned 1625–49), moved steadily toward returning to Roman Catholicism, even though they were the "supreme governors" of the Church of England. In 1649 the strongly Puritan Parliament raised its own army to overthrow and execute Charles. During the ten years of the English Commonwealth, the Church of England was disestablished (that is, was no longer the official government-supported church), and other Protestant groups such as Baptists and Quakers enjoyed toleration.

In 1660, Parliament restored the monarchy with Charles II as king. The Church of England was again established, and any group not abiding by the Book of Common Prayer could be liable to arrest. Many "nonconforming" ministers spent at least some time in prison. Among them were John Bunyan, who wrote much of *The Pilgrim's Progress* (published in 1678) while in jail.

Charles II was succeeded by his son James II in 1685. James openly embraced Roman Catholicism and was soon deposed in favor of his daughter Mary and her husband (and first cousin), William of Orange. Their reign began in 1689 with the Toleration Act, which allowed other Protestant groups freedom of religion as long as their ministers and meetinghouses were registered with the government. Althought Catholics and Unitarians were not included, it was hoped that at last religious and political struggles were over.

One minority group displeased with the new rulers included nine Church of England bishops and several hundred clergy who felt their oaths of loyalty to James II could not be so easily swept away by an act of Parliament. They refused to swear a new oath to Mary and William and so lost the right to hold office in church or nation. These "nonjurors" (from Latin *jurare*, swear) formed a schismatic church that lasted more than a century.

Mary and her sister Anne (queen 1702–14) were at least descendants of James II. But William and Mary were childless, Anne's children died young, and other children of James II were excluded from the succession as Catholics. When Anne died, she was followed by George I, a German-born (and German-speaking) great-grandson of Charles I. Among those who refused the Oath of Allegiance to George (creating a new generation of nonjurors) was William Law.

One result of this religious and political fighting was a general distaste for any hint of extremism in religion. It was fine to attend worship and give something to charity now and then. But sufficient devotion to change one's life from the norm for one's class was at best in poor taste and at worst could become enthusiasm, a chargeable offense. Moderation was the key. Law took his stand against this attitude, calling instead for the pursuit of Christian perfection through a devout and holy life.

Another result was a philosophical quest for a common ground of religion through reason and study of human nature. Deism denied revelation (seeing Jesus as a natural philosopher) and denounced ritual as superstition. Law, on the other hand, insisted that devotion was a reasonable consequence of beginning any sort of religious life.

In Law's time, the class structure in England was firmly entrenched. One's class was a given, an instance of divine Providence. Law perceived class, wealth, and gender as one's state and therefore static, unchanging. Though Law was aware of the problems faced by the poor, he did not criticize the system at all. Instead, he counted on the charity of a devout upper class to ease the conditions of the lower classes.

Law's Life

William Law was born in 1686 in King's Cliffe, Northamptonshire, England. He was the fourth of eight children of Thomas Law and his wife, Margaret. Thomas was the town grocer and sufficiently prosperous to be considered a gentleman.

In 1705, before he left home to study at Emmanuel College, Cambridge, Law drew up a set of rules for living that indicate severity and idealism were already part of his character. He graduated in 1708, became a fellow (instructor) at the college in 1711 and received his Master of Arts the next year. In

1714, when George I came to the throne, Law refused to take the Oath of Allegiance. As a nonjuror, Law was banned from teaching, from serving as a pastor in the Church of England, and from holding public office.

Law published his first pamphlet in 1717, the first of three open letters to the bishop of Bangor defending the nonjurors' positions. They were popular and brought Law some fame. He assured publication of these and other writings by giving the printer all profits from the first edition. Profit from later editions went to Law.

In 1723, Law became tutor to Edward Gibbon (father of historian Edward Gibbon, who wrote *The Decline and Fall of the Roman Empire*), both at the Gibbon home in Putney (near London) and at Emmanuel College when Gibbon went there. He remained part of the Gibbon household for the next fifteen years, long after Edward's studies were completed.

Law's writing continued with a major work on Christian perfection in 1726 followed two years later by *A Serious Call to a Devout and Holy Life, Adapted to the State and Condition of All Orders of Christians,* certainly his best-known work. Among those strongly influenced by this book were John and Charles Wesley, then beginning the group of devout students at Oxford that they called the Holy Club and detractors called Methodists. Both Wesleys visited and corresponded with Law.

About 1734, Law began reading the works of Jacob Boehme, called Behmen in the English editions of Law's day. Boehme (1575–1624) was a German shoemaker and mystic who claimed that his knowledge came not from study but from direct experience of God. Law found Boehme fascinating and integrated Boehme's mystical theology with his own practical devotion. Law's later works, such as *The Spirit of Prayer* (1749) and *The Spirit of Love* (1752), show the transformation Boehme made in Law's thought.

Law finally left the Gibbon home in 1738 and lived briefly in London before returning to King's Cliffe and the house his father had owned. Soon after Law moved there, Mrs. Elizabeth Hutcheson, widow of a member of Parliament, and Miss Hester Gibbon, older sister of Edward, asked Law to serve as their "chaplain, instructor, and almoner" (that is, to take charge of making charitable gifts on their behalf). At first the two women lived in a house several miles from King's Cliffe, but in 1744 they moved in with Law. There they tried to put into practice the devout life of which Law had written. Each woman was wealthy, with several thousand pounds of annual income probably far exceeding what Law earned from his writing. They gave away most (perhaps as much as 90 percent) of this income in direct charity and in support of two schools (one for boys and one for girls) and a library they established in King's Cliffe. The school buildings also included apartments for aged widows. Some of the neighbors complained that the copious amount of charity was bringing spongers into the community and placing Law in "competition" with the charity of the local parish church.

Law died in King's Cliffe on April 9, 1761, a few

days after finishing *An Humble, Earnest, and Affectionate Address to the Clergy*, a renewed call for devotion and religious experience in contrast to overemphasis on reason and the pursuit of a ministerial career.

FURTHER READING

Many of Law's works are most easily available in electronic format on the Internet or on CD-ROM. *A Serious Call* and some other works are also available in various print editions.

A. Keith Walker's *William Law: His Life and Thought* (SPCK, 1973) intermixes biography with critical summaries of Law's writings and was very helpful in preparing this introduction.

The Imitation of Christ by Thomas à Kempis (easily available in a variety of editions) strongly influenced Law's early spiritual formation. So did the writings of Nicolas Malebranche and Jeremy Taylor. Jacob Boehme's key writings were gathered in *The Way to Christ*, available in English from Paulist Press.

NOTE ON THE TEXT

All selections are from a 1906 edition of *A Serious Call* as reproduced in The AGES Digital Library CD-ROM, *The Master Christian Library*. The selections have been abridged (Law can become repetitive when driving home a point) and edited for punctuation, grammar, vocabulary, and inclusive language. Scripture quotes have been changed to the New Revised Standard Version.

Devout Life

From Chapter 1

William Law published A Serious Call to a Devout and Holy Life *in 1728. In these opening paragraphs, he defines what he means by a devout life.*

Devotion is neither private nor public prayer. But prayers, whether private or public, are particular parts or instances of devotion. Devotion signifies a life given or devoted to God.

Devout people, therefore, live no longer according to their own will or the way and spirit of the world but solely according to the will of God. They consider God in everything, serve God in everything, make all the parts of their ordinary lives parts of their piety by doing everything in the name of God and under such rules as conform to God's glory.

We readily acknowledge that God alone is to be the rule and measure of our prayers. In them we are to look wholly to God and act wholly for God. We are to pray only in such a manner, for such things, and for such ends as are suitable to God's glory.

Now let any find out the reason why they are to be strictly pious in their prayers, and they will find the same as strong a reason to be as strictly pious in all the other parts of their lives. For there is no other reason why our prayers should be according to the will of God, why they should have nothing in them but what is wise, and holy, and heavenly than this: that our lives may be of the same nature, full of the same wisdom, holiness, and heavenly tempers, and that we may live to God in the same spirit that we pray to God. Were it not our strict duty to live by reason and to devote all the actions of our lives to God, were it not absolutely necessary to walk before God in wisdom and holiness and all heavenly conversation, doing everything in God's name and for God's glory, there would be no excellency or wisdom in the most heavenly prayers. No, such prayers would be absurdities. They would be like prayers for wings when it was no part of our duty to fly.

It is for lack of knowing or at least considering this that we see such a mixture of the ridiculous in the lives of many people. You see them strict as to some times and places of devotion. But when the church service is over, they are just like those who seldom or never come there. In their way of life, their manner of spending their time and money, their cares and fears, their pleasures and indulgences, their labor and diversions, they are like the rest of the world. This makes the loose part of the world generally make a joke of those who are devout because they see their devotion goes no farther than their prayers, and that when they are over, they live no more to God till the time of prayer returns again. Instead they live by the same humor and fancy and in as full enjoyment of all the follies of life as other people. This is the reason why they are the joke and scorn of careless and worldly people: not because they are really devoted to God, but because they appear to have no other devotion but that of occasional prayers.

And indeed nothing can be imagined more absurd in itself than wise and sublime and heavenly prayers added to a life of vanity and folly, where neither labor nor diversions, neither time nor money, are under the direction of the wisdom and heavenly tempers of our prayers. If we were to see a man claiming to act wholly with regard to God in everything that he did, who would neither spend time nor money nor take any labor or diversion but so far as he could act according to strict principles of reason and piety, and yet at the same time neglect all prayer, public or private, should we not be amazed at such a man and wonder how he could have so much folly along with so much religion?

Yet this is as reasonable as for any person to claim strictness in devotion, to be careful in observing times and places of prayer, and yet letting the rest of his life, his time and labor, his talents and money, be disposed of without any regard to strict rules of piety and devotion. For it is as great an absurdity to suppose holy prayers and divine petitions without a holiness of life suitable to them, as to suppose a holy and divine life without prayers.

The short of the matter is this: either reason and religion prescribe rules and ends to all the ordinary actions of our lives, or they do not. If they do, then it is as necessary to govern all our actions by those rules as it is to worship God. For if religion teaches us anything concerning eating and drinking or spending our time and money; if it teaches us how we are to have contempt for the world; if it tells us what tempers we are to have in common life, how we are to be disposed toward all people, and how we are to behave toward the sick, the poor, the old, the destitute; if it tells us whom we are to treat with a particular love or to regard with a particular esteem; if it tells us how we are to treat our enemies and how we are to mortify and deny ourselves; then they must be very weak that can think these parts of religion are not to be observed with as much exactness as any doctrines that relate to prayers.

SEEKING PERFECTION

From Chapter 3

Here Law suggests that meditating on the virtues we would like to have at the hour of death will guide us to seek them now.

The measure of our love to God seems in justice to be the measure of our love of every virtue. We are to love and practice it with all our hearts, with all our souls, with all our minds, and with all our strength. And when we cease to live with this regard to virtue, we live below our nature. Instead of being able to plead our infirmities, we stand chargeable with negligence.

It is for this reason that we are exhorted to work out our salvation with fear and trembling. Unless our hearts and passions are eagerly bent upon the work of our salvation; unless holy fears animate our endeavors and keep our consciences strict and tender about every part of our duty, constantly examining how we live and how fit we are to die; we shall in all probability fall into a state of negligence and sit down in such a course of life as will never carry us to the rewards of heaven.

And whoever considers that a just God can make such allowances only as are suitable to divine justice, that our works are all to be examined by fire, will find that fear and trembling are proper tempers for those who are drawing near so great a trial.

And indeed there is no probability that any should do all the duty that God expects or make the progress in piety that the holiness and justice of God require but those who are constantly afraid of falling short of it.

Now this is not intended to possess people's minds with a scrupulous anxiety and discontent in the service of God but to fill them with a just fear of living in sloth and idleness and in the neglect of such virtues as they will want at the day of judgment. It is to excite them to an earnest examination of their lives, to such zeal and care and concern for Christian perfection as they use in any matter that has gained their hearts and affections. It is only desiring them to be so apprehensive of their state, so humble in the opinion of themselves, so earnest after higher degrees of piety, and so fearful of falling short of happiness as the great apostle Saint Paul was, when he wrote to the Philippians: "Not that I have already obtained this or have already reached the goal; . . . but this one thing I do: forgetting what lies behind and straining forward to what lies ahead, I press on toward the goal for the prize of the heavenly call of God in Christ Jesus." And then he added, "Let those of us then who are mature be of the same mind."

The Apostle thought it necessary for those who were in his state of perfection to be "of the same mind," that is, laboring, pressing, and aspiring after some degree of holiness to which they had not then arrived. Surely it is much more necessary for us, who are laboring under great imperfections, to be earnest and striving after such degrees of a holy and divine life as we have not yet attained.

The best way for any to know how much they ought to aspire after holiness is to consider, not how much will make their present lives easy, but how much they think will make them easy at the hour of death.

Now any who dare be so serious as to put this question to themselves will be forced to answer that at death all will wish that they had been as perfect as human nature can be.

Is not this, therefore, sufficient to put us not only upon wishing, but laboring after all the perfection that we shall then lament the lack of? Is it not excessive folly to be content with such a course of piety as we already know cannot content us at a time when we shall so desire it as to have nothing else to comfort us? How can we carry a severer condemnation against ourselves than to believe that, at the hour of death, we shall want the virtues of the saints and wish that we had been among the first servants of God and yet take no methods of arriving at their height of piety while we are alive?

This is an absurdity that we can easily pass over at present, while the health of our bodies, the passions of our minds, the noise and hurry and pleasures and business of the world lead us on with eyes that see not and ears that hear not. But at death, it will set itself before us in a dreadful magnitude. It will haunt us like a dismal ghost, and the conscience will never let us take our eyes from it.

We see in worldly matters what a torment self-condemnation is, and how hardly any are able to forgive themselves when they have brought themselves into any calamity or disgrace purely by their own folly. The affliction is made doubly tormenting because they are forced to charge it all to themselves, as their own acts and deeds against the nature and reason of things and contrary to the advice of all their friends.

Now from this we may in some degree guess how terrible the pain of that self-condemnation will be when any shall find themselves in the miseries of death under the severity of a self-condemning conscience, charging all their distress to their own folly and madness against the sense and reason of their own minds, against all the doctrines and precepts of religion, and contrary to all the instructions, calls, and warnings of both God and people.

BUSINESS

From Chapter 4

Law often presents character sketches as either positive or negative examples. Often the character's name helps to understand the portrait. Here Calidus (Latin for hot*) is so hot to get ahead in business that he has little time for God except during business emergencies.*

Calidus has traded more than thirty years in the greatest city of the kingdom. He has been so many years constantly increasing his trade and his fortune. Every hour of the day is with him an hour of business. Though he eats and drinks very heartily, yet every meal seems to be in a hurry. He would say grace if he had time. Calidus ends every day at the tavern though he is not free to be there until nearly nine o'clock. He is always forced to drink a good hearty glass to drive thoughts of business out of his head and make his spirits drowsy enough for sleep. He does business all the time that he is rising and has settled several matters before he can get to his countingroom. His prayers are a short ejaculation or two. He never misses them in stormy, tempestuous weather because he has always something or other at sea. Calidus will tell you with great pleasure that he has been in this hurry for many years, and that it might have killed him long ago, except that it has been a rule with him to get out of town every Saturday and make Sunday a day of quiet and good refreshment in the country.

He is now so rich that he would leave off his business and amuse his old age with building and furnishing a fine house in the country. But he is afraid he should grow melancholy if he quit his business. He will tell you with great gravity that it is a dangerous thing for a man who has been used to getting money ever to stop. If thoughts of religion happen at any time to steal into his head, Calidus contents himself with thinking that he never was a friend to heretics and infidels, that he has always been civil to the minister of his parish, and that he has very often given something to the charity schools.

Now this way of life is at such a distance from all the doctrine and discipline of Christianity that no one can live in it through ignorance or frailty. Calidus can no more imagine that he is born again of the Spirit; that he is a new creation in Christ; that he lives here as an alien and exile, setting his mind on things above and laying up treasures in heaven—he can no more imagine this than he can think that he has been all his life an apostle, working miracles and preaching the gospel.

It must admitted that businesspeople in general, especially in great towns, are too much like Calidus. You see them all the week buried in business, unable to think of anything else. Then they spend Sunday in idleness and refreshment, in wandering into the country, in such visits and jovial meetings as make it often the worst day of the week.

Now they do not live like this because they cannot support themselves with less care and application to business but because they want to grow rich in their trades and to maintain their families in some such figure and degree of finery as a reasonable Christian life has no occasion for. Take away this temper and then people of all trades will find themselves at leisure to live every day like Christians, to be careful of every duty of the gospel, to live in a visible course of religion, and to be every day strict observers of both private and public prayer.

Now the only way to do this is for people to consider their trade as something they are obliged to devote to the glory of God, something they are to do only in such a manner that they may make it a duty to God. Nothing can be right in business that is not under these rules.

It is therefore absolutely certain that no Christians are to enter any farther into business, or for any other ends, than such as they can in singleness of heart offer to God as a reasonable service. For the Son of God has redeemed us for this end only: that we should, by a life of reason and piety, live to the glory of God. This is the only rule and measure for every order and state of life. Without this rule, the most lawful employment becomes a sinful state of life.

# MIRANDA'S LIFE

From Chapter 8

The centerpiece of the first half of A Serious Call *is the portrait of Miranda, whose name means* wonderful. *She and her sister Flavia (*extravagant*) are women who have maintained their independence by remaining single and living on endowment income. But while Flavia wastes her wealth on self-centered indulgence, Miranda is a model of Christian charity and devotion.*

Miranda is a sober, reasonable Christian. As soon as she was mistress of her time and fortune, her first thought was how she might best fulfill everything that God required of her in the use of them and how she might make the best and happiest use of this short life. She depends upon the truth of what our blessed Lord has said, that "there is need of only one thing," and therefore makes her whole life one continual labor after it. She has only one reason for doing or not doing, for liking or not liking anything, and that is the will of God. She is not so weak as to pretend to add what is called the fine lady to the true Christian. Miranda thinks too well to be taken with the sound of such silly words. She has renounced the world to follow Christ in the exercise of humility, charity, devotion, abstinence, and heavenly affections. That is Miranda's fine breeding.

While she was under her mother, she was forced to be genteel, to live in ceremony, to sit up late at nights, to be in the folly of every fashion, and to always visit on Sundays. She was forced to go patched and loaded with a burden of finery to the Holy Sacrament, to be in every polite conversation, to hear profanity at the playhouse and wanton songs and love intrigues at the opera, and to dance at public places so that fops and rakes might admire the fineness of her shape and the beauty of her motions. The remembrance of this way of life makes her exceedingly careful to atone for it by a contrary behavior.

Miranda does not divide her duty between God, her neighbor, and herself. She considers all as due to God. So she does everything in God's name and for God's sake. This makes her consider her fortune as the gift of God that is to be used, as is everything that belongs to God, for the wise and reasonable ends of a Christian and holy life. Her fortune, therefore, is divided between herself and several poor people, and she has only her part of relief from it. She thinks it the same folly to indulge herself in needless, vain expenses as to give to other people to spend in the same way. Therefore as she will not give a poor man money to see a puppet show, neither will she allow herself any to spend in the same manner. She thinks it very proper to be as wise as she expects poor men should be. For it is a folly and a crime in a poor man, says Miranda, to waste what is given him in foolish trifles, while he lacks meat, drink, and clothes. And is it less folly or less a crime in me to spend that money in silly diversions that might be so much better spent in imitation of the divine goodness, in works of kindness and charity toward my fellow creatures and fellow Christians?

Except for her food, she never spent as much as ten pounds a year upon herself. If you were to see her, you would wonder what poor body it was that was so surprisingly neat and clean. She has but one rule that she observes in her dress: to be always clean and in the cheapest things. Everything about her resembles the purity of her soul. She is always clean without, because she is always pure within.

Every morning sees her early at her prayers. She rejoices in the beginning of every day because it begins all her pious rules of holy living and brings the fresh pleasure of repeating them. She seems to be as a guardian angel to those who dwell about her. With her prayers she blesses the place where she dwells and makes intercession with God for those who are asleep.

When you see her at work, you see the same wisdom that governs all her other actions. She is doing something that is necessary for herself or necessary for others who want to be assisted. There is scarcely a poor family in the neighborhood that does not wear something or other that has had the labor of her hands. Her wise and pious mind neither wants the amusement nor can bear with the folly of idle and impertinent work. She can allow no such folly as this by day because she has to answer for all her actions at night. When there is no wisdom to be observed in the employment of her hands, when there is no useful or charitable work to be done, Miranda will work no more. At her table she lives strictly by this rule of Holy Scripture, "Whether you eat or drink, or whatever you do, do everything for the glory of God." This makes her begin and end every meal as she begins and ends every day: with acts of devotion. She eats and drinks only for the sake of living. With such regular abstinence every meal is an exercise of self-denial. She humbles her body every time that she is forced to feed it. If Miranda were to run a race for her life, she would submit to a diet that was proper for it. But since the race set before her is a race of holiness, purity, and heavenly affection that she is to finish in a corrupt, disordered body of earthly passions, so her everyday diet has only this one end: to make her body fitter for this spiritual race.

The Holy Scriptures, especially the New Testament, are her daily study. She reads them with watchful attention, constantly casting an eye upon herself and trying herself by every doctrine that is there. When she has the New Testament in her hand, she supposes herself at the feet of our Savior and his apostles and makes everything that she learns of them so many laws of her life. She receives their sacred words with as much attention and reverence as if she saw their persons and knew that they were just come from heaven to teach her the way that leads to it.

She is sometimes afraid that she pays too much money for books because she cannot forbear buying all practical books of any note, especially such as enter into the heart of religion and describe the inward holiness of the Christian life. But of all human writings the lives of pious persons and eminent saints are her greatest delight. She searches them as for hidden treasure, hoping to find some secret of holy living, some uncommon degree of piety she may make her own. By this means Miranda has her head and her heart so stored with all the principles of wisdom and holiness, she is so full of the one main business of life, that she finds it difficult to converse upon any other subject. If you are in her company when she thinks it proper to talk, you must be made wiser and better, whether you will or no.

 MIRANDA'S CHARITY

From Chapter 8

After describing Miranda's personal conduct, he turns to her use of money for charitable purposes.

To tell of her charity would be to relate the history of every day for twenty years. For so long her fortune has all been spent that way. She has set up about twenty poor tradesmen who had failed in their businesses and saved as many from failing. She has educated several poor children and put them in a way of honest employment. As soon as any laborer is confined at home with sickness, she sends him, until he recovers, twice the value of his wages so that he may have one part to give to his family as usual and the other to provide things needed for his sickness.

If a family seems too large to be supported by the labor of those who can work in it, she pays their rent and gives them something yearly toward their clothing. By this means, there are several poor families that live in a comfortable manner and are from year to year blessing her in their prayers.

If any poor men or women are more than ordinarily wicked and reprobate, Miranda has her eye upon them. She watches their time of need and adversity. And if she can discover that they are in any great straits or affliction, she gives them speedy relief. She has this care for this sort of people because she once saved a very dissolute person from being carried to prison, who immediately became a true penitent.

There is nothing in the character of Miranda more to be admired than this temper. For this tenderness of affection toward the most abandoned sinners is the highest example of a divine and godlike soul.

Miranda is a constant relief to poor people in their misfortunes and accidents. There are sometimes little misfortunes that happen to them that they could never be able to overcome by themselves. The death of a cow or a horse or some little robbery would keep them in distress all their lives. She does not allow them to grieve under such accidents. She immediately gives them the full value of their loss and makes use of it as a means of raising their minds toward God.

She has a great tenderness for older people who have grown past their labor. The parish allowance to such people is very seldom a comfortable maintenance. For this reason they are the constant objects of her care. She adds so much to their allowance as to exceed the wages they got when they were young. This she does to comfort the infirmities of their age so that, being free from trouble and distress, they may serve God in peace and tranquillity of mind. She has generally a large number of this kind who, by her charities and exhortations to holiness, spend their last days in great piety and devotion.

Miranda never wants compassion, even for common beggars—especially those who are old or sick or full of sores or lack eyes or limbs. She hears their complaints with tenderness, gives them some proof of her kindness, and never rejects them with hard or reproachful language for fear of adding affliction to her fellow creatures.

It may be, says Miranda, that I may often give to those who do not deserve it or who will make an ill use of my alms. But what then? Is not this the very method of divine goodness? Does not God make the "sun rise on the evil and on the good"? Is not this the very goodness that is recommended to us in Scripture, that, by imitating it, we may be children of our Father in heaven, who "sends rain on the righteous and on the unrighteous"? And shall I withhold a little money or food from my fellow creature for fear he should not be good enough to receive it of me? Do I beg of God to deal with me not according to my merit but according to God's own great goodness; and shall I be so absurd as to withhold my charity from a poor brother because he may perhaps not deserve it? Shall I use a measure toward him that I pray God never to use toward me?

Besides, where has the Scripture made merit the rule or measure of charity? On the contrary, the Scripture says, "If your enemies are hungry, feed them; if they are thirsty, give them something to drink."

Now this plainly teaches us that the merit of persons is to be no rule of our charity. We are to do acts of kindness to those that least of all deserve it. For if I am to love and do good to my worst enemies and be charitable to them despite all their malice, surely merit is no measure of charity. If I am not to withhold my charity from such bad people who are at the same time my enemies, surely I am not to deny alms to poor beggars whom I know to be neither bad people nor any way my enemies.

You will perhaps say that by this means I encourage people to be beggars. But the same thoughtless objection may be made against all kinds of charities, since they may encourage people to depend upon them. The same may be said against forgiving our enemies, for it may encourage people to do us hurt. The same may be said even against the goodness of God: by pouring blessings on the evil and on the good, on the unjust and on the just, evil and unjust people are encouraged in their wicked ways. The same may be said against clothing the naked or giving medicine to the sick: that may encourage people to neglect themselves and be careless of their health. But when the love of God dwells in you, when it has enlarged your heart and filled you with mercy and compassion, you will make no more such objections.

This is the spirit and life of the devout Miranda. When she dies, she must shine among apostles and saints and martyrs. She must stand among the first servants of God and be glorious among those who have fought the good fight and finished their course with joy.

PRAYER AND DEVOTION

From Chapter 10

After the special case of Miranda, Law goes on to argue that devotion, like prayer, is for all people in any walk of life.

It is granted that prayer is a duty that belongs to all states and conditions of people. If we inquire into the reason why no state of life is to be excused from prayer, we shall find it as good a reason why every state of life is to be made a state of piety and holiness in all its parts.

For we pray and glorify God with hymns and psalms of thanksgiving because we are to live wholly for God and glorify God in all possible ways. It is not because the praises of words or forms of thanksgiving are more particularly parts of piety or more the worship of God than other things. But it is because they are possible ways of expressing our dependence, our obedience, and our devotion to God. Now if the reason for verbal praises and thanksgiving to God is that we are to live for God in all possible ways, then it plainly follows that we are equally obliged to worship and glorify God in all other actions that can be turned into acts of piety and obedience to God. And as actions are of much more significance than words, it must be a much more acceptable worship to glorify God in all the actions of our common life than with any little form of words at any particular times.

Prayer and Devotion — 33

Thus, if God is to be worshiped with forms of thanksgiving, those who make it a rule to be content and thankful in every part and accident of life, because it comes from God, praise God in a much higher manner than those who have some set time for singing psalms. Those who dare not say an ill-natured word or do an unreasonable thing because they consider God as everywhere present perform a better devotion than those who dare not miss church. Living in the world as a stranger and a pilgrim, using all its enjoyments as if we used them not and making all our actions so many steps toward a better life, is offering a better sacrifice to God than any forms of holy and heavenly prayers.

To be humble in all our actions, to avoid every appearance of pride and vanity, to be meek and lowly in our words, actions, dress, behavior, and designs, in imitation of our blessed Savior, is to worship God in a higher manner than those who have only certain times to fall low on their knees in devotions. Those who content themselves with necessities in order to give the remainder to those that lack it and who dare not to spend any money foolishly, considering it as a talent from God that must be used according to God's will, praise God with something that is more glorious than songs of praise.

Those who have appointed times for the use of wise and pious prayers perform a proper instance of devotion. But those who allow themselves no times or places or actions but those strictly conformable to wisdom and holiness worship the Divine nature with the most true and substantial devotion. For who does not know that it is better to be pure and holy than to talk about purity and holiness? No, who does not know that people are to be reckoned no more pure or holy or just than they are pure and holy and just in the common course of their lives? But if this is plain, then it is also plain that it is better to be holy than to have holy prayers.

Prayers, therefore, are so far from being a sufficient devotion that they are the smallest parts of it. We are to praise God with words and prayers because such praise is a possible way of glorifying God. But then as words are but small things in themselves and times of prayer are but little if compared with the rest of our lives, so devotion that consists in times and forms of prayer is but a very small thing if compared to devotion that appears in every other part and circumstance of our lives.

Bended knees, while you are clothed with pride; heavenly petitions, while you are hoarding up treasures upon earth; holy devotions, while you live in the follies of the world; prayers of meekness and charity, while your heart is the seat of pride and resentment; hours of prayer, while you give up days and years to idle diversions, impertinent visits, and foolish pleasures—all are as absurd and unacceptable services to God as forms of thanksgiving from a person who lives in moping and discontent.

Unless the common course of our lives is according to the common spirit of our prayers, our prayers are so far from being a real or sufficient degree of devotion that they become an empty lip service or, what is worse, a notorious hypocrisy.

Since we are to make the spirit and temper of our prayers the common spirit and temper of our lives, this may convince us that all orders of people are to labor and aspire after the same utmost perfection of the Christian life. For as all Christians are to use the same holy and heavenly devotions and with the same earnestness to pray for the Spirit of God, so is it a sufficient proof that all orders of people are, to the utmost of their power, to make their lives agreeable to the one Spirit for whom they are all to pray.

DISCIPLINE

From Chapter 11

In this selection Law addresses the concern that following Christian disciplines in our lives will make them boring and uncomfortable.

Most people confess that religion preserves us from a great many evils and helps us in many respects to a more happy enjoyment of ourselves. But then they imagine that this is true only of such a moderate share of religion as gently restrains us from the excesses of our passions. They suppose that the strict rules and restraints of an exalted piety are such contradictions to our nature as must make our lives dull and uncomfortable.

This objection supposes that religion, moderately practiced, adds much to the happiness of life but that such heights of piety as the perfection of religion requires have a contrary effect.

It supposes, therefore, that it is happy to be kept from the excesses of envy, but unhappy to be kept from other degrees of envy. That it is happy to be delivered from a boundless ambition, but unhappy to be without a more moderate ambition. It supposes, also, that the happiness of life consists in a mixture of virtue and vice, a mixture of ambition and humility, charity and envy, heavenly affection and covetousness.

All this is as absurd as to suppose that it is happy to be free from excessive pains, but unhappy to be without more moderate pains; or that the happiness of health consists in being partly sick and partly well.

If religion restrains only the excesses of revenge but lets the spirit still live within you in lesser instances, your religion may have made your life a little more outwardly decent but not made you at all happier or easier in yourself. But if you have once sacrificed all thoughts of revenge in obedience to God and are resolved to return good for evil at all times in order to render yourself more like God and fitter for God's mercy in the kingdom of love and glory, this is a height of virtue that will make you feel its happiness.

Piety requires us to renounce no ways of life where we can act reasonably and offer what we do to the glory of God. All ways of life—all satisfactions and enjoyments—that are within these bounds are no way denied us by the strictest rules of piety. Whatever you can do or enjoy as in the presence of God, as God's servant, as God's rational creature that has received reason and knowledge from God, and all that you can do in conformity to a rational nature and the will of God—all this is allowed by the laws of piety. Will you think that your life will be uncomfortable unless you may displease God, be a fool, and act contrary to the reason and wisdom that God has implanted in you?

As for those satisfactions we dare not offer to a holy God, that are invented only by the folly and corruption of the world, that inflame our passions and sink our souls into grossness and sensuality and render us incapable of the Divine favor either here or hereafter—surely it can be no uncomfortable state of life to be rescued by religion from such self-murder and to be rendered capable of eternal happiness.

Let us suppose a person destitute of the knowledge we have from our senses, placed somewhere alone by himself in the midst of a variety of things he did not know how to use: bread, wine, water, gold dust, iron chains, gravel, garments, fire, etc. Let us suppose that he has no knowledge of the right use of these things or any direction from his senses how to quench his thirst or satisfy his hunger or make any use of the things about him. In his thirst, he puts gold dust into his eyes. When his eyes smart, he puts wine into his ears. In his hunger, he puts gravel into his mouth. In pain, he loads himself with the iron chains. Feeling cold, he puts his feet in the water. Being frightened by the fire, he runs away from it. Being weary, he makes a seat of his bread. Through his ignorance of the right use of the things that are about him, he will vainly torment himself while he lives and at last die, blinded with dust, choked with gravel, and loaded with irons. Let us suppose that some good being came to him and showed him the nature and use of all the things that were about him and gave him such strict rules of using them as would certainly, if observed, make him the happier for all that he had and deliver him from the pains of hunger and thirst and cold.

Now could you with any reason affirm that those strict rules of using those things that were about him had rendered that poor man's life dull and uncomfortable?

Now this is in some measure a representation of the strict rules of religion. They only relieve our ignorance, save us from tormenting ourselves, and teach us to use everything about us to our proper advantage.

We are placed in a world full of a variety of things. Our ignorance makes us use many of them as absurdly as the man who put dust in his eyes to relieve his thirst or put on chains to remove pain.

Religion, therefore, comes in to our relief and gives us strict rules of using all things that are about us, so that by using them suitably to our own nature and the nature of the things we may have always the pleasure of receiving a right benefit from them.

SEEING CLEARLY

From Chapter 13

Law hopes that by careful observation of the people and events around them, people will be inspired to change their lives, just as well-born Eugenius is shocked into repentance by the death of Octavius.

Let us only intend to see and hear, and then the whole world becomes a book of wisdom and instruction to us. All that is regular in the order of nature, all that is accidental in the course of things, all the mistakes and disappointments that happen to us, and all the miseries and errors that we see in other people become so many plain lessons of advice to us. They teach us, with as much assurance as an angel from heaven, that we can in no way raise ourselves to any true happiness but by turning all our thoughts, wishes, and endeavors after the happiness of another life.

It is this right use of the world that I would lead you into by directing you to turn your eyes upon every shape of human folly. From that you may draw fresh arguments and motives of living to the best and greatest purposes of your creation.

If you would only carry with you this intention of profiting by the follies of the world and of learning the greatness of religion from the littleness and vanity of every other way of life, you would find every day, every place, and every person, a fresh proof of the wisdom of those who choose to live wholly to God. You would then often return home the wiser, the better, and the more strengthened in religion by everything that has fallen in your way.

Octavius is a learned, ingenious man, well versed in most parts of literature and no stranger to any kingdom in Europe. The other day, being just recovered from a lingering fever, he began to talk thus to his friends: "My glass is almost run out, and your eyes see how many marks of age and death I bear. I plainly feel myself sinking away faster than any bystanders imagine. I fully believe that one year more will conclude my reckoning."

The attention of his friends was much raised by such a declaration. They expected to hear something truly excellent from so learned a man, who had only a year longer to live. Octavius proceeded in this manner: "For these reasons, my friends, I have left off all taverns. The wine of those places is not good enough for me in this decay of nature. I must now be particular in what I drink. I cannot pretend to do as I have done and therefore am resolved to furnish my own cellar with a little of the very best, though it cost me ever so much.

"I must also tell you, my friends, that age forces a man to be wise in many other respects and makes us change many of our opinions and practices.

"You know how much I have liked a large acquaintance. I now condemn it as an error. Three or four cheerful, diverting companions are all that I now desire. I find that in my present infirmities if I am left alone or to solemn company, I am not so easy to myself."

A few days after Octavius had made this declaration to his friends, he relapsed into his former illness and was committed to a nurse, who closed his eyes before his fresh parcel of wine came in.

Young Eugenius, who was present at this discourse, went home a new man, with full resolutions of devoting himself wholly to God.

"I never," says Eugenius, "was so deeply affected with the wisdom and importance of religion as when I saw how poorly and meanly the learned Octavius was to leave the world through the lack of it.

"How often I had envied his great learning, his skill in languages, his knowledge of antiquity, his address, and his fine manner of expressing himself upon all subjects! But when I saw how poorly it all ended, what was to be the last year of such a life, and how foolishly the master of all these accomplishments was then forced to talk, for lack of being acquainted with the joys and expectations of piety, I was thoroughly convinced that there was nothing to be envied or desired but a life of true piety, nor anything so poor and comfortless as a death without it."

Young Eugenius was thus edified and instructed in the present case. If you are so fortunate as to have anything of his thoughtful temper, you will meet with variety of instruction of this kind. You will find that arguments for the wisdom and happiness of a strict piety offer themselves in all places and appeal to all your senses in the plainest manner.

You will find that all the world preaches to an attentive mind. If you have but ears to hear, almost everything you meet teaches you some lesson of wisdom.

But now, if to these admonitions and instructions that we receive from our senses and from an experience of the state of human life—if to these we add the lights of religion, those great truths the Son of God has taught us, it will be then as much beyond all doubt that there is but one happiness for a person, as that there is but one God.

For since religion teaches us that our souls are immortal, that piety and devotion will carry them to an eternal enjoyment of God, and that carnal, worldly tempers will sink them into an everlasting misery with damned spirits, what gross nonsense and stupidity it is to give the name of joy or happiness to anything but what carries us to this joy and happiness in God!

NEGOTIUS

From Chapter 13

In the portrait of Negotius (businessman), Law hopes to show how being a good, sober, honest person is not the same as being devout and how true devotion and business might go together.

Negotius is a temperate, honest man. He served his time under a master of great trade but has, by his own management, made it a more substantial business than ever it was before. The general good of trade seems to Negotius to be the general good of life. Whom he admires or what he commends or condemns, either in church or in state, is admired, commended, or condemned with some regard to trade.

As money is continually pouring in upon him, so he often lets it go in various kinds of expense and generosity, sometimes in ways of charity.

He has given a fine set of bells to a church in the country. There is much expectation that he will some time or other make a more beautiful front to the markethouse than has yet been seen in any place. For it is the generous spirit of Negotius to do nothing in a cheap way.

If you ask what has secured Negotius from all scandalous vices, it is the same thing that has kept him from all strictness of devotion: his great business. He has always had too many important things in his head to allow him either to fall into any courses of debauchery or to feel the necessity of an inward, solid piety.

For this reason he hears of the pleasures of debauchery and the pleasures of piety with the same indifference. He has no more desire of living in the one than in the other because neither of them consists with that turn of mind and multiplicity of business that are his happiness.

If Negotius were asked what he drives at in life, he would be as much at a loss for an answer as if he were asked what any other person is thinking. For though he always seems to himself to know what he is doing and has many things in his head that are the motives of his actions, yet he cannot tell you of any one general end in life that he has chosen with deliberation as being truly worthy of all his labor and pains. The thing that seems to give Negotius the greatest life and spirit and to be most in his thoughts is an expectation that he shall die richer than any of his business ever did.

Most people, when they think of happiness, think of Negotius, in whose life every instance of happiness is supposed to meet. He is sober, prudent, rich, prosperous, generous, and charitable.

Let us now, therefore, look at this condition in another, but truer light.

Suppose that this same Negotius was a painstaking, hardworking man, every day deep in a variety of affairs, and that he neither drank nor debauched but was sober and regular in his business. Suppose that he grew old in this course of trading and that the end and design of all this labor, and care, and application to business was only this: that he might die possessed of more than one hundred thousand pairs of boots and spurs.

Now if this were really the case, I believe it would be readily granted that a life of such business was as poor and ridiculous as any that can be invented. But it would puzzle anyone to show that people who have spent all their time and thoughts in business and hurry that they might die, as it is said, worth one hundred thousand pounds are any wiser than one who has taken the same pains to have as many pairs of boots and spurs when he leaves the world.

For the only end of life is to die as free from sin and exalted in virtue as we can. Naked we came and naked we are to return and to stand trial before Christ and his holy angels for everlasting happiness or misery. Then what can it possibly signify what we had or did not have in this world? What can it signify what we call the things that we leave behind, whether we call them one hundred thousand pounds or one hundred thousand pairs of boots and spurs?

Now it is easy to see the folly of a life spent to furnish a man with such a number of boots and spurs. For when he has got all his boots, his soul is to go to its own place among separate spirits and his body be laid by in a coffin till the last trumpet calls him to judgment. There the inquiry will be how humbly, how devoutly, how purely, how meekly, how piously, how charitably, how heavenly we have spoken, thought, and acted while we were in the body. How can we say that those who have worn out their lives in raising one hundred thousand pounds have acted wiser than one who has had the same care to procure one hundred thousand of anything else?

But suppose that Negotius, when he first entered into business, happened to read the gospel with attention and eyes open and found that he had a much greater business on his hands than that to which he had served an apprenticeship. Suppose that he had discovered that his soul was more to him than his body; that it was better to grow in the virtues of the soul than to have a large body or a full purse; better to be fit for heaven than to have a variety of fine houses upon the earth; better to secure everlasting happiness than to have plenty of things that he cannot keep; better to live in habits of humility, piety, devotion, charity, and self-denial than to die unprepared for judgment; better to be most like our Savior or some eminent saint than to excel all the tradesmen in the world in business and bulk of fortune. Suppose that Negotius, believing these things to be true, entirely devoted himself to God at his first setting out in the world, resolving to pursue his business no farther than was consistent with great devotion, humility, and self-denial and for no other ends but to provide himself with a sober subsistence and to do all the good that he could to the souls and bodies of his fellow creatures.

Suppose, therefore, that instead of the continual hurry of business, he was frequent in his retirements and a strict observer of all the hours of prayer; that, instead of restless desires after more riches, his soul had been full of the love of God and heavenly affection, constantly watching against worldly tempers and always aspiring after divine grace; that, instead of worldly cares and contrivances, he was busy in fortifying his soul against all approaches of sin; that, instead of costly show and expensive generosity of a splendid life, he loved and exercised all instances of humility and lowliness; that, instead of great treats and full tables, his house furnished only sober refreshment to those who wanted it. Let it be supposed that his contentment kept him free from all kinds of envy; that his piety made him thankful to God in all crosses and disappointments; that his charity kept him from being rich by a continual distribution to all objects of compassion. Now, had this been the Christian spirit of Negotius, can anyone say that he had lost the true joy and happiness of life by thus conforming to the spirit and living up to the hopes of the gospel? Can it be said that a life made exemplary by such virtues as these that keep heaven always in our sight, that both delight and exalt the soul here and prepare it for the presence of God hereafter, must be poor and dull if compared to that of heaping up riches that can neither stay with us nor we with them?

 # SOUL AND BODY

From Chapter 15

In the last half of A Serious Call, Law writes about topics for prayer throughout the day. The first topic, for prayer on rising at 6:00 A.M., is praise. After giving examples of spoken prayers, he urges readers to begin by singing or chanting a psalm so that the body joins the mind in prayer.

The soul and the body are so united that each has power over the other in its actions. Certain thoughts and sentiments in the soul produce such and such motions and actions in the body. On the other hand, certain motions and actions of the body have the same power of raising such and such thoughts and sentiments in the soul. As singing is the natural effect of joy in the mind, so it is as truly a natural cause of raising joy in the mind.

As devotion of the heart naturally breaks out into outward acts of prayer, so outward acts of prayer are natural means of raising the devotion of the heart.

If we simply consider human nature, we shall find that singing or chanting psalms is as proper and necessary to raise our hearts to a delight in God as prayer is proper and necessary to excite in us the spirit of devotion. Every reason for one is in all respects as strong a reason for the other.

If, therefore, you would know the reason and necessity of singing psalms, you must consider the reason and necessity of praising and rejoicing in God. Singing psalms is as much the true exercise and support of the spirit of thanksgiving as prayer is the true exercise and support of the spirit of devotion. You may as well think that you can be devout as you ought without the use of prayer as that you can rejoice in God as you ought without the practice of singing psalms. This singing is as much the natural language of praise and thanksgiving as prayer is the natural language of devotion.

This union of our souls and bodies is the reason both why we have so little and why we have so much power over ourselves. It is owing to this union that we have so little power over our souls. We cannot prevent the effects of external objects upon our bodies or command outward causes. So we cannot always command the inward state of our minds. As outward objects act upon our bodies without our leave, so our bodies act upon our minds by the laws of the union of the soul and the body. So you see it is owing to this union that we have so little power over ourselves.

On the other hand, it is owing to this union that we have so much power over ourselves. Our souls, in a great measure, depend upon our bodies, and we have great power over our bodies. We can command our outward actions and oblige ourselves to such habits of life as naturally produce habits in the soul. We can mortify our bodies and remove ourselves from objects that inflame our passions. So we have a great power over the inward state of our souls. Again, we can force ourselves to outward acts of reading, praying, singing, and the like. All these bodily actions have an effect upon the soul. As they naturally tend to form such and such tempers in our hearts, so by being masters of these outward, bodily actions, we have great power over the inward state of the heart. So it is owing to this union that we have so much power over ourselves.

Now from this you may also see the necessity and benefit of singing psalms and of all the outward acts of religion. For if the body has so much power over the soul, it is certain that all such bodily actions as affect the soul are of great weight in religion. Not as if there were any true worship or piety in the actions themselves, but because they are proper to raise and support the spirit that is true worship of God.

This doctrine may easily be carried too far. By calling in too many outward means of worship, it may degenerate into superstition. On the other hand, some have fallen into the contrary extreme. For because religion is justly placed in the heart, some have pursued that notion so far as to renounce vocal prayer and other outward acts of worship and have resolved all religion into quietism or mystic intercourse with God in silence.

Now these are two extremes equally prejudicial to true religion. You ought not to say that I encourage quietism by placing religion in the heart. Neither ought you to say that I encourage superstition by showing the benefit of outward acts of worship.

If we would truly prostrate our souls before God, we must accustom our bodies to postures of lowliness. If we desire true favors of devotion, we must make prayer the frequent labor of our lips. If we would banish all pride and passion from our hearts, we must force ourselves to all outward actions of patience and meekness. If we would feel inward motions of joy and delight in God, we must practice all the outward acts of it and make our voices call upon our hearts.

Now, therefore, you may plainly see the reason and necessity of singing psalms. Outward actions are necessary to support inward tempers. Therefore, the outward act of joy is necessary to raise and support the inward joy of the mind.

If any people were to leave off prayer because they seldom find the motions of their hearts answering the words they speak, you would charge them with great absurdity. Now this is very much the case as to singing psalms. People often sing without finding any inward joy suitable to the words they speak. Therefore, they are careless of it or wholly neglect it, not considering that they act as absurdly as one who neglected prayer because his heart was not enough affected with it. For it is certain that this singing is as much the natural means of raising emotions of joy in the mind as prayer is the natural means of raising devotion.

Humility and Pride

From Chapter 16

For prayer at 9:00 A.M., Law suggests humility as the appropriate topic. The example about Caecus (blind), who is unable to see himself truly, is taken from later in the chapter than the first part of this selection.

This virtue is so essential to the right state of our souls that there is no pretending to a reasonable or pious life without it. We may as well think to see without eyes or live without breath as to live in the spirit of religion without the spirit of humility.

Although it is the soul and essence of all religious duties, it is, generally speaking, the least understood, the least regarded, the least intended, the least desired and sought after of all other virtues among all sorts of Christians.

No people have more occasion to be afraid of the approaches of pride than those who have made some advances in a pious life. Pride can grow as well upon our virtues as our vices and steal upon us on all occasions.

Every good thought that we have and every good action that we do lays us open to pride and exposes us to the assaults of vanity and self-satisfaction.

It is not only the beauty of our persons, the gifts of fortune, our natural talents, and the distinctions of life, but even our devotions and alms, our fasting and humiliations, expose us to fresh and strong temptations of this evil spirit.

And it is for this reason that I so earnestly advise all devout persons to begin every day in this exercise of humility, so that they may go on in safety under the protection of this good guide and not fall a sacrifice to their own progress in those virtues that are to save humankind from destruction.

Humility does not consist in having a worse opinion of ourselves than we deserve or in abasing ourselves lower than we really are. But as all virtue is founded in truth, so humility is founded in a true and just sense of our weakness, misery, and sin. Those who rightly feel and live in this sense of their condition live in humility.

—

Caecus is a rich man, of good breeding and very fine parts. He is fond of dress and curious about the smallest matters that can add any ornament to his person. He is haughty and imperious to all his inferiors, is very full of everything that he says or does, and never imagines it possible for such a judgment as his to be mistaken. He can bear no contradiction and discovers the weakness of your understanding as soon as you oppose him. He changes everything in his house, his habit, and his equipage as often as anything more elegant comes in his way. Caecus would have been very religious but that he always thought he was so.

There is nothing so odious to Caecus as a proud man. The misfortune is that in this he is so very quick to judge that he discovers in almost everybody some strokes of vanity.

On the other hand, he is exceedingly fond of humble and modest persons. "Humility," says he, "is so amiable a quality that it forces our esteem wherever we meet with it. There is no possibility of despising the meanest person that has it or of esteeming the greatest man that lacks it."

Caecus no more suspects himself to be proud than he suspects his want of sense. And the reason is thtat he always finds himself so in love with humility and so enraged at pride.

It is very true, Caecus. You speak sincerely when you say you love humility and abhor pride. You are no hypocrite. You speak the true sentiments of your mind. But then take this along with you, Caecus, that you love humility and hate pride only in other people. You never once in your life thought of any other humility or of any other pride than what you have seen in other people.

The case of Caecus is a common case. Many people live in all the instances of pride and indulge every vanity that can enter into their minds and yet never suspect themselves to be governed by pride and vanity because they know how much they dislike proud people and how mightily they are pleased with humility and modesty wherever they find them.

You must therefore act by a quite contrary measure and reckon yourself only so far humble as you impose every instance of humility upon yourself and never call for it in other people. You must be such an enemy to pride that you never spare it in yourself or censure it in other persons.

Now to set out well in the practice of humility, you must take it for granted that you are proud and have been more or less infected with this unreasonable temper all your life.

You should believe also that it is your greatest weakness, that your heart is most subject to it, that it is so constantly stealing upon you that you have reason to watch and suspect its approaches in all your actions.

For this is what most people—especially new beginners in a pious life—may with great truth think of themselves.

If, therefore, you find it disagreeable to your mind to entertain this opinion of yourself and that you cannot put yourself among those who want to be cured of pride, you may be as sure as if an angel from heaven had told you that you have not only much but all your humility to seek.

For you can have no greater sign of a more confirmed pride than when you think that you are humble enough. Those who think they love God enough show themselves to be complete strangers to that holy passion. So those who think they do not have humility enough show that they are not so much as beginners in the practice of true humility.

INTERCESSION

From Chapter 21

Law commends universal love as the topic for prayer at noon. This general love becomes specific through intercessory prayer that softens our hearts toward those for whom we pray. The example of Susurrus, the whispering gossip, is taken from the end of the chapter.

A frequent intercession with God, earnestly beseeching God to forgive the sins of all humankind, to bless them with providence, enlighten them with the Spirit, and bring them to everlasting happiness, is the divinest exercise in which the human heart can be engaged.

Be daily, therefore, on your knees, praying for others in such forms and with such length, importunity, and earnestness as you use for yourself. You will find all little, ill-natured passions die away and your heart grow great and generous, delighting in the common happiness of others as you used only to delight in your own.

For those who pray daily to God that all may be happy in heaven take the likeliest way to make themselves wish for and delight in the happiness of all on earth. It is hardly possible for you to beseech and entreat God to make anyone happy in the highest enjoyments of God's glory to all eternity and yet be troubled to see him or her enjoy the much smaller gifts of God in this short and low state of human life.

How strange and unnatural it would be to pray to God to grant health and a longer life to a sick man and at the same time to envy him the poor pleasure of agreeable medicines! Yet this would be no more strange or unnatural than to pray to God that your neighbor may enjoy the highest degrees of God's mercy and favor and yet at the same time envy her the little credit and reputation she has among her fellow creatures.

When you have once accustomed your heart to a serious performance of this holy intercession, you have done a great deal to render it incapable of spite and envy and to make it naturally delight in the happiness of all people.

This is the natural effect of a general intercession for all humankind. But the greatest benefits are then received when it descends to particular instances.

You should always change and alter your intercessions according to what the needs and necessities of your neighbors or friends seem to require, beseeching God to deliver them from such and such particular evils or to grant them this or that particular gift or blessing. Such intercessions, besides the great charity of them, would have a mighty effect upon your heart, disposing you to every other good office and to the exercise of every other virtue toward such persons as have so often a place in your prayers.

This would make it pleasant to you to be courteous, civil, and gracious to all about you, and unable to say or do a rude or hard thing to those for whom you had accustomed yourself to be so kind and compassionate in your prayers.

For there is nothing that makes us love a person so much as praying for him or her. When you can once do this sincerely for anyone, you have fitted your soul for the performance of everything that is kind and civil toward that person. This will fill your heart with a generosity and tenderness that will give you a better and sweeter behavior than anything that is called fine breeding and good manners.

By considering yourself an advocate with God for your neighbors and friends, you would never find it hard to be at peace with them. It would be easy to you to bear with and forgive those for whom you particularly implored divine mercy and forgiveness.

Such prayers among neighbors and friends would unite them to one another in the strongest bonds of love and tenderness. Such prayers would exalt and ennoble their souls and teach them to consider one another in a higher state, as members of a spiritual society, created for the enjoyment of the common blessings of God and fellow heirs of the same future glory.

—

Susurrus is a pious, temperate, good man, remarkable for abundance of excellent qualities. There is no one more constant at worship or whose heart is more affected with it. His charity is so great that he almost starves himself to be able to give greater alms to the poor.

Yet Susurrus had a prodigious failing along with these great virtues: a mighty inclination to hear and discover all the defects and infirmities of all about him. You were welcome to tell him anything of anybody, provided that you did not do it in the style of an enemy. If you would only whisper anything gently, though it were ever so bad in itself, Susurrus was ready to receive it.

When he visits, you generally hear him relating how sorry he is for the defects and failings of such a neighbor. He is always letting you know how tender he is of the reputation of his neighbor, how reluctant to say what he is forced to say, and how gladly he would conceal it if it could be concealed.

Susurrus had such a tender, compassionate manner of relating the most prejudicial things about his neighbor that he even seemed—both to himself and to others—to be exercising Christian charity at the same time that he was indulging a whispering, evil-speaking temper.

Susurrus once whispered to a particular friend in great secrecy something too bad to be spoken of publicly. He ended with saying how glad he was that it had not yet taken wind and that he had some hopes it might not be true, though the suspicions were very strong. His friend made him this reply:

"You say, Susurrus, that you are glad it has not yet taken wind and that you have some hope it may not prove true. Go home, therefore, to your closet and pray to God for this man in such a manner and with such earnestness as you would pray for yourself on a similar occasion.

"Beseech God to interpose in his favor, to save him from false accusers, and to bring all those to shame who wound him by uncharitable whispers and secret stories, like those that stab in the dark. And when you have made this prayer, then you may, if you please, go tell the same secret to some other friend that you have told to me."

Susurrus was exceedingly affected with this rebuke and felt its force upon his conscience in as lively a manner as if he had seen the books opened at the day of judgment.

All other arguments might have been resisted. But it was impossible for Susurrus either to reject or to follow this advice without being equally self-condemned in the highest degree.

From that time to this, he has constantly accustomed himself to this method of intercession. His heart is so entirely changed by it that he can now no more privately whisper anything to the prejudice of another than he can openly pray to God to do people hurt.

Whispering and evil-speaking now hurt his ears like oaths and curses. He has appointed one day in the week to be a day of penance as long as he lives, to humble himself before God in the sorrowful confession of his former guilt.

RESIGNATION TO GOD'S WILL

From Chapter 22

Resignation or self-abandonment is the topic for prayer at 3:00 P.M.

Whether we consider the infinite goodness of God that cannot choose amiss for us or our own great ignorance of what is most advantageous to us, there can be nothing so reasonable and pious as to have no will but God's and to desire nothing for ourselves in our persons, our state, and condition but what the good providence of God appoints for us.

Further, as the good providence of God introduces us into the world, putting us into such states and conditions of life as are most appropriate to us, so the same unerring wisdom orders all events and changes in the whole course of our lives in such a manner as to render them the fittest means to exercise and improve our virtue.

Nothing hurts us, nothing destroys us, but the ill use of that liberty with which God has entrusted us.

We are as sure that nothing happens to us by chance as that the world itself was not made by chance. We are as certain that all things happen and work together for our good as that God is goodness itself.

This is not cheating or soothing ourselves into any false content or imaginary happiness. It is a satisfaction grounded upon as great a certainty as the being and attributes of God.

For if we are right in believing God to act over us with infinite wisdom and goodness, we cannot carry our notions of conformity and resignation to the divine will too high. Nor can we ever be deceived by thinking best for us what God has brought upon us.

For the providence of God is not more concerned in the government of night and day and the variety of seasons than in the common course of events that seem most to depend upon mere human wills. It is as strictly right to look upon all worldly accidents and changes, all the various turns and alternations in your life, to be as truly the effects of Divine providence as the rising and setting of the sun or the alternations of the seasons of the year. As you are, therefore, always to adore the wisdom of God in the direction of these things, so it is the same reasonable duty always to magnify God as equally director of everything that happens to you in the course of your life.

This holy resignation and conformity of your will to the will of God is so much the true state of piety that I hope you will think it proper to make this hour of prayer a constant season of asking God for so great a gift. By thus constantly praying for it, your heart may be habitually disposed toward it and always in a state of readiness to look at everything as God's and to consider God in everything. Then everything that happens to you may be received in the spirit of piety and made a means of exercising some virtue.

There is nothing that so powerfully governs the heart, that so strongly excites us to wise and reasonable actions, as a true sense of God's presence. But as we cannot see or apprehend the essence of God, so nothing will so constantly keep us under a lively sense of the presence of God as this holy resignation that attributes everything to God and receives everything as from God.

If we could see a miracle from God, how our thoughts would be affected with holy awe and veneration of God's presence! But if we consider everything as God's doing, either by order or by permission, we shall then be affected with common things as they would be who saw a miracle.

For there is nothing to affect you in a miracle except that it is the action of God and tells of God's presence. So when you consider God as acting in all things and all events, then all things will become holy to you, like miracles, and fill you with the same awe-filled sentiments of the divine presence.

Now you must not reserve the exercise of this pious temper to any particular times or occasions or fancy how resigned you will be to God if such and such trials should happen. For this is amusing yourself with the notion or idea of resignation instead of the virtue itself.

Do not therefore please yourself with thinking how piously you would act and submit to God in a plague or famine or persecution. Be intent upon the perfection of the present day. And be assured that the best way to show true zeal is to make little things the occasions of great piety.

Begin therefore in the smallest matters and most ordinary occasions, and accustom your mind to the daily exercise of this pious temper in the lowest occurrences of life. And when a contempt, an affront, a little injury, loss, or disappointment, or the smallest events of every day continually raise your mind to God in proper acts of resignation, then you may justly hope that you shall be numbered among those who are resigned and thankful to God in the greatest trials and afflictions.

CONFESSION

From Chapter 23

Evening prayer at 6 P.M. is a time for confession. As love must be made specific through intercession, so repentance must lead to confession of particular sins through a review of the day's activities. (Note: Law also briefly suggests that prayer before going to sleep be a meditation on the inevitability of death, commending oneself to God's care.)

Evening repentance that brings all the actions of the day to account is not only necessary to wipe off the guilt of sin but is also the most certain way to amend and perfect our lives.

For it is only such a repentance that touches the heart, awakens the conscience, and leaves horror and hatred of sin upon the mind.

For instance, if it should happen that upon any particular evening all that you could charge yourself with should be a hasty, negligent performance of your devotions or too much time spent in an impertinent conversation; if the unreasonableness of these things were fully reflected upon and acknowledged; if you were then to condemn yourself before God for them and implore God's pardon and assisting grace, then what could be so likely a means to prevent your falling into the same faults the next day?

Or if you should fall into them again the next day, yet if they were again brought to the same examination and condemnation in the presence of God, their happening again would be such a proof to you of your own folly and weakness, would cause such pain and remorse in your mind and fill you with such shame and confusion at yourself as would in all probability make you exceedingly desire greater perfection.

Now in the case of repeated sins this would be the certain benefit that we should receive from this examination and confession. The mind would be made humble, full of sorrow and deep compunction, and by degrees, forced into amendment.

A formal, general confession that is considered only as an evening duty, that overlooks the particular mistakes of the day, and is the same whether the day is spent ill or well has little or no effect upon the mind. People may use such a daily confession and still go on sinning and confessing all their lives without any remorse of mind or true desire of amendment.

For if your own particular sins are left out of your confession, your confessing of sin in general has no more effect upon your mind than if you had confessed only that all people in general are sinners. And there is nothing in any confession to show that it is yours unless it is a self-accusation, not of sin in general or such as is common to all others, but of such particular sins as are your own proper shame and reproach.

No other confession but one that discovers and accuses your own particular guilt can be an act of true sorrow or real concern at your condition. And a confession that is without this sorrow and compunction of heart has nothing in it either to atone for past sins or to produce in you any true reformation and amendment of life.

To proceed: in order to make this examination more beneficial, everyone should follow a certain method in it. Every individual has something particular to her or his nature, stronger inclinations to some vices than others, some infirmities that stick closer and are harder to be conquered than others. It is as easy for each of us to know this of ourselves as to know whom we like or dislike. So it is highly necessary that these particularities of our natures and tempers should never escape a severe trial at our evening repentance. I say a severe trial because nothing but a rigorous severity against these natural tempers is sufficient to conquer them.

They are the right eyes that are not to be spared but plucked out and cast from us. For as they are the infirmities of nature, so they have the strength of nature and must be treated with great opposition or they will soon be too strong for us.

He, therefore, who knows himself most of all subject to anger and passion must be very exact and constant in his examination of this temper every evening. He must find out every slip that he has made of that kind whether in thought, word, or action. He must shame and reproach and accuse himself before God for everything that he has said or done in obedience to his passion. He must no more allow himself to forget the examination of this temper than to forget his whole prayers.

Again, if you find that vanity is your prevailing temper, always pushing you to adorn your person and catching after everything that compliments or flatters your abilities, never spare or forget this temper in your evening examination. Confess to God every vanity of thought or word or action that you have been guilty of, and put yourself to all the shame and confusion for it that you can.

In this manner should all people act with regard to the chief frailty to which their nature most inclines them. And though it should not immediately do all that they would wish, yet by a constant practice, it would certainly in a short time produce its desired effect.

Further, as all states and employments of life have their particular dangers and temptations and expose people more to some sins than others, so everyone who wishes to improve should make it a necessary part of this evening examination to consider how he or she has avoided or fallen into such sins as are most common to this state of life.

For as our business and condition of life have great power over us, so nothing but such watchfulness can secure us from those temptations to which they daily expose us.

The poor, from their condition of life, are always in danger of repining and uneasiness. The rich are most exposed to sensuality and indulgence, businesspersons to lying and unreasonable gains, scholars to pride and vanity. So in every state of life we should always in our self-examination have a strict eye upon those faults to which our state of life most of all exposes us.

Again, it is reasonable to suppose that all good people have entered into or at least proposed to themselves some method of holy living and set themselves some such rules to observe as are not common to other people and known only to themselves. So it should be a constant part of their nightly recollection to examine how and in what degree they have observed them and to reproach themselves before God for every neglect of them.

By rules, I here mean such rules as relate to the proper ordering of our time and the business of our common life. Such rules prescribe a certain order to all that we are to do: our business, devotion, self-discipline, readings, retirements, conversation, meals, refreshments, sleep, and the like.

Now as good rules relating to all these things are certain means of great improvement and such as all serious Christians must propose to themselves, so they will hardly ever be observed to any purpose unless they are made the constant subject of our evening examination.

Last, you are not to content yourself with a hasty general review of the day, but you must enter upon it with deliberation. Begin with the first action of the day, and proceed step by step through every particular matter that you have been concerned in. So you will let no time, place, or action be overlooked.

An examination thus managed will in a little time make you as different from yourself as a wise person is different from an idiot. It will give you such a newness of mind, such a spirit of wisdom and desire of perfection, as you were an entire stranger to before.

Appendix

Reading Spiritual Classics for Personal and Group Formation

Many Christians today are searching for more spiritual depth, for something more than simply being good church members. That quest may send them to the spiritual practices of New Age movements or of Eastern religions such as Zen Buddhism. Christians, though, have their own long spiritual tradition, a tradition rich with wisdom, variety, and depth.

The great spiritual classics testify to that depth. They do not concern themselves with mystical flights for a spiritual elite. Rather, they contain very practical advice and insights that can support and shape the spiritual growth of any Christian. We can all benefit by sitting at the feet of the masters (both male and female) of Christian spirituality.

Reading spiritual classics is different from most of the reading we do. We have learned to read to master a text and extract information from it. We tend to read quickly, to get through a text. And we summarize as we read, seeking the main point. In reading spiritual classics, though, we allow the text to master and form us. Such formative reading goes more slowly, more reflectively, allowing time for God to speak to us through the text. God's word for us may come as easily from a minor point or even an aside as from the major point.

Formative reading requires that you approach the text in humility. Read as a seeker, not an expert. Don't demand that the text meet your expectations for what an "enlightened" author should write. Humility means accepting the author as another imperfect human, a product of his or her own time and situation. Learn to celebrate what is foundational in an author's writing without being overly disturbed by what is peculiar to the author's life and times. Trust the text as a gift from both God and the author, offered to you for your benefit—to help you grow in Christ.

To read formatively, you must also slow down. Feel free to reread a passage that seems to speak specially to you. Stop from time to time to reflect on what you have been reading. Keep a journal for these reflections. Often the act of writing can itself prompt further, deeper reflection. Keep your notebook open and your pencil in hand as you read. You might not get back to that wonderful insight later. Don't worry that you are not getting through an entire passage—or even the first paragraph! Formative reading is about depth rather than breadth, quality rather than quantity. As you read, seek God's direction for your own life. Timeless truths have their place but may not be what is most important for your own formation here and now.

As you read the passage, you might keep some of these questions running through your mind:

- How is what I'm reading true of my own life? Where does it reflect my own *experience*?

- How does this text challenge me? What new *direction* does it offer me?
- What must I change to put what I am reading into practice? How can I *incarnate* it, let this word become flesh in my life?

You might also devote special attention to sections that upset you. What is the source of the disturbance? Do you want to argue theology? Are you turned off by cultural differences? Or have you been skewered by an insight that would turn your life upside down if you took it seriously? Let your journal be a dialogue with the text.

If you find yourself moving from reading the text to chewing over its implications to praying, that's great! Spiritual reading is really the first step in an ancient way of prayer called *lectio divina* or "divine reading." Reading leads naturally into reflection on what you have read (meditation). As you reflect on what the text might mean for your life, you may well want to ask for God's help in living out any new insights or direction you have perceived (prayer). Sometimes such prayer may lead you further into silently abiding in God's presence (contemplation). And, of course, the process is only really completed when it begins to make a difference in the way we live (incarnation).

As good as it is to read spiritual classics in solitude, it is even better to join with others in a small group for mutual formation or "spiritual direction in common." This is *not* the same as a study group that

talks about spiritual classics. A group for mutual formation would have similar goals as for an individual's reading: to allow the text to shine its light on the *experiences* of the group members, to suggest new *directions* for their lives and practical ways of *incarnating* these directions. Such a group might agree to focus on one short passage from a classic at each meeting (even if members have read more). Discussion usually goes much deeper if all the members have already read and reflected on the passage before the meeting and bring their journals.

Such groups need to watch for several potential problems. It is easy to go off on a tangent (especially if it takes the focus off the members' own experience and onto generalities). At such times a group leader might bring the group's attention back to the text: "What does our author say about that?" Or, "How do we experience that in our own lives?" When a group member shares a problem, others may be tempted to try to "fix" it. This is much less helpful than sharing similar experiences and how they were handled (for good or ill). "Sharing" someone else's problems (whether that person is in or out of the group) should be strongly discouraged.

One person could be designated as leader, to be responsible for opening and closing prayers; to be the first to share or respond to the text; and to keep notes during the discussion to highlight recurring themes, challenges, directives, or practical steps. These responsibilities could also be shared among several members of the group or rotated.

For further information about formative reading of spiritual classics, try *A Practical Guide to Spiritual Reading* by Susan Annette Muto. *Shaped by the Word* by Robert Mulholland (Upper Room Books®) covers formative reading of the Bible. *Good Things Happen: Experiencing Community in Small Groups* by Dick Westley is an excellent resource on forming small groups of all kinds.

LOVING GOD THROUGH THE DARKNESS

Selected Writings of
JOHN OF THE CROSS

Upper Room Spiritual Classics® — Series 3

Selected, edited, and introduced by
Keith Beasley-Topliffe

**Loving God through the Darkness:
Selected Writings of John of the Cross**

Copyright © 2000 by Upper Room Books™
All rights reserved.

No part of this book may be used or reproduced in any manner whatsoever without written permission of the publisher except in the case of brief quotations embodied in critical articles or reviews. For information, write Upper Room Books,™ 1908 Grand Avenue, Nashville, Tennessee 37212.

The Upper Room® Website: http://www.upperroom.org

UPPER ROOM,® UPPER ROOM BOOKS™ and design logos are trademarks owned by the Upper Room,® Nashville, Tennessee. All rights reserved.

Scripture quotations are from the New Revised Standard Version of the Bible Copyright © 1989 by the Division of Christian Education of the National Council of Churches of Christ in the USA. Used by permission. All rights reserved.

Excerpts from *The Collected Works of St. John of the Cross* translated by Kieran Kavanaugh and Otilio Rodriguez 1979, 1991, by Washington Province of Discalced Carmelites. ICS Publications, 2131 Lincoln Road, N.E., Washington, D.C. 20002, U.S.A.

Cover design: Gore Studio, Inc.
Interior design and layout: Nancy J. Cole

First printing: 2000

Library of Congress Cataloging-in-Publication Data

John of the Cross, Saint, 1542–1591.
  [Selections. English. 2000]
  Loving God through the darkness : selected writings of John of
the Cross / selected, edited, and introduced by Keith Beasley-Topliffe.
    p. cm. — (Upper Room spiritual classics. Series 3)
  ISBN 0-8358-0904-8
  1. Spiritual life—Catholic Church. I. Beasley-Topliffe, Keith.
II. Title. III. Series.
BX2179.J63213 2000   99-37741
248.2'2—dc21   CIP

Printed in the United States of America

TABLE OF CONTENTS

Introduction	5
One Dark Night	12
John's Purpose in Writing	14
Light and Dark	18
Detachment	23
Climbing the Mountain	27
The Nature of Union with God	32
Spiritual Detachment	36
Openness to a New Kind of Prayer	39
The Prayer of Beginners	42
Spiritual Pride	45
Spiritual Gluttony	50
Signs of God's Call to Contemplation	54
Accepting God's Guidance	59
Prayer of Proficients	63
Light in the Night	67
The Ladder of Love	71
Appendix: Reading Spiritual Classics for Personal and Group Formation	76

INTRODUCTION

When we are beginning to grow as Christians, our love of God is inevitably mixed up with other loves. We love other people, our country, our possessions. We love the blessings God gives us, even the good feelings we get from prayer.

If we are to continue to grow, we must become detached from these loves so that we can move toward loving God alone. John of the Cross, a Carmelite monk who lived in Spain during the sixteenth century, described this process of detachment as a dark night of the soul. This night has both active and passive aspects: things we do to lay aside attachments and things God does in our souls to wean us from them. He uses biblical stories and vivid metaphors to explain both the process and the need for it, offering guidance for beginners and those far along the spiritual path.

JOHN'S WORLD

Spain in the sixteenth century was a nation in turmoil. Granada, the last Moorish stronghold, fell in 1492. A land where Jew, Christian, and Muslim once lived together fairly peacefully became exclusively Christian. Jews and Muslims had to leave or convert. Thirteen years earlier, the Spanish Inquisition had been formed, in part, to test the sincerity of such forced conversions and weed out all whose faith did not conform to official Roman Catholic teachings.

After the beginnings of the Protestant Reformation in 1517, the Inquisition also examined any who insisted on the primacy of grace or the priesthood of all believers. On the other hand, the Spanish king was interested in church reform, particularly reform movements in monastic orders. Innovative spiritual leaders could find themselves in the midst of the ongoing power struggle between church and crown.

The Carmelite Order to which John belonged began with a group of pilgrims who founded a community on Mount Carmel in the Holy Land near the beginning of the thirteenth century. When Muslim victories forced them to leave, they brought their way of life back to Western Europe. They were granted recognition in 1247 as an order dedicated to prayer and teaching. A few years later, the Order of Carmelite Sisters began. Both orders spread through France, Spain, Italy, and England. In 1562, Teresa of Avila, a Carmelite nun, began a reform movement, establishing new Carmelite convents with a stricter observance of the order's rule and a greater emphasis on prayer. Because one aspect of their stricter rule was wearing sandals rather than shoes, they were called "discalced," or shoeless. Six years later Teresa was ready to extend the reform to the men. John was one of the three monks in the first monastery established.

John was highly educated and his writings reflect his learning. Of particular importance for his descriptions of the spiritual life is the understanding of the mind, described in terms of faculties. According to John, the mind has three primary (or higher) faculties: the will, the intellect, and the memory, all operating more or less independently. Together these form the human spirit. So John can talk of the will being united to God while the intellect is distracted by many thoughts. When the memory and the intellect are quieted and brought back into alignment with the will, this is "recollection." These primary faculties were supported by the five exterior senses as well as three interior ones. *Phantasy* forms internal images based on external or supernatural sensory impressions. *Sense memory* stores such impressions and images. *Imagination* uses these images to form new images for things not directly experienced. Learning to ignore the constant clamor of all these senses is another, more basic sort of recollection. John's distinction between the purification of the senses and the purification of the spirit is based on this understanding.

John's Life

John was born as Juan de Yepes in 1542 in Fontiveros, Castile. He was the third son of Gonzalo de Yepes and Catalina Alvarez. Gonzalo had been disinherited by his wealthy silk merchant father for marrying beneath his station. When he died, two years after John's birth, Catalina's trade as a weaver kept the family alive, even if in grave poverty. The middle brother, Luis, died when John was five, and John remained small (an inch less than five feet tall and thin) for his whole life.

When the family moved to Medina del Campo, John was able to study at a local school for orphans. After showing little promise in other trades, John began to help out in a hospital. The administrator recognized his intelligence and caring and arranged for him to study further with the Jesuits while continuing to assist at the hospital. When he was twenty-one (1563, the year after the beginning of Teresa's reform), John became a novice in the Carmelite Order, taking the name John of Saint Matthias. Following his final vows, he was sent to the University of Salamanca for four years. In 1567 he was ordained and returned to Medina to celebrate his first Mass. Teresa was in town, establishing her second Medina convent. When they met, John decided to join her reform. John was twenty-five years old, Teresa fifty-two. After completing his education, he went to Valladolid for several months to learn from Teresa.

On November 28, 1568, John and two others started the first friars' house of the reform. John was subprior and novice master and took the new name John of the Cross. Over the next few years he worked to establish the reform. In 1572, Teresa was recalled to her home convent in Avila to be prioress. She asked John to be vicar and confessor for the convent as well as her own spiritual director.

In 1575, the General Chapter of the Carmelite Order, meeting in Italy and without benefit of leaders from Spain, demanded an end to the reform and the return of all discalced Carmelites into the regular Carmelite houses. With the Spanish king Philip II supporting the reform, John continued at Avila, ignoring the demand. On December 2, 1577, though, he was abducted and taken to the Carmelite monastery in Toledo where he was confined in a six-by-ten-foot room for about nine months. He spent his time in prayer and in composing poetry about the love between the soul and God. Eventually a new jailer allowed him pen and ink to write down the poems. In August 1578, he decided to escape. John loosened the screws of the lock until one night he was able to break the door open, run down the hall to a window, and escape by means of a rope made from torn mattress covers. Friends got him to safety in Andalusia (southern Spain), where the Carmelite leadership was more sympathetic to the reform. John became vicar of a discalced monastery, El Calvario in Sierra del Segura. There he continued to offer spiritual direction to people from all walks of life and to write poetry (including the poem "One Dark Night"). He also planned and started a discalced college in Baeza where he served as rector from 1579 to 1582. During that time Teresa's reform was officially confirmed by the pope, and the discalced were free to establish new houses for men and women.

In 1582 (a few months before Teresa's death) John became prior of Los Martires in Granada. There he designed the monastery gardens and an aqueduct for the monastery. Over the course of the next six years he wrote four books on the spiritual life as prolonged commentaries on his poems. Two were on "One Dark Night" and the others were on "The Spiritual Canticle" and "The Living Flame of Love." In 1585 he became vicar provincial for Andalusia and spent much of his time overseeing new foundations.

In 1588, John became prior in Segovia. Three years later, after a disagreement over the governing of the order, John was removed from all offices. He offered to go to Mexico, but first went to La Penuela in the mountains of Andalusia. After a couple of months, he became ill. In September 1591, John went to the discalced house in Ubeda for medical care. He died there on December 14, just after the stroke of midnight. He was canonized in 1726. Two hundred years later Pope Pius XI declared him a Doctor of the Church.

FURTHER READING

The Collected Works of Saint John of the Cross, translated by Kieran Kavanaugh and Otilio Rodriguez (rev. ed. ICS Publications, 1991), is the best modern translation and the basis for these selections. More extensive selections from this translation are available in the Paulist Press volume on John of the Cross. Some of the main works are also available as separate paperbacks from Image Books in an older translation by E. Allison Peers.

The best short biography and introduction to John is the introduction to the Kavanaugh and Rodriguez translation. Two books by Susan Muto offer excellent commentary to help modern readers understand John's teaching: *John of the Cross for Today: The Ascent* and *John of the Cross for Today: The Dark Night*, both from Ave Maria Press.

The works of Teresa of Avila (also translated by Kavanaugh and Rodriguez and available from ICS Publications) are the ideal complement to reading John of the Cross. Other important influences on John include Bernard of Clairvaux, Thomas Aquinas, and Francisco de Osuna.

NOTE ON THE TEXT

These selections are taken from the Kavanaugh and Rodriguez translations of *The Ascent of Mount Carmel* and *The Dark Night of the Soul*. They have been edited primarily for length. Scripture quotations have been conformed to the New Revised Standard Version where possible.

# ONE DARK NIGHT

John wrote this poem shortly after his escape from imprisonment in 1578. His two treatises on the dark night of the soul begin as commentaries on the poem, although John never gets beyond the third stanza. Note that the Spanish words translated "Lover" and "Beloved" are the masculine and feminine forms of the same adjective and do not imply the active and passive connotations of the English words.

Songs of the soul that rejoices in having reached the high state of perfection, which is union with God, by the path of spiritual negation.

> One dark night,
> fired with love's urgent longings
> —ah, the sheer grace!—
> I went out unseen,
> my house being now all stilled.
>
> In darkness and secure,
> by the secret ladder, disguised,
> —ah, the sheer grace!—
> in darkness and concealment,
> my house being now all stilled.
>
> On that glad night,
> in secret, for no one saw me,
> nor did I look at anything,
> with no other light or guide
> than the one that burned in my heart.

This guided me
more surely than the light of noon
to where he was awaiting me
—him I knew so well—
there in a place where no one appeared.

O guiding night!
O night more lovely than the dawn!
O night that has united
the Lover with his Beloved,
transforming the Beloved in her Lover.

Upon my flowering breast
which I kept wholly for him alone,
there he lay sleeping,
and I caressing him
there in a breeze from the fanning cedars.

When the breeze blew from the turret,
as I parted his hair,
it wounded my neck
with its gentle hand,
suspending all my senses.

I abandoned and forgot myself,
laying my face on my Beloved;
all things ceased; I went out from myself,
leaving my cares
forgotten among the lilies.

JOHN'S PURPOSE IN WRITING

From T*he Ascent of Mount Carmel*, Prologue, Sections 3–8

About 1579, John created a sketch of "The Mount of Perfection" that showed the "negative path" of self-denial he taught. The Ascent of Mount Carmel, written a year or so later, begins as a commentary on both the sketch and the poem "The Dark Night." In this introductory passage, John explains the need for understanding the dark night of the soul, especially on the part of spiritual directors.

I am not undertaking this arduous task because of any particular confidence in my own abilities. Rather, I am confident that the Lord will help me explain this matter because it is extremely necessary to so many souls. Even though these souls have begun to walk along the road of virtue, and our Lord desires to place them in the dark night that they may move on to the divine union, they do not advance. The reason for this may be that sometimes they do not want to enter the dark night or allow themselves to be placed in it, or that sometimes they misunderstand themselves and are without suitable and alert directors who will show them the way to the summit. God gives many souls the talent and grace for advancing, and should they desire to make the effort they would arrive at this high state. And so it is sad to see them continue in their lowly method of communion with God because they do not want or know how to advance, or because they receive no direction on breaking away from the methods of beginners. Even if our Lord finally comes to their aid to the extent of making them advance without these helps, they reach the summit much later, expend more effort, and gain less merit, because they do not willingly adapt themselves to God's work of placing them on the pure and reliable road leading to union. Although God does lead them—since he can do so without their cooperation—they do not accept his guidance. In resisting God who is conducting them, they make little progress and fail in merit because they do not apply their wills; as a result they must endure greater suffering. Some souls, instead of abandoning themselves to God and cooperating with him, hamper him by their indiscreet activity or their resistance. They resemble children who kick and cry and struggle to walk by themselves when their mothers want to carry them; in walking by themselves they make no headway, or if they do, it is at a child's pace.

With God's help, then, we will propose doctrine and counsel for beginners and proficients that they may understand or at least know how to practice abandonment to God's guidance when he wants them to advance.

It will happen to individuals that while they are being conducted by God along a sublime path of dark contemplation and aridity, in which they feel lost and filled with darknesses, trials, conflicts, and temptations, they will meet someone who, in the style of Job's comforters, will proclaim that all of this is due to melancholia, depression, or temperament, or to some hidden wickedness, and that as a result God has forsaken them. Therefore the usual verdict is that these individuals must have lived an evil life since such trials afflict them.

Other directors will tell them that they are falling back since they find no satisfaction or consolation as they previously did in the things of God. Such talk only doubles the trial of a poor soul. It will happen that the soul's greatest suffering will be caused by the knowledge of its own miseries. That it is full of evil and sin is as clear as day to it, and even clearer, for, as we shall say further on, God is the author of this enlightenment in the night of contemplation. And when this soul finds someone who agrees with what it feels (that these trials are all its own fault), its suffering and distress grow without bounds. And this suffering usually becomes worse than death.

With divine help we will discuss all this: how individuals should behave; what method the confessor should use in dealing with them; signs to recognize this purification of the soul that we call the dark night; whether it is the purification of the senses or of the spirit; and how we can discern whether this affliction is caused by melancholia or some other deficiency of sense or spirit.

Some souls or their confessors may think that God is leading them along this road of the dark night of spiritual purgation, but perhaps this will not be so.

What they suffer will be due to one of these deficiencies. Likewise, many individuals think they are not praying when, indeed, their prayer is deep. Others place high value on their prayer while it amounts to little more than nothing.

Some people—and it is sad to see them—work and tire themselves greatly, and yet go backward; they look for progress in what brings no progress but instead hinders them. Others, in peace and tranquillity, continue to advance well. Some others let themselves be encumbered by the very consolations and favors God bestows on them for the sake of their advancing, and they advance not at all.

We will also discuss many other experiences of those who walk along this road: joys, afflictions, hopes, and sorrows—some of these originating from the spirit of perfection, others from the spirit of imperfection. Our goal will be to explain, with God's help, all these points so that those who read this book will in some way discover the road they are walking along, and the one they ought to follow if they want to reach the summit of this mount.

Readers should not be surprised if this doctrine on the dark night—through which a soul advances toward God—appears somewhat obscure. This, I believe, will be the case as they begin to read, but as they read on they will understand it better since the latter parts will explain the former. Then, if they read this work a second time, the matter will seem clearer and the doctrine sounder.

LIGHT AND DARK

From *The Ascent of Mount Carmel*, Book 1, Chapter 4

In this selection, John explains the importance of stripping away all worldly attachments.

The necessity to pass through this dark night (the mortification of the appetites and denial of pleasure in all things) to attain divine union with God arises from the fact that all of a person's attachments to creatures are pure darkness in God's sight. Clothed in these affections, people are incapable of the enlightenment and dominating fullness of God's pure and simple light.

The reason, as we learn in philosophy, is that two contraries cannot coexist in the same subject. Darkness, which is an attachment to creatures, and light, which is God, are contraries and bear no likeness toward each other, as Saint Paul teaches in his letter to the Corinthians, "What fellowship is there between light and darkness?" Consequently, the light of divine union cannot be established in the soul until these affections are eradicated.

For a better proof of this, it ought to be kept in mind that an attachment to a creature makes a person equal to that creature; the stronger the attachment, the closer is the likeness to the creature and the greater the equality, for love effects a likeness between the lover and the beloved. Anyone who loves a creature, then, is as low as that creature and in some way even lower because love not only equates but even subjects the lover to the loved creature.

All creatures of heaven and earth are nothing when compared to God, as Jeremiah points out: "I looked on the earth, and lo, it was waste and void; and to the heavens, and they had no light." By saying that he saw an empty earth, he meant that all its creatures were nothing and that the earth too was nothing. In stating that he looked up to the heavens and beheld no light, he meant that all the heavenly luminaries were pure darkness in comparison to God. All creatures considered in this way are nothing, and a person's attachments to them are less than nothing since these attachments are an impediment to and deprive the soul of transformation in God—just as darkness is nothing and less than nothing since it is a privation of light. In no way, then, is such a person capable of union with the infinite being of God. There is no likeness between what is not and what is. To be particular, here are some examples.

All the beauty of creatures compared to the infinite beauty of God is the height of ugliness. As Solomon says in Proverbs: "Charm is deceitful, and beauty is vain." So a person attached to the beauty of any creature is extremely ugly in God's sight. A soul so unsightly is incapable of transformation into the beauty that is God.

All the grace and elegance of creatures compared to God's grace is utter coarseness and crudity.

That is why a person captivated by this grace and elegance of creatures becomes highly coarse and crude in God's sight. Someone like this is incapable of the infinite grace and beauty of God.

Compared to the infinite goodness of God, all the goodness of the creatures of the world can be called wickedness. Nothing is good but God alone. Those who set their hearts on the good things of the world become extremely wicked in the sight of God. Since wickedness does not comprehend goodness, such persons will be incapable of union with God, who is supreme goodness.

All the world's wisdom compared to the wisdom of God is pure and utter ignorance, as Saint Paul writes to the Corinthians: "God's foolishness is wiser than human wisdom." Those, therefore, who value their knowledge and ability as a means of reaching union with the wisdom of God are highly ignorant in God's sight and will be left behind, far away from this wisdom. Ignorance does not grasp what wisdom is. In God's sight those who think they have some wisdom are very ignorant. The Apostle says of them in writing to the Romans: "Claiming to be wise, they became fools."

Only those who set aside their own knowledge and walk in God's service like unlearned children receive wisdom from God. This is the wisdom about which Saint Paul taught the Corinthians: "If you think that you are wise in this age, you should become fools so that you may become wise." Accordingly, to reach union with the wisdom of God, a person must advance by unknowing rather than by knowing.

All the delights and satisfactions of the will in the things of the world compared to all the delight that is God are intense suffering, torment, and bitterness. Those who link their hearts to these delights, then, deserve in God's eyes intense suffering, torment, and bitterness. They will not be capable of attaining the delights of the embrace of union with God, since they merit suffering and bitterness.

All the wealth and glory of creation compared to the wealth that is God is utter poverty and misery in the Lord's sight. The person who loves and possesses these things is completely poor and miserable before God and will be unable to attain the richness and glory of transformation in God.

Divine Wisdom, with pity for these souls that become ugly, abject, miserable, and poor because of their love for worldly things, which in their opinion are rich and beautiful, exclaims in Proverbs: "To you, O people, I call, and my cry is to all that live. O simple ones, learn prudence; acquire intelligence, you who lack it. Hear, for I will speak noble things . . . Riches and honor are with me, enduring wealth and prosperity. My fruit is better than gold, even fine gold, and my yield than choice silver. I walk in the way of righteousness, along the paths of justice, endowing with wealth those who love me, and filling their treasuries."

Divine Wisdom speaks, here, to all those who are attached to the things of the world. She tells them that she is dealing with great things, not small things, as they are. The riches and glory they love are with her and in her, not where they think. Lofty riches and justice are present in her. Although in their opinion the things of this world are riches, she tells them to bear in mind that her riches are more precious, that the fruit found in them will be better than gold and precious stones, and that what she begets in souls has greater value than cherished silver, which signifies every kind of affection possible in this life.

DETACHMENT

From *The Ascent of Mount Carmel*, Book 1, Chapter 5, Sections 3–8

In this passage, John uses several biblical examples as allegories of the spiritual need for detachment before we can be open to receive God's blessings.

We have a figure of this in Exodus where we read that God did not give the children of Israel the heavenly manna until they exhausted the flour brought from Egypt. The meaning here is that first a total renunciation is needed, for this bread of angels is disagreeable to the palate of anyone who wants to taste human food. Persons feeding on other strange tastes not only become incapable of the divine Spirit, but even greatly anger the divine Majesty because in their aspirations for spiritual food they are not satisfied with God alone, but mix with these aspirations a desire and affection for other things. This is likewise apparent in the same book of sacred Scripture where it states that the people, discontented with that simple food, requested and craved meat, and seriously angered our Lord because of their desire to commingle a food so base and coarse with one so high and simple that, even though simple, contained the savor and substance of all foods. Consequently, while morsels of manna were yet in their mouths, the wrath of God descended on them, as David also says, spouting fire from heaven and reducing thousands of them to ashes. For God thought it shameful for them to crave other food while he was giving them heavenly food.

Oh, if spiritual persons knew how much spiritual good and abundance they lose by not attempting to raise their appetites above childish things, and if they knew to what extent, by not desiring the taste of these trifles, they would discover in this simple spiritual food the savor of all things! The Israelites did not perceive the taste of every other food that was contained in the manna, because their appetite was not centered on this manna alone. They were unsuccessful in deriving from the manna all the taste and strength they were looking for, not because the manna didn't have these but because of their craving for other foods. Similarly, those who love something together with God undoubtedly make little of God, for they weigh in the balance with God an object far distant from God, as we have said.

This was also indicated when God ordered Moses to climb to the top of the mountain. He did this that Moses might be able to speak to him. He commanded Moses not only to ascend alone and leave the children of Israel below, but to rule against even the pasturing of beasts on the mountainside. The meaning is that those who ascend this mount of perfection to converse with God must not only renounce all things by leaving them at the bottom, but also restrict their appetites (the beasts) from pasturing on the mountainside, on things that are not purely God. For in God, or in the state of perfection, all appetites cease.

We also have a striking figure of this in Genesis. When the patriarch Jacob desired to ascend Mount Bethel to build an altar to offer sacrifice to God, he first ordered his people to do three things: destroy all strange gods; purify themselves; and change their garments.

Those desiring to climb to the summit of the mount in order to become an altar for the offering of a sacrifice of pure love and praise and reverence to God must first accomplish these three tasks perfectly. First, they must cast out strange gods, all alien affections and attachments. Second, by denying these appetites and repenting of them—through the dark night of the senses—they must purify themselves of the residue. Third, in order to reach the top of this high mount, their garments must be changed. By means of the first two works, God will substitute new garments for the old. The soul will be clothed in a new understanding of God in God (through removal of the old understanding) and in a new love of God in God, once the will is stripped of all the old cravings and satisfactions. And God will vest the soul with new knowledge when the other old ideas and images are cast aside. He causes all that is of the old self, the abilities of one's natural being, to cease, and he attires all the faculties with new supernatural abilities. As a result, one's activities, once human, now become divine. This is achieved in the state of union when the soul, in which God alone dwells, has no other function than that of an altar on which God is adored in praise and love.

God allows nothing else to dwell together with him. We read, consequently, in 1 Kings that when the Philistines put the ark of the covenant in a temple with their idol, the idol was hurled to the ground at the dawn of each day and broken into pieces. The only appetite God permits and wants in his dwelling place is the desire for the perfect fulfillment of his law and the carrying of the cross of Christ. Scripture teaches that God ordered nothing else to be placed in the ark where the manna was than the Law and the rod of Moses (signifying the cross). Those who have no other goal than the perfect observance of the Lord's law and the carrying of the cross of Christ will be true arks, and they will bear within themselves the real manna, which is God, when they possess perfectly, without anything else, this law and this rod.

CLIMBING THE MOUNTAIN

From The Ascent of Mount Carmel, Book 1,
Chapter 13, Sections 3–13

Here John spells out what detachment from creatures and sensory gratification involves. In doing so he quotes some of the annotations from the sketch "The Mount of Perfection."

First, have habitual desire to imitate Christ in all your deeds by bringing your life into conformity with his. You must then study his life in order to know how to imitate him and behave in all events as he would.

Second, in order to be successful in this imitation, renounce and remain empty of any sensory satisfaction that is not purely for the honor and glory of God. Do this out of love for Jesus Christ. In his life he had no other gratification, nor desired any other, than the fulfillment of his Father's will, which he called his meat and food.

For example, if you are offered the satisfaction of hearing things that have no relation to the service and glory of God, do not desire this pleasure or the hearing of these things. When you have an opportunity for the gratification of looking upon objects that will not help you love God more, do not desire this gratification of sight. And if in speaking there is a similar opportunity, act in the same way. And so on with all the senses insofar as you can duly avoid such satisfaction. If you cannot except the experience of this satisfaction, it will be sufficient to have no desire for it.

By this method you should endeavor, then, to leave the senses as though in darkness, mortified and empty of that satisfaction. With such vigilance you will gain a great deal in a short time.

Many blessings flow when the four natural passions (joy, hope, fear, and sorrow) are in harmony and at peace. The following maxims contain a complete method for mortifying and pacifying them. If put into practice these maxims will give rise to abundant merit and great virtues.

> Endeavor to be inclined always:
> not to the easiest, but to the most difficult;
> not to the most delightful, but to the most distasteful;
> not to the most gratifying, but to the less pleasant;
> not to what means rest for you, but to hard work;
> not to the consoling, but to the unconsoling;
> not to the most, but to the least;
> not to the highest and most precious, but to the lowest and most despised;
> not to wanting something, but to wanting nothing.

Do not go about looking for the best of temporal things, but for the worst, and, for Christ, desire to enter into complete nakedness, emptiness, and poverty in everything in the world.

You should embrace these practices earnestly and try to overcome the repugnance of your will toward them. If you sincerely put them into practice with order and discretion, you will discover in them great delight and consolation.

These counsels if truly carried out are sufficient for entry into the night of senses. But, to ensure that we give abundant enough counsel, here is another exercise that teaches mortification of concupiscence of the flesh, concupiscence of the eyes, and pride of life, which, as Saint John says, reign in the world and give rise to all the other appetites.

First, try to act with contempt for yourself and desire that all others do likewise.

Second, endeavor to speak in contempt of yourself and desire all others to do so.

Third, try to think lowly and contemptuously of yourself and desire that all others do the same.

As a conclusion to these counsels and rules it would be appropriate to repeat the verses in The Ascent of the Mount, which are instructions for climbing to the summit, the high state of union. Although in the drawing we admittedly refer to the spiritual and interior aspect, we also deal with the spirit of imperfection existent in the sensory and exterior part of the soul, as is evident by the two ways, one on each side of the path that leads to perfection. Consequently these verses will here bear reference to the sensory part. Afterward, in the second division of this night, they may be interpreted in relationship to the spiritual part.

The verses are:

> To reach satisfaction in all
> desire satisfaction in nothing.
> To come to possess all
> desire the possession of nothing.
> To arrive at being all
> desire to be nothing.
> To come to the knowledge of all
> desire the knowledge of nothing.

> To come to enjoy what you have not
> you must go by a way in which you enjoy not.
> To come to the knowledge you have not
> you must go by a way in which you know not.
> To come to the possession you have not
> you must go by a way in which you possess not.
> To come to be what you are not
> you must go by a way in which you are not.

> When you delay in something
> you cease to rush toward the all.
> For to go from the all to the all
> you must deny yourself of all in all.

And when you come to the possession of the all you must possess it without wanting anything. Because if you desire to have something in all your treasure in God is not purely your all.

In this nakedness the spirit finds its quietude and rest. For in coveting nothing, nothing tires it by pulling it up and nothing oppresses it by pushing it down, because it is in the center of its humility. When it covets something, by this very fact it tires itself.

THE NATURE OF UNION WITH GOD

From *The Ascent of Mount Carmel*, Book 2, Chapter 5, Sections 3–4, 6–7

In the second book of The Ascent, John moves from discussing detachment (the first part of the dark night or night of the senses) to faith (the second part or night of the spirit). Since the stated purpose of passing through the dark night is to reach union with God, John pauses to explain what he means by such union.

To understand the nature of this union, one should first know that God sustains every soul and dwells in it substantially, even though it may be that of the greatest sinner in the world. This union between God and creatures always exists. By it he conserves their being so that if the union should end they would immediately be annihilated and cease to exist. Consequently, in discussing union with God we are not discussing the substantial union that always exists, but the soul's union with and transformation in God that does not always exist, except when there is likeness of love. We will call it the union of likeness; and the former, the essential or substantial union. The union of likeness is supernatural; the other, natural. The supernatural union exists when God's will and the soul's are in conformity, so that nothing in the one is repugnant to the other. When the soul rids itself completely

THE NATURE OF UNION WITH GOD — 33

of what is repugnant and unconformed to the divine will, it rests transformed in God through love.

Ridding oneself of what is repugnant to God's will should be understood not only of one's acts but of one's habits as well. Not only must actual voluntary imperfections cease, but habitual imperfections must be annihilated too.

No creature, none of its actions and abilities, can reach or encompass God's nature. Consequently, a soul must strip itself of everything pertaining to creatures and of its actions and abilities (of its understanding, satisfaction, and feeling) so that when everything unlike and unconformed to God is cast out, it may receive the likeness of God. And the soul will receive this likeness because nothing contrary to the will of God will be left in it. Thus it will be transformed in God.

It is true that God is ever present in the soul, as we said, and thereby bestows and preserves its natural being by his sustaining presence. Yet he does not always communicate supernatural being to it. He communicates supernatural being only through love and grace, which not all souls possess. And those who do, do not possess them in the same degree. Some have attained higher degrees of love; others remain in lower degrees. To the soul that is more advanced in love, more conformed to the divine will, God communicates himself more. A person who has reached complete conformity and likeness of will has attained total supernatural union and transformation in God.

Manifestly, then, the more that individuals through attachment and habit are clothed with their own abilities and with creatures, the less disposed they are for this union. For they do not afford God full opportunity to transform their souls into the supernatural. As a result, individuals have nothing more to do than to strip their souls of these natural contraries and dissimilarities so that God, who is naturally communicating himself to them through nature, may do so supernaturally through grace.

Here is an example that will provide a better understanding of this explanation. A ray of sunlight shining on a smudgy window is unable to illumine that window completely and transform it into its own light. It could do this if the window were cleaned and polished. The less the film and stains are wiped away, the less the window will be illumined; and the cleaner the window is, the brighter will be its illumination. The extent of illumination is not dependent on the ray of sunlight but on the window. If the window is totally clean and pure, the sunlight will so transform and illumine it that to all appearances the window will be identical with the ray of sunlight and shine just as the sun's ray. Although obviously the nature of the window is distinct from that of the sun's ray (even if the two seem identical), we can assert that the window is the ray or light of the sun by participation. The soul on which the divine light of God's being is ever shining, or better, in which it is ever dwelling by nature, is like this window, as we have affirmed.

The Nature of Union with God — 35

A soul makes room for God by wiping away all the smudges and smears of creatures, by uniting its will perfectly to God's; for to love is to labor to divest and deprive oneself for God of all that is not God. When this is done the soul will be illumined by and transformed in God. And God will so communicate his supernatural being to the soul that it will appear to be God himself and will possess what God himself possesses.

When God grants this supernatural favor to the soul, so great a union is that all the things of both God and the soul become one in participant transformation, and the soul appears to be God more than a soul. Indeed, it is God by participation. Yet truly, its being (even though transformed) is naturally as distinct from God's as it was before, just as the window, although illuminated by the ray, has being distinct from the ray's.

SPIRITUAL DETACHMENT

From *The Ascent of Mount Carmel*, Book 2, Chapter 7, Sections 4, 5, 8

Our activity during the night of the spirit is to detach ourselves from our need for spiritual feelings and consolations—to learn to love God for God alone, not for how God blesses us or makes us feel.

Obviously one's journey must not merely exclude the hindrance of creatures but also embody a dispossession and annihilation in the spiritual part of one's nature. Our Lord, for our instruction and guidance along this road, imparted that wonderful teaching—I think it is possible to affirm that the more necessary the doctrine the less it is practiced by spiritual persons—that I will quote fully and explain in its genuine and spiritual sense because of its importance and relevance to our subject. He states in the eighth chapter of Saint Mark: "If any want to become my followers, let them deny themselves and take up their cross and follow me. For those who want to save their life will lose it, and those who lose their life for my sake, and for the sake of the gospel, will save it."

Oh, who can make this counsel of our Savior on self-denial understandable, and practicable, and attractive, that spiritual persons might become aware of the difference between the method many of them think is good and the one that ought to be used in traveling this road! They are of the opinion that any kind of withdrawal from the world or reformation of life suffices. Some are content with a certain degree of virtue, perseverance in prayer, and mortification, but never achieve the nakedness, poverty, selflessness, or spiritual purity (which are all the same) about which the Lord counsels us here. For they still feed and clothe their natural selves with spiritual feelings and consolations instead of divesting and denying themselves of these for God's sake. They think denial of self in worldly matters is sufficient without annihilation and purification in the spiritual domain. It happens that, when some of this solid, perfect food (the annihilation of all sweetness in God—the pure spiritual cross and nakedness of Christ's poverty of spirit) is offered them in dryness, distaste, and trial, they run from it as from death and wander about in search only of sweetness and delightful communications from God. Such an attitude is not the hallmark of self-denial and nakedness of spirit but the indication of a spiritual sweet tooth. Through this kind of conduct they become, spiritually speaking, enemies of the cross of Christ.

A genuine spirit seeks rather the distasteful in God than the delectable, leans more toward suffering than toward consolation, more toward dryness and affliction than toward sweet consolation. It knows that this is the significance of following Christ and denying self, that the other method is perhaps a seeking of self in God—something entirely contrary to love. Seeking oneself in God is the same as looking for the caresses and consolations of God. Seeking God in oneself entails not only the desire to do without these consolations for God's sake, but also the inclination to choose for love of Christ all that is most distasteful whether in God or in the world; and this is what loving God means.

I should like to persuade spiritual persons that the road leading to God does not entail a multiplicity of considerations, methods, manners, and experiences—though in their own way these may be a requirement for beginners—but demands only the one thing necessary: true self-denial, exterior and interior, through the surrender of self both to suffering for Christ and to annihilation in all things. In the exercise of this self-denial everything else, and even more, is discovered and accomplished. If one fails in this exercise, the root and sum total of all the virtues, the other methods would amount to no more than going around in circles without getting anywhere, even were one to enjoy considerations and communications as lofty as those of the angels.

A person makes progress only by imitating Christ, who is the Way, the Truth, and the Life. No one goes to the Father but through him, as he states himself in Saint John. Accordingly, I would not consider any spirituality worthwhile that wants to walk in sweetness and ease and run from the imitation of Christ.

OPENNESS TO A NEW KIND OF PRAYER

From *The Ascent of Mount Carmel*, Book 2, Chapter 12, Sections 6–8

One of the turning points in the dark night of the spirit is God's call to move to contemplative prayer, prayer that abides in God's presence without the intellectual activity of meditation on a scriptural passage or event. Here John discusses the need to be open to this call.

Many spiritual persons, after having exercised themselves in approaching God through images, forms, and meditations suitable for beginners, err greatly if they do not determine, dare, or know how to detach themselves from these palpable methods to which they are accustomed. For God then wishes to lead them to more spiritual, interior, and invisible graces by removing the gratification derived from discursive meditation. They still try to hold on to these methods, desiring to travel the road of consideration and meditation, using images as before. They think they must always act in this way. Striving hard to meditate, they draw out little satisfaction or none at all. Rather, aridity, fatigue, and restlessness of soul increase in the measure they strive through meditation for that former sweetness, now unobtainable. They will no longer taste that sensible food, as we said, but rather will enjoy another food, more delicate, interior, and spiritual. Not by working with the imagination will they acquire this spiritual nourishment but by pacifying the soul, by leaving it to its more spiritual quiet and repose.

The more spiritual they are, the more they discontinue trying to make particular acts with their faculties, for they become more engrossed in one general, pure act. Once the faculties reach the end of their journey, they cease to work, just as we cease to walk when we reach the end of our journey. If everything consisted in going, one would never arrive; and if everywhere we found means, when and where could we enjoy the end and goal?

It is sad to see many disturb the soul when it desires to abide in this calm and repose of interior quietude, where it is filled with God's peace and refreshment. Desiring to make it retrace its steps and turn back from the goal in which it now reposes, they draw the soul out to more exterior activity, to considerations, which are the means. They do this with strong repugnance and reluctance in the soul. The soul wants to remain in that peace, which it does not understand, as in its rightful place. People suffer if, after laboring to reach their place of rest, they are forced to return to their labors.

Since these individuals do not understand the mystery of this new experience, they imagine themselves to be idle and doing nothing. Thus in their struggle with considerations and discursive meditations they disturb their quietude. They become filled with aridity and trial because of efforts to get satisfaction by means no longer apt. We can say that the more intense their efforts, the less will be their gain. The more they persist at meditation, the worse their state becomes because they drag the soul farther away from spiritual peace. They resemble one who abandons the greater for the lesser, turns back on a road already covered and wants to redo what is already done.

The proper advice for these individuals is that they must learn to abide in that quietude with a loving attentiveness to God and pay no heed to the imagination and its work. At this stage, as was said, the faculties are at rest and do not work actively but passively, by receiving what God is effecting in them. If at times the soul puts the faculties to work, it should not use excessive efforts or studied reasonings, but it should proceed with gentleness of love, moved more by God than by its own abilities, as we will explain later.

This explanation should be sufficient at present for those who want to make progress. They will understand the appropriateness and necessity of detaching oneself at the required time and season from all these methods, ways, and uses of the imagination.

THE PRAYER OF BEGINNERS

From *The Dark Night of the Soul*, Book 1, Chapter 1

The Ascent ends abruptly in the midst of a discussion of purifying the will during the active night of the spirit. In The Dark Night of the Soul, written in 1584–85, John begins a new discussion of the dark night. He starts by describing those who are just beginning to pray with regular times of meditation.

Souls begin to enter this dark night when God, gradually drawing them out of the state of beginners (those who practice meditation on the spiritual road), begins to place them in the state of proficients (those who are already contemplatives), so that by passing through this state they might reach that of the perfect, which is the divine union of the soul with God. We should first mention here some characteristics of beginners, for the sake of a better explanation and understanding of the nature of this night and of God's motive for placing the soul in it. Although our treatment of these things will be as brief as possible, it will help beginners understand the feebleness of their state and take courage and desire that God place them in this night where the soul is strengthened in virtue and fortified for the inestimable delights of the love of God. And, although we will be delayed for a moment, it will be for no longer than our discussion of this dark night requires.

It should be known, then, that God nurtures and caresses the soul, after it has been resolutely converted to his service, like a loving mother who warms her child with the heat of her bosom, nurses it with good milk and tender food, and carries and caresses it in her arms. But as the child grows older, the mother withholds her caresses and hides her tender love; she rubs bitter aloes on her sweet breast and sets the child down from her arms, letting it walk on its own feet so that it may put aside the habits of childhood and grow accustomed to greater and more important things. The grace of God acts just as a loving mother by re-engendering in the soul new enthusiasm and fervor in the service of God. With no effort on the soul's part, this grace causes it to taste sweet and delectable milk and to experience intense satisfaction in the performance of spiritual exercises, because God is handing the breast of his tender love to the soul, just as if it were a delicate child.

The soul finds its joy, therefore, in spending lengthy periods at prayer, perhaps even entire nights; its penances are pleasures; its fasts, happiness; and the sacraments and spiritual conversations are its consolations. Although spiritual persons do practice these exercises with great profit and persistence, and are very careful about them, spiritually speaking, they conduct themselves in a very weak and imperfect manner. Since their motivation in their spiritual works and exercises is the consolation and satisfaction they experience in them, and since they have not been conditioned by the arduous struggle of practicing virtue, they possess many faults and imperfections in the discharge of their spiritual activities. Assuredly, since everyone's actions are in direct conformity with the habit of perfection that has been acquired, and since these persons have not had time to acquire those firm habits, their work must of necessity be feeble, like that of weak children. For a clearer understanding of this and of how truly imperfect beginners are, insofar as they practice virtue readily because of the satisfaction attached to it, we will describe, using the seven capital vices as our basis, some of the numerous imperfections beginners commit. Thus we will clearly see how very similar their deeds are to those of children. The benefits of the dark night will become evident, since it cleanses and purifies the soul of all these imperfections.

SPIRITUAL PRIDE

From *The Dark Night of the Soul*, Book 1, Chapter 2, Sections 1–7

John explains the traps beginners can fall into as spiritual analogues of the seven deadly sins: pride, avarice, lust, anger, gluttony, envy, and sloth. Here he discusses spiritual pride.

These beginners feel so fervent and diligent in their spiritual exercises and undertakings that a certain kind of secret pride is generated in them that begets a complacency with themselves and their accomplishments, even though holy works do of their very nature cause humility. Then they develop a somewhat vain—at times very vain—desire to speak of spiritual things in others' presence, and sometimes even to instruct rather than be instructed; in their hearts they condemn others who do not seem to have the kind of devotion they would like them to have, and sometimes they give expression to this criticism like the Pharisee who despised the publican while he boasted and praised God for the good deeds he himself accomplished.

The devil, desiring the growth of pride and presumption in these beginners, often increases their fervor and readiness to perform such works, and other ones, too. For he is quite aware that all these works and virtues are not only worthless for them, but even become vices. Some of these persons become so evil-minded that they do not want anyone except themselves to appear holy. By both word and deed they condemn and detract others whenever the occasion arises, seeing the little splinter in their brother's eye and failing to consider the wooden beam in their own eye; they strain at the other's gnat and swallow their own camel.

And when at times their spiritual directors, their confessors, or their superiors disapprove their spirit and method of procedure, they feel that these directors do not understand, or perhaps that this failure to approve derives from a lack of holiness, since they want these directors to regard their conduct with esteem and praise. So they quickly search for some other spiritual advisor more to their liking, someone who will congratulate them and be impressed by their deeds; and they flee, as they would death, those who attempt to place them on the safe road by forbidding these things—and sometimes they even become hostile toward such spiritual directors. Frequently, in their presumption, they make many resolutions but accomplish very little. Sometimes they want others to recognize their spirit and devotion, and as a result occasionally contrive to make some manifestations of it, such as movements, sighs, and other ceremonies; sometimes, with the assistance of the devil, they experience raptures, more often in public than in private, and they are quite pleased, and often eager, for others to take notice of these.

Sometimes they minimize their faults, and at other times they become discouraged by them, since they felt they were already saints, and they become impatient and angry with themselves, which is yet another fault. They are often extremely anxious that God remove their faults and imperfections, but their motive is personal peace rather than God. They fail to realize that were God to remove their faults they might very well become more proud and presumptuous. They dislike praising anyone else, but they love to receive praise, and sometimes they even seek it. In this they resemble the foolish virgins who had to seek oil from others when their own lamps were extinguished.

But souls who are advancing in perfection at this time act in an entirely different manner and with a different quality of spirit. They receive great benefit from their humility, by which they not only place little importance on their deeds, but also take very little self-satisfaction from them. They think everyone else is far better than they are, and usually possess a holy envy of them and would like to emulate their service of God. Since they are truly humble, their growing fervor and the increased number of their good deeds and the gratification they receive from them only cause them to become more aware of their debt to God and the inadequacy of their service to him, and thus the more they do, the less satisfaction they derive from it. Their charity and love make them want to do so much for God that what they actually do accomplish seems as nothing. This loving solicitude goads them, preoccupies them, and absorbs them to such an extent that they never notice what others do or do not accomplish, but if they should, they then think, as I say, that everyone is better than they. They think they themselves are insignificant, and want others to think this also and to belittle and slight their deeds. Moreover, even though others do praise and value their works, these souls are unable to believe them; such praises seem strange to them.

These souls humbly and tranquilly long to be taught by anyone who might be a help to them. This desire is the exact opposite of that other desire we mentioned above, of those who want to be themselves the teachers in everything. When these others notice that someone is trying to give them some instruction, they themselves take the words from their very mouths as though they already know everything. Yet these humble souls, far from desiring to be anyone's teacher, are ready to take a road different from the one they are following, if told to do so. For they do not believe they could ever be right themselves. They rejoice when others receive praise, and their only sorrow is that they do not serve God as these others do. Because they consider their deeds insignificant, they do not want to make them known. They are even ashamed to speak of them to their spiritual directors because they think these deeds are not worth mentioning. They are more eager to speak of their faults and sins, and reveal these to others, than of their virtues. They have an inclination to seek direction from one who will have less esteem for their spirit and deeds. Such is the characteristic of a pure and simple and true spirit, one very pleasing to God. Since the wise Spirit of God dwells within these humble souls, he moves them to keep these treasures hidden, and to manifest only their faults. God gives this grace to the humble, together with the other virtues, just as he denies it to the proud.

SPIRITUAL GLUTTONY

From *The Dark Night of the Soul*, Book 1, Chapter 6, Sections 1, 5–8

Here John discusses spiritual gluttony as seeking sweetness through prayer, worship, and other devotional activities.

A great deal can be said on spiritual gluttony, the fourth vice. There are hardly any persons among these beginners, no matter how excellent their conduct, who do not fall into some of the many imperfections of this vice. These imperfections arise because of the delight beginners find in their spiritual exercises. Many, lured by the delight and satisfaction procured in their religious practices, strive more for spiritual savor than for spiritual purity and discretion; yet it is this purity and discretion that God looks for and finds acceptable throughout a soul's entire spiritual journey. Besides the imperfection of seeking after these delights, the sweetness these persons experience makes them go to extremes and pass beyond the mean in which virtue resides and is acquired. Some, attracted by the delight they feel in their spiritual exercises, kill themselves with penances, and others weaken themselves by fasts and, without the counsel or command of another, overtax their weakness; indeed, they try to hide these penances from the one to whom they owe obedience in such matters. Some even dare perform these penances contrary to obedience.

In receiving Communion they spend all their time trying to get some feeling and satisfaction rather than humbly praising and reverencing God dwelling within them. And they go about this in such a way that, if they do not procure any sensible feeling and satisfaction, they think they have accomplished nothing. As a result they judge very poorly of God and fail to understand that the sensory benefits are the least among those that this most blessed sacrament bestows, for the invisible grace it gives is a greater blessing. God often withdraws sensory delight and pleasure so that souls might set the eyes of faith on this invisible grace. Not only in receiving Communion, but in other spiritual exercises as well, beginners desire to feel God and taste him as if he were comprehensible and accessible. This desire is a serious imperfection and, because it involves impurity of faith, is opposed to God's way.

They have the same defect in their prayer, for they think the whole matter of prayer consists in looking for sensory satisfaction and devotion. They strive to procure this by their own efforts, and tire and weary their heads and their faculties. When they do not get this sensible comfort, they become very disconsolate and think they have done nothing. Because of their aim they lose true devotion and spirit, which lie in distrust of self and in humble and patient perseverance so as to please God. Once they do not find delight in prayer, or in any other spiritual exercise, they feel extreme reluctance and repugnance in returning to it and sometimes even give it up. For after all, as was mentioned, they are like children who are prompted to act not by reason but by pleasure. All their time is spent looking for satisfaction and spiritual consolation; they can never read enough spiritual books, and one minute they are meditating on one subject and the next on another, always hunting for some gratification in the things of God. God very rightly and discreetly and lovingly denies this satisfaction to these beginners. If he did not, they would fall into innumerable evils because of their spiritual gluttony and craving for sweetness. This is why it is important for these beginners to enter the dark night and be purged of this childishness.

Those who are inclined toward these delights have also another serious imperfection, which is that they are weak and remiss in treading the rough way of the cross. A soul given up to pleasure naturally feels aversion toward the bitterness of self-denial.

These people incur many other imperfections because of this spiritual gluttony, of which the Lord in time will cure them through temptations, aridities, and other trials, which are all a part of the dark night. So as not to be too lengthy, I do not want to discuss these imperfections any more, but only point out that spiritual sobriety and temperance beget another very different quality, one of mortification, fear, and submissiveness in all things. Individuals thereby become aware that the perfection and value of their works do not depend on quantity or the satisfaction found in them but on knowing how to practice self-denial in them. These beginners ought to do their part in striving after this self-denial until God in fact brings them into the dark night and purifies them. In order to get to our discussion of this dark night, I am passing over these imperfections hurriedly.

SIGNS OF GOD'S CALL TO CONTEMPLATION

From *The Dark Night of the Soul*, Book 1, Chapter 9

Again John discusses the soul's need to move beyond meditation to contemplation. Here he gives some of the signs that God is calling the soul to make in this transition.

Because these aridities may not proceed from the sensory night and purgation, but from sin and imperfection, or weakness and lukewarmness, or some bad humor or bodily indisposition, I will give some signs here for discerning whether the dryness is the result of this purgation or of one of these other defects. I find there are three principal signs for knowing this.

The first is that since these souls do not get satisfaction or consolation from the things of God, they do not get any from creatures either. Since God puts a soul in this dark night in order to dry up and purge its sensory appetite, he does not allow it to find sweetness or delight in anything. Through this sign it can in all likelihood be inferred that this dryness and distaste is not the outcome of newly committed sins and imperfections. If this were so, some inclination or propensity to look for satisfaction in something other than the things of God would be felt in the sensory part, for when the appetite is allowed indulgence in some imperfection, the soul immediately feels an inclination toward it, little or great in proportion to the degree of its satisfaction and attachment. Yet, because the want of satisfaction in earthly or heavenly things could be the product of some indisposition or melancholic humor, which frequently prevents one from being satisfied with anything, the second sign or condition is necessary.

The second sign for the discernment of this purgation is that the memory ordinarily turns to God solicitously and with painful care, and the soul thinks it is not serving God but turning back, because it is aware of this distaste for the things of God. There is a notable difference between dryness and lukewarmness. The lukewarm are very lax and remiss in their will and spirit, and have no solicitude about serving God. Those suffering from the purgative dryness are ordinarily solicitous, concerned, and pained about not serving God. Even though the dryness may be furthered by melancholia or some other humor—as it often is—it does not thereby fail to produce its purgative effect in the appetite, for the soul will be deprived of every satisfaction and concerned only about God. If this humor is the entire cause, everything ends in displeasure and does harm to one's nature, and there are none of these desires to serve God that accompany the purgative dryness. Even though in this purgative dryness the sensory part of the soul is very cast down, slack, and feeble in its actions because of the little satisfaction it finds, the spirit is ready and strong.

The reason for this dryness is that God transfers his goods and strength from sense to spirit. Since the sensory part of the soul is incapable of the goods of spirit, it remains deprived, dry, and empty. Thus, while the spirit is tasting, the flesh tastes nothing at all and becomes weak in its work. But through this nourishment the spirit grows stronger and more alert, and becomes more solicitous than before about not failing God. If in the beginning the soul does not experience this spiritual savor and delight, but dryness and distaste, the reason is the novelty involved in this exchange. Since its palate is accustomed to these other sensory tastes, the soul still sets its eyes on them. And since, also, its spiritual palate is neither purged nor accommodated for so subtle a taste, it is unable to experience the spiritual savor and good until gradually prepared by means of this dark and obscure night.

Yet, as I say, when these aridities are the outcome of the purgative way of the sensory appetite, the spirit feels the strength and energy to work, which are obtained from the substance of that interior food, even though in the beginning it may not experience the savor, for the reason just mentioned. This food is the beginning of a contemplation that is dark and dry to the senses. Ordinarily this contemplation, which is secret and hidden from the very one who receives it, imparts to the soul, together with the dryness and emptiness it produces in the senses, an inclination to remain alone and in quietude. And the soul will be unable to dwell on any particular thought, nor will it have the desire to do so. If those in whom this occurs know how to remain quiet, without care or solicitude about any interior or exterior work, they will soon in that unconcern and idleness delicately experience the interior nourishment. If the soul desires or tries to experience it, it cannot do so. It is like air that escapes when one tries to grasp it in one's hand.

Now in this state of contemplation, when the soul leaves discursive meditation and enters the state of proficients, it is God who works in it. He therefore binds the interior faculties and leaves no support in the intellect, nor satisfaction in the will, nor remembrance in the memory. At this time a person's own efforts are of no avail, but are an obstacle to the interior peace and work God is producing in the spirit through that dryness of sense. Since this peace is something spiritual and delicate, its fruit is quiet, delicate, solitary, satisfying, and peaceful, and far removed from all the other gratifications of beginners, which are very palpable and sensory.

The third sign follows from this one: the powerlessness, in spite of one's efforts, to meditate and make use of the imagination, the interior sense, as was one's previous custom. At this time God does not communicate through the senses as before, by means of the discursive analysis and synthesis of ideas, but begins to communicate through pure spirit by an act of simple contemplation in which there is no discursive succession of thought. The exterior and interior senses of the lower part of the soul cannot attain to this contemplation. As a result the imaginative power and phantasy can no longer rest in any consideration or find support in it.

From the third sign it can be deduced that this dissatisfaction of the faculties is not the fruit of any bad humor. If it were, people would be able with a little care to return to their former exercises and find support for their faculties when that humor passed away, for it is by its nature changeable. In the purgation of the appetite this return is not possible, because on entering it the powerlessness to meditate always continues. It is true, though, that at times in the beginning the purgation of some souls is not continuous in such a way that they are always deprived of sensory satisfaction and the ability to meditate. Perhaps, because of their weakness, they cannot be weaned all at once. Nevertheless, if they are to advance, they will ever enter farther into the purgation and leave farther behind their work of the senses.

ACCEPTING GOD'S GUIDANCE

From *The Dark Night of the Soul*, Book 1, Chapter 10

Here John emphasizes that spiritual progress is at God's direction, not our own, and in God's own time. We need to understand how God leads the soul to avoid becoming impatient or turning back from God's call.

At the time of the aridities of this sensory night, God makes the exchange we mentioned by withdrawing the soul from the life of the senses and placing it in that of spirit—that is, he brings it from meditation to contemplation—where the soul no longer has the power to work or meditate with its faculties on the things of God. Spiritual persons suffer considerable affliction in this night, owing not so much to the aridities they undergo as to their fear of having gone astray. Since they do not find any support or satisfaction in good things, they believe there will be no more spiritual blessings for them and that God has abandoned them. They then grow weary and strive, as was their custom, to concentrate their faculties with some satisfaction on a subject of meditation, and they think that if they do not do this and do not feel that they are at work, they are doing nothing. This effort of theirs is accompanied by an interior reluctance and repugnance on the part of the soul, for it would be pleased to dwell in that quietude and idleness without working with the faculties. They consequently impair God's work and do not profit by their own. In searching for spirit, they lose the spirit that was the source of their tranquillity and peace. They are like someone who turns from what has already been done in order to do it again, or like one who leaves a city only to re-enter it, or they are like a hunter who abandons the prey in order to go hunting again. It is useless, then, for the soul to try to meditate because it will no longer profit by this exercise.

If there is no one to understand these persons, they either turn back and abandon the road or lose courage, or at least they hinder their own progress because of their excessive diligence in treading the path of discursive meditation. They fatigue and overwork themselves, thinking that they are failing because of their negligence or sins. Meditation is now useless for them because God is conducting them along another road, which is contemplation and is very different from the first, for the one road belongs to discursive meditation and the other is beyond the range of the imagination and discursive reflection.

Those who are in this situation should feel comforted; they ought to persevere patiently and not be afflicted. Let them trust in God who does not fail those who seek him with a simple and righteous heart; nor will he fail to impart what is needful for the way until getting them to the clear and pure light of love. God will give them this light by means of that other night, the night of spirit, if they merit that he place them in it. The attitude necessary in the night of sense is to pay no attention to discursive meditation since this is not the time for it. They should allow the soul to remain in rest and quietude even though it may seem obvious to them that they are doing nothing and wasting time, and even though they think this disinclination to think about anything is due to their laxity. Through patience and perseverance in prayer, they will be doing a great deal without activity on their part. All that is required of them here is freedom of soul, that they liberate themselves from the impediment and fatigue of ideas and thoughts, and care not about thinking and meditating. They must be content simply with a loving and peaceful attentiveness to God, and live without the concern, without the effort, and without the desire to taste or feel him. All these desires disquiet the soul and distract it from the peaceful, quiet, and sweet idleness of the contemplation that is being communicated to it.

And even though more scruples come to the fore concerning the loss of time and the advantages of doing something else, since it cannot do anything or think of anything in prayer, the soul should endure them peacefully, as though going to prayer means remaining in ease and freedom of spirit. If individuals were to desire to do something themselves with their interior faculties, they would hinder and lose the goods that God engraves on their souls through that peace and idleness. If a model for the painting or retouching of a portrait should move because of a desire to do something, the artist would be unable to finish and the work would be spoiled. Similarly, any operation, affection, or thought a soul might cling to when it wants to abide in interior peace and idleness would cause distraction and disquietude, and make it feel sensory dryness and emptiness. The more a person seeks some support in knowledge and affection the more the soul will feel the lack of these, for this support cannot be supplied through these sensory means.

Accordingly, such persons should not mind if the operations of their faculties are being lost to them; they should desire rather that this be done quickly so they may be no obstacle to the operation of the infused contemplation God is bestowing, so they may receive it with more peaceful plenitude and make room in the spirit for the enkindling and burning of the love that this dark and secret contemplation bears and communicates to the soul. For contemplation is nothing else than a secret and peaceful and loving inflow of God, which, if not hampered, fires the soul in the spirit of love.

PRAYER OF PROFICIENTS

From *The Dark Night of the Soul*, Book 2, Chapters 3–4

At last John is ready to describe the passive night of the spirit. He begins with a description of prayer as experienced by proficients: those who have moved from meditation to contemplation, but are still far from perfection. As part of this, he offers this third explanation of the first stanza of the poem.

These souls, then, are now proficients. Their senses have been fed with sweet communications so that, allured by the gratification flowing from the spirit, they could be accommodated and united to the spirit. These two parts thus united and conformed are jointly prepared to suffer the rough and arduous purgation of the spirit that awaits them. In this purgation, these two portions of the soul will undergo complete purification, for one part is never adequately purged without the other. The real purgation of the senses begins with the spirit. Hence the night of the senses we explained should be called a certain reformation and bridling of the appetite rather than a purgation. The reason is that all the imperfections and disorders of the sensory part are rooted in the spirit and from it receive their strength. All good and evil habits reside in the spirit and until these habits are purged, the senses cannot be completely purified of their rebellions and vices.

In this night that follows both parts are jointly purified. This was the purpose of the reformation of the first night and the calm that resulted from it: that the sensory part, united in a certain way with the spirit, might undergo purgation and suffering with greater fortitude. Such is the fortitude necessary for so strong and arduous a purgation that if the lower part in its weakness is not reformed first, and afterward strengthened in God through the experience of sweet and delightful communion with him, it has neither the fortitude nor the preparedness to endure it.

These proficients are still very lowly and natural in their communion with God and in their activity directed toward him because the gold of the spirit is not purified and illumined. They still think of God and speak of him as little children, and their knowledge and experience of him are like those of little children, as Saint Paul asserts. The reason is that they have not reached perfection, which is union of the soul with God. Through this union, as fully grown, they do mighty works in the spirit since their faculties and works are more divine than human, as we will point out. Wishing to strip them in fact of this old self and clothe them with the new, which is created according to God in the newness of sense, as the Apostle says, God divests the faculties, affections, and senses, both spiritual and sensory, interior and exterior. He leaves the intellect in darkness, the will in aridity, the memory in emptiness, and the affections in supreme affliction, bitterness, and anguish by depriving the soul of the feeling and satisfaction it previously obtained from spiritual blessings. For this privation is one of the conditions required that the spiritual form, which is the union of love, may be introduced into the spirit and united with it. The Lord works all of this in the soul by means of a pure and dark contemplation, as is indicated in the first stanza. Although we explained this stanza in reference to the first night of the senses, the soul understands it mainly in relation to this second night of the spirit, since this night is the principal purification of the soul. With this in mind, we will quote it and explain it again.

> One dark night,
> fired with love's urgent longings
> —ah, the sheer grace!—
> I went out unseen,
> my house being now all stilled.

Understanding this stanza now to refer to contemplative purgation or nakedness and poverty of spirit (which are all about the same), we can thus explain it, as though the soul says: Poor, abandoned, and unsupported by any of the apprehensions of my soul (in the darkness of my intellect, the distress of my will, and the affliction and anguish of my memory), left to darkness in pure faith, which is a dark night for these natural faculties, and with my will touched only by sorrows, afflictions, and longings of love of God, I went out from myself. That is, I departed from my low manner of understanding, and my feeble way of loving, and my poor and limited method of finding satisfaction in God. I did this unhindered by either the flesh or the devil.

This was great happiness and a sheer grace for me, because through the annihilation and calming of my faculties, passions, appetites, and affections, by which my experience and satisfaction in God were base, I went out from my human operation and way of acting to God's operation and way of acting. That is: My intellect departed from itself, changing from human and natural to divine. For united with God through this purgation, it no longer understands by means of its natural vigor and light, but by means of the divine wisdom to which it was united. And my will departed from itself and became divine. United with the divine love, it no longer loves in a lowly manner, with its natural strength, but with the strength and purity of the Holy Spirit; and thus the will does not operate humanly in relation to God. The memory, too, was changed into presentiments of eternal glory. And finally, all the strength and affections of the soul, by means of this night and purgation of the old self, are renewed with divine qualities and delights.

LIGHT IN THE NIGHT

From *The Dark Night of the Soul*, Book 2, Chapter 9, Sections 1–4

In this stage of the dark night, the soul can begin to hope for dawn and to experience the light of union with God.

It remains to be said, then, that even though this happy night darkens the spirit, it does so only to impart light concerning all things; and even though it humbles individuals and reveals their miseries, it does so only to exalt them; and even though it impoverishes and empties them of all possessions and natural affection, it does so only that they may reach out divinely to the enjoyment of all earthly and heavenly things, with a general freedom of spirit in them all. That elements be commingled with all natural compounds, they must be unaffected by any particular color, odor, or taste, and thus they can concur with all colors, odors, and tastes. Similarly, the spirit must be simple, pure, and naked as to all natural affections, actual and habitual, in order to be able to communicate freely in fullness of spirit with the divine wisdom in which, on account of the soul's purity, the delights of all things are tasted to a certain eminent degree. Without this purgation the soul would be wholly unable to experience the satisfaction of all this abundance of spiritual delight. Only one attachment or one particular object to which the spirit is actually or habitually bound is enough to hinder the experience or reception of the delicate and intimate delight of the spirit of love that contains eminently in itself all delights.

Because of their one attachment to the food and fleshmeat they had tasted in Egypt, the children of Israel were unable to get any taste from the delicate bread of angels—the manna of the desert, which, as Scripture says, contained all savors and was changed to the taste each one desired. Similarly the spirit, still affected by some actual or habitual attachment or some particular knowledge or any other apprehension, is unable to taste the delights of the spirit of freedom. The reason is that the affections, feelings, and apprehensions of the perfect spirit, because they are divine, are of another sort and are so eminent and so different from the natural that their actual and habitual possession demands the annihilation and expulsion of the natural affections and apprehensions; for two contraries cannot coexist in one subject. Hence, so the soul may pass on to these grandeurs, this dark night of contemplation must necessarily annihilate it first and undo it in its lowly ways by putting it into darkness, dryness, conflict, and emptiness. For the light imparted to the soul is a most lofty divine light that transcends all natural light and does not belong naturally to the intellect.

That the intellect reach union with the divine light and become divine in the state of perfection, this dark contemplation must first purge and annihilate it of its natural light and bring it actually into obscurity. It is fitting that this darkness last as long as is necessary for the expulsion and annihilation of the intellect's habitual way of understanding, which was a long time in use, and that divine light and illumination take its place. Since that strength of understanding was natural to the intellect, the darkness it here suffers is profound, frightful, and extremely painful. This darkness seems to be substantial darkness, since it is felt in the deep substance of the spirit. The affection of love that is bestowed in the divine union of love is also divine, and consequently very spiritual, subtle, delicate, and interior, exceeding every affection and feeling of the will and every appetite. The will, as a result, must first be purged and annihilated of all its affections and feelings in order to experience and taste, through union of love, this divine affection and delight, which is so sublime and does not naturally belong to the will. The soul is left in a dryness and distress proportional to its habitual natural affections (whether for divine or human things), so that every kind of demon may be debilitated, dried up, and tried in the fire of this divine contemplation, as when Tobias placed the fish heart in the fire, and the soul may become pure and simple, with a palate purged and healthy and ready to experience the sublime and marvelous touches of divine love. After the expulsion of all actual and habitual obstacles, it will behold itself transformed in these divine touches.

Furthermore, in this union for which the dark night is a preparation, the soul in its communion with God must be endowed and filled with a certain glorious splendor embodying innumerable delights. These delights surpass all the abundance the soul can possess naturally, for nature, so weak and impure, cannot receive these delights. As a result the soul must first be set in emptiness and poverty of spirit and purged of every natural support, consolation, and apprehension, earthly and heavenly. Thus empty, it is truly poor in spirit and stripped of the old self, and thereby able to live that new and blessed life which is the state of union with God, attained by means of this night.

 THE LADDER OF LOVE

From *The Dark Night of the Soul*, Book 2, Chapters 19–20

Near the end of The Dark Night, *John offers another metaphor of the spiritual journey: a ladder of love reaching from beginning to union. It is based on a work attributed—incorrectly—to Bernard of Clairvaux. This selection is severely abridged in order to show the basic progression of all ten steps.*

We mentioned that there are ten successive steps on this ladder of love by which the soul ascends to God. The first step of love makes the soul sick in an advantageous way. The bride speaks of this step of love when she says: "I adjure you, O daughters of Jerusalem, if you find my beloved, tell him this: I am faint with love." Yet this sickness is not unto death but for the glory of God, because in this sickness the soul's languor pertains to sin and to all the things that are not God. As a sick person changes color and loses appetite for all foods, so on this step of love the soul changes the color of its past life and loses its appetite for all things. It becomes unable then to find satisfaction, support, consolation, or a resting place in anything. The soul therefore begins immediately to ascend from this step to the next.

The second step causes a person to search for God unceasingly. When the bride was languishing, she added: "I will rise now and . . . seek him whom my soul loves." Searching for him in all things, it pays heed to nothing until it finds him. Since the soul is here convalescing and gaining strength in the love found in this second step, it immediately begins to ascend to the third through a certain degree of new purgation in the night.

The third step of this loving ladder prompts the soul to the performance of works and gives it fervor that it might not fail. The royal prophet exclaims: "Happy are those who fear the LORD, who greatly delight in his commandments." If fear, a child of love, produces this eagerness in the soul, what will love itself do? On this step the soul thinks the great works it does for the Beloved are small; its many works, few; the long time spent in his service, short. It believes all of this because of the fire of love in which it is now burning. One reason for this effect is that love is teaching them what God deserves; another is that because the works they perform for God are many and they know them to be wanting and imperfect, they are confused and pained by them all. On this third step the soul is far removed from vainglory, presumption, and the practice of condemning others. And thus one acquires the courage and strength to ascend to the fourth step.

On the fourth step of this ladder of love a habitual yet unwearisome suffering is engendered on account of the Beloved. As Saint Augustine says: "Love makes all burdensome and heavy things nearly nothing." The spirit possesses so much energy on this step that it brings the flesh under control and takes as little account of it as would a tree of one of its leaves. The soul in no way seeks consolation or satisfaction either in God or in anything else; neither does it desire or ask favors of God, for it is clearly aware that it has already received many from him. All its care is directed toward how it might give some pleasure to God and render him some service because of what he deserves and the favors he has bestowed, even though the cost might be high.

On the fifth step the desire of the lover to apprehend and be united with the Beloved is so ardent that any delay, no matter how slight, is long, annoying, and tiresome. The soul is ever believing that it is finding its Beloved; and when it sees its desire frustrated, which is at almost every step, it faints in its longing, as the psalmist declares: "My soul longs, indeed it faints for the courts of the LORD." On this step the lover must either see its love or die.

The sixth step makes the soul run swiftly toward God and experience many touches in him. It runs without fainting by reason of its hope. The love that has invigorated it makes it fly swiftly. The prophet Isaiah also speaks of this step: "Those who wait for the LORD shall renew their strength, they shall mount up with wings like eagles, . . . they shall walk and not faint."

The seventh step of the ladder gives the soul an ardent boldness. At this stage love neither profits by the judgment to wait nor makes use of the counsel to retreat, neither can it be curbed through shame. For the favor God now gives it imparts an ardent daring. Hence the Apostle says: "[Love] believes all things, hopes all things, endures all things."

The eighth step of love impels the soul to lay hold of the Beloved without letting go, as the bride proclaims: "I found him whom my soul loves. I held him and would not let him go." Although the soul satisfies its desire on this step of union, it does not do so continually. Some manage to get to it, but soon turn back and leave it. If one were to remain on this step, a certain glory would be possessed in this life, and so the soul rests on it for only short periods of time. After this step comes the ninth, which is that of the perfect.

The ninth step of love causes the soul to burn gently. The Holy Spirit produces this gentle and delightful ardor by reason of the perfect soul's union with God. We cannot speak of the goods and riches of God a person enjoys on this step because even were we to write many books about them the greater part would remain unsaid.

The tenth and last step of this secret ladder of love assimilates the soul to God completely because of the clear vision of God that a person possesses at once on reaching it. After arriving at the ninth step in this life, the soul departs from the body. Saint Matthew says: "Blessed are the pure in heart, for they will see God." As we mentioned, this vision is the cause of the soul's complete likeness to God. Saint John says: "We will be like him," not because the soul will have as much capacity as God—this is impossible—but because all it is will become like God. Thus it will be called, and shall be, God through participation.

Thus, by means of this mystical theology and secret love, the soul departs from itself and all things and ascends to God. For love is like a fire that always rises upward as though longing to be engulfed in its center.

APPENDIX

Reading Spiritual Classics for Personal and Group Formation

Many Christians today are searching for more spiritual depth, for something more than simply being good church members. That quest may send them to the spiritual practices of New Age movements or of Eastern religions such as Zen Buddhism. Christians, though, have their own long spiritual tradition, a tradition rich with wisdom, variety, and depth.

The great spiritual classics testify to that depth. They do not concern themselves with mystical flights for a spiritual elite. Rather, they contain very practical advice and insights that can support and shape the spiritual growth of any Christian. We can all benefit by sitting at the feet of the masters (both male and female) of Christian spirituality.

Reading spiritual classics is different from most of the reading we do. We have learned to read to master a text and extract information from it. We tend to read quickly, to get through a text. And we summarize as we read, seeking the main point. In reading spiritual classics, though, we allow the text to master and form us. Such formative reading goes more slowly, more reflectively, allowing time for God to speak to us through the text. God's word for us may come as easily from a minor point or even an aside as from the major point.

Formative reading requires that you approach the text in humility. Read as a seeker, not an expert. Don't demand that the text meet your expectations for what an "enlightened" author should write. Humility means accepting the author as another imperfect human, a product of his or her own time and situation. Learn to celebrate what is foundational in an author's writing without being overly disturbed by what is peculiar to the author's life and times. Trust the text as a gift from both God and the author, offered to you for your benefit—to help you grow in Christ.

To read formatively, you must also slow down. Feel free to reread a passage that seems to speak specially to you. Stop from time to time to reflect on what you have been reading. Keep a journal for these reflections. Often the act of writing can itself prompt further, deeper reflection. Keep your notebook open and your pencil in hand as you read. You might not get back to that wonderful insight later. Don't worry that you are not getting through an entire passage—or even the first paragraph! Formative reading is about depth rather than breadth, quality rather than quantity. As you read, seek God's direction for your own life. Timeless truths have their place but may not be what is most important for your own formation here and now.

As you read the passage, you might keep some of these questions running through your mind:

- How is what I'm reading true of my own life? Where does it reflect my own *experience*?

- How does this text challenge me? What new *direction* does it offer me?
- What must I change to put what I am reading into practice? How can I *incarnate* it, let this word become flesh in my life?

You might also devote special attention to sections that upset you. What is the source of the disturbance? Do you want to argue theology? Are you turned off by cultural differences? Or have you been skewered by an insight that would turn your life upside down if you took it seriously? Let your journal be a dialogue with the text.

If you find yourself moving from reading the text to chewing over its implications to praying, that's great! Spiritual reading is really the first step in an ancient way of prayer called *lectio divina* or "divine reading." Reading leads naturally into reflection on what you have read (meditation). As you reflect on what the text might mean for your life, you may well want to ask for God's help in living out any new insights or direction you have perceived (prayer). Sometimes such prayer may lead you further into silently abiding in God's presence (contemplation). And, of course, the process is only really completed when it begins to make a difference in the way we live (incarnation).

As good as it is to read spiritual classics in solitude, it is even better to join with others in a small group for mutual formation or "spiritual direction in common." This is *not* the same as a study group that talks about spiritual classics. A group for mutual formation would have similar goals as for an individual's reading: to allow the text to shine its light on the *experiences* of the group members, to suggest new *directions* for their lives and practical ways of *incarnating* these directions. Such a group might agree to focus on one short passage from a classic at each meeting (even if members have read more). Discussion usually goes much deeper if all the members have already read and reflected on the passage before the meeting and bring their journals.

Such groups need to watch for several potential problems. It is easy to go off on a tangent (especially if it takes the focus off the members' own experience and onto generalities). At such times a group leader might bring the group's attention back to the text: "What does our author say about that?" Or, "How do we experience that in our own lives?" When a group member shares a problem, others may be tempted to try to "fix" it. This is much less helpful than sharing similar experiences and how they were handled (for good or ill). "Sharing" someone else's problems (whether that person is in or out of the group) should be strongly discouraged.

One person could be designated as leader, to be responsible for opening and closing prayers; to be the first to share or respond to the text; and to keep notes during the discussion to highlight recurring themes, challenges, directives, or practical steps. These responsibilities could also be shared among several members of the group or rotated.

For further information about formative reading of spiritual classics, try *A Practical Guide to Spiritual Reading* by Susan Annette Muto. *Shaped by the Word* by Robert Mulholland (Upper Room Books®) covers formative reading of the Bible. *Good Things Happen: Experiencing Community in Small Groups* by Dick Westley is an excellent resource on forming small groups of all kinds.